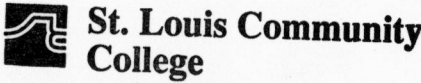

UNEARTHLY
VISIONS

**Recent Titles in Contributions to the
Study of Science Fiction and Fantasy**

UNEARTHLY

VISIONS

APPROACHES TO SCIENCE FICTION AND FANTASY ART

EDITED BY GARY WESTFAHL, GEORGE SLUSSER, AND KATHLEEN CHURCH PLUMMER

CONTRIBUTIONS TO THE STUDY OF SCIENCE FICTION AND FANTASY, NO. 98
DONALD PALUMBO, SERIES ADVISER

GREENWOOD PRESS
WESTPORT, CONNECTICUT • LONDON

Library of Congress Cataloging-in-Publication Data

Unearthly visions : approaches to science fiction and fantasy art / edited by Gary
Westfahl, George Slusser, and Kathleen Church Plummer.
    p. cm.—(Contributions to the study of science fiction and fantasy, ISSN 0193–
6875 ; no. 98)
  Includes bibliographical references and index.
  ISBN 0–313–31705–4 (alk. paper)
  1. Fantastic, The, in art. 2. Science fiction—Illustrations. 3. Fantasy
fiction—Illustrations. I. Westfahl, Gary. II. Slusser, George Edgar. III. Plummer,
Kathleen Church, 1943– . IV. Series.
N8217.F28U54 2002
704.9′4980938762—dc21   2001040561

British Library Cataloguing in Publication Data is available.

Library of Congress Catalog Card Number: 2001040561
ISBN: 0–313–31705–4
ISSN: 0193–6875

First published in 2002

Greenwood Press, 88 Post Road West, Westport, CT 06881
An imprint of Greenwood Publishing Group, Inc.
www.greenwood.com

Printed in the United States of America

The paper used in this book complies with the
Permanent Paper Standard issued by the National
Information Standards Organization (Z39.48–1984).

10 9 8 7 6 5 4 3 2 1

Copyright Acknowledgments

The editors and publisher gratefully acknowledge permission to quote from the following:

From "The Gernsback Continuum" by William Gibson, which first appeared in *Universe 11*, ©
1981 by Terry Carr. Used by permission of the author and Martha Millard Literary Agency.

To reprint " 'Getting It Right': A Reflection on Titans and Technology" by Gregory Benford. Copyright 2001 by Abbenford Associates.

Contents

Part II. Approaches to Fantasy Art

Acknowledgments

We must first thank the many people who contributed to the long process of assembling this volume, including Eric S. Rabkin, the late Frank McConnell, Gladys Murphy, Sheryl Lewis, Darian Daries, Susan Korn, Sara Fitzpatrick, David Clayton, Cuyler Brooks, William G. Contento, Mark Owings, Bud Webster, and especially Donald E. Palumbo. For guidance and assistance during the final stages of preparation, we thank George F. Butler, his colleagues at Greenwood Press, and our copyeditor Terri M. Jennings. We also thank the Martha Millard Literary Agency, representing William Gibson, for permission to quote extensively from Gibson's story "The Gernsback Continuum," as well as friends, family members, and colleagues too numerous to name who have provided encouragement and support while we worked on completing this project.

Introduction: The Iconology of Science Fiction and Fantasy Art

George Slusser

A symposium on science fiction and fantasy art is long overdue. Perhaps the delay is due to the daunting nature of the task, for here there is no canon or established corpus of works. Gary Westfahl sets down a "history" of sf art, only to abolish it with the flick of a finger, warning that such neat schema are always biased (especially in this vast field of works, where generalizations are always hasty, and artists always to be found who successfully defy whatever "style" seems in favor). Ensuing papers in the sf section focus on types or themes—architectural or environmental art, space art—and on a significant individual artist—Richard M. Powers. The same pattern works for fantasy art. John Clute maps the field, then ensuing chapters focus on specific situations or writers—such as the Tolkien universe and Frank Frazetta. Apparently breaking the pattern, yet actually following it in his own way, John Grant employs the ancient tradition of the parable to raise provocative questions about the assumptions we usually make in examining fantasy art, useful points to ponder for anyone preparing to examine the field.

This volume then maps, and in doing so points the way to a *method* of approaching the welter of images and artists, as suggested by Grant's phrase "archeological fieldwork." In fact, what is needed is an iconography of sf and fantasy images, an exhaustive catalog of all the covers, illustrations, dust jackets found in a comprehensive science fiction collection—photographed, scanned, or otherwise preserved as images—which will be around when the original source or artifact is gone. This alone would be miraculous; but it is not the first step. There must first be an *iconology* of sf and fantasy art—that is, an interpretative system that organizes images according to fundamental, widely shared formal categories—generally meta-historical and mythical categories. I would like to offer some thoughts on what such an iconology would be. How might one determine the fundamental icons or visual forms of sf/fantasy art? What is the dynamic by which these basic forms interact and transform? To answer these questions, however, one must define in what way sf and fantasy images *are* icons. To do this, one needs first to examine its relationship to modern canonical art.

The Science of Images

Sf and fantasy art do not just "borrow" images and techniques from canonical art, though such borrowings clearly exist. What it rather does, on the deeper level, is redirect the impetus of science, whose role in the way the physical world is represented begins to be felt, in radical ways, as early as the mid-nineteenth century. If one wishes, one could say there are two "science fiction" art forms. The first of these, following the rise of positivist science, particularly in France, works to break down or dissolve the dominant icons of traditional painting in the name of more basic analytical categories, such as "light," "color," and ultimately relativity. The result of all these refocusings was to challenge the classic iconic system centered on the human form. Take the example of impressionism. Painters like Claude Monet and Pierre-Auguste Renoir set about to analyze the effects of variations in a single element, light, on the representation of reality. In his famous "haystacks," Monet set a series of canvases in a field facing the haystack, an object obviously not chosen for its relevance to any particular human myth or story. He would paint the object from, say, 9:00 a.m. to 10:00 a.m. on canvas one, then shift with the light to canvas two, and so on during the day, following the course of natural atmospheric change. Other painters, like Monet, Hilaire Degas, and Paul Cézanne, sketched in nature, then recomposed their canvases in the workshop. Degas offers paintings of ballet dancers—human forms and not haystacks. His scenes, however, are not recomposed in traditional manner, in the studio in accordance with rules of perspective that place the human form at the center of a composition. Instead of a pose we have (the influence of photography is clear) a "snapshot," figures presented from a contingent angle, with parts of bodies cut by margins—a view of things in motion stopped at random. Human forms are flecks of color and light in Monet's landscapes. Renoir's humans are vulgar, often with bestial faces; these forms however are "decomposed" in flickerings of light, shadow, color. These are works of art in a new sense— because they reveal deeper, non-human systems of order beneath the surface of human activities and pretensions, forms that do not correspond to conventional human centered canons of symmetry, texture, or "beauty."

It was however the "formalizations" of Cézanne that, according to Sam Hunter, "virtually remade painting."[1] The artist reworked paintings made of landscapes of Provence until what emerged from the surface detail were underlying structures of lines and volumes. In a painting like "Still Life: Jar, Cup, and Fruit," he offers a purely geometrical play of rectangles, triangles, and circles. By rearranging objects according to their own, internal, formal logic, he unifies in single frontal plane what are (if we seek to draw the lines of force) multiple visual "points of view," thus, as Hunter says, shattering "all painting formulas based on traditional Renaissance perspective" (118). This is the beginning of cubist art, and the multi-perspectival paintings of Pablo Picasso—consummate "modern" works of art, that aim at transforming the way we see reality, replacing the human perspective with those of relativity and other scientific theories. The result is the removal of the human form, as normatively and conventionally perceived and depicted, from its role as central icon of Western art. Here is the true "science art," but what it has produced is (to our human eye) increasingly abstract products, "underlying" forms and dynamics, but with no identifiable human beings left to inhabit them.

But, for human viewers, the human form as icon is not abolished so easily. To such viewers, the positivist analysis of art leads to paralyzing dilemma. Lezlek Kolakowski, in his essay "The Two Eyes of Spinoza," sets forth the situation out of which sf art seems to have emerged. Benedict Spinoza, who in the seventeenth century was already telling us to study "human actions and desires as if [one] were dealing with lines, planes and bodies," could be the spiritual father of positivist science. Even so, as Kolakowski claims, this apostle of dehumanized unitarianism still, like all humans, has two eyes. Where one eye perceives a world order that is comprised of a single substance, subsuming mankind into nature, and making nature and God one and indistinguishable, the other eye still sees as a human does. As such, this eye laments that "to the world it is indifferent that we are a part of it . . . [that] there is no providence in the world . . . no protection, no reward and punishment, no good and evil . . . nature [and thus God] is not interested in our constructions." Under the gaze of Spinoza's scientific eye, humans are seen to engage in "powerless but self-deceiving self-observation, thanks to which we dream in our pitiful pride that we ourselves are the creative source of the mechanical motion which the totality of our physical actions exhaust."[2] The latter, to some, is a good description of sf and fantasy art—all powerless dreams of grandeur, proud self-deceptions. And yet, if Spinoza has a second eye, does not art deserve the same, an eye that seeks to relocate the human icon at the center of its field of technological artifacts and transformations?

The Images of Science

The representations of science fiction and fantasy art are, respectively, of the future and the past—not the present, which is the field of representation of canonical visual arts. There may be idealized, or allegorical worlds, but as in the paintings of Hieronymus Bosch and Pieter Breughel, the basis or "tenor" of the represented world is in general the artist's contemporary landscape. In terms of medium, however, the future of modern art on canvas is at best the wall of a museum, where images remain trapped in their frames. Sf and fantasy art, in contrast, is mobile and protean. It paints on an increasing variety of "canvases." First, there are black-and-white story illustrations, squeezed around titles and text inside the covers of magazines. Then we have color covers, offering a crude array of primary tints. Restraints abound here too. Frank R. Paul, for example, on the large folio-size covers of *Amazing Stories*, had to work around title lettering that ran from mid-left to upper-right, vertical to horizontal, forcing him to counterweight his images in the bottom right portion of the cover. The cover images proliferated, from pulp magazine to digest, to dust jackets and paperback covers. Though these covers begin as paintings, they are transferred to, and disseminated by, this mass distribution format. In a Philip K. Dick sense, not only in many instances are the original paintings lost, but artists' images migrate to so many venues (from sf magazines to astronomy magazines, popular science magazines, etc.), that the artist loses track of where and when a given painting appeared. For example, when the Eaton Collection acquired the effects of artist Maurice Dolens, there were no paintings; indeed, the only record of decades of his work was a collection of slides, many of which had no information as to title, origin, or date(s) of appearance. Paul's famous Cities of Tomorrow paintings, from the back covers of early 1940s *Amazing Stories*, have found themselves on covers and centerfolds of architecture magazines (*Arts + Architecture*, Summer 1984). They draw in the print medium from numerous sf covers; the lateral thrust of such future cities creates a tradition of film sets from *Just Imagine* (1931) to *Blade Runner* (1982) and beyond. Images from sf covers have moved into an increasing variety of domains—buildings, airplane design, urban planning, domestic appliances, animation films, role-playing games, and virtual reality constructs. These images are as widespread for our culture as was the ensemble of images and media that comprised the Gothic cathedral. If, as Brian W. Aldiss claims, the origin of sf and fantasy art is the Gothic, then it is *this* Gothic he must mean, in its totality of sculptured programs, bas reliefs, statues on pillars and cornices, gargoyles, and stained glass windows.

For the Romantics, cathedrals were replaced by "sublime" vistas of nature—vast forests, mountains, ice floes. Their vastness was reinforced by the spatiotemporal panoramas of geology, paleontology, ultimately evolutionary theory itself, that linked the expanses of past and future, and give us works like H. G. Wells's *The Time Machine*. Technology enforced these inhuman vistas. There was William Wordsworth's London and its mighty terrifying heart; or Emile Zola's Paris, with its monstrous metal distillery in *L'Assommoir*, or the ruthless excavations, Georges Haussmann's carving new thoroughfares and districts in *La Curée*; or Jules Verne's stultifying *Paris au XXe Siècle*. In the engravings in Verne novels (perhaps the first example of illustrated narratives), it is the fabulous, futuristic machines—rockets, submarines, flying ships—that dominate the human figures. They are dressed in contemporary garb, relegated to second or third rank in terms of size and volume. Sf art, then (Westfahl is correct in locating its *focused* beginnings in Hugo Gernsback's *Amazing*), represents a gradual process of reinstating the human form, as primary icon, in this dehumanized landscape we inherited from the visions of nineteenth-century science and technology. It was the latter who dredged up monstrous images from past and future—from the former, lost "races" and dinosaurs that time forgot, now made accessible by technological advancement, or H. P. Lovecraft's ancient race (and John W. Campbell, Jr.'s "things" in "Who Goes There!"); from the latter, the monstrous bivalves on the Time Traveller's terminal beach. Given such vistas, the problem sf and fantasy artists alike faced, perhaps for the first time since the cave painters of Lascaux, was to redefine what the human norm might be, to re-calibrate a "measure of man" in past and future worlds at a time when (through the eyes of canonical art) science was well on its way to abolishing not just the centrality but the *presence* of the human form in the vast sweep of macrocosmic and microcosmic events. Sf art exploits the paradox of our scientific age, where science works against the glory of man, yet remains a profoundly human activity. After all, for whose sake (from whose "point of view") does science redefine the limits of knowledge, if not ours, the reader, and viewer of images?

We need only slightly realign Isaac Asimov's famous definition of sf to have a definition of sf art: It is the form of painting that represents the impact of scientific and technological advancement on human beings. Fantasy art is easily included, for in our new era of time-folds and alternate universes, to "advance" may mean going back to bygone "heroic" times—witness Edgar Rice Burroughs's John Carter on Mars. In all events, this art form itself advances in the sense that it is an ongoing engagement of the scientific and cultural imagination with unfolding possibilities of the century, measuring and remeasuring, over and over, the size, proportion, and position of human figures *in relation to* other categories of being, both past and future—machines, cities, planets, organisms, mental or "invisible" phenomena, nonorganic "life" forms, and finally the void itself, the darkness of the infinitely large or small. But the purpose of sf art, in stark opposition to the "erasures" of canonical art, is to revision a human face or form in this dark canvas of modern science. Precisely, these artists play the game begun by Blaise Pascal, when in his humanist mathematics he redefines mankind as an inverse proportionality between the "two Infinities."[3] Pascal speaks as God, and each sf artist easily claims this role for himself in his works: "If he [mankind] exalt himself, I humble him; if he humble himself, I exalt him; and always I contradict him, till he understands that he is an incomprehensible monster."[4] Just as the act of understanding never reaches rest or finality in such a dynamic, so does the act of repositioning. In the ever shifting compositional play of proportionality that is sf/fantasy art, the human form, or its surrogate or analog, must abide, if only in some radically decentered position or form. In the words of Stanislaw Lem's Snow, human beings want mirrors, especially in dehumanizing surroundings. Sf art responds to this need, restoring familiar images at the heart of the unfamiliar, offering persistence of icons against the unvisualizable. The "city" at the end of Chris Marker's *Le Jetée* (1962) offers an example. We see an uninhabitable maze of abstract lines. Yet it is presided over by disembodied human heads, which, because they do not speak, retain a purely iconic role. In like manner, the images of the "time shots," or single, isolated frames, are both frames out of time, and virtual icons, forms that wait to be "animated" by the human act of telling this story of a logically impossible love.

Borrowings, Revisionings

Sf and fantasy art has borrowed techniques from modernist canonical art, but it is wrong to see here nothing but second-rate imitation. On the contrary, sf art has readapted or "revisioned" aspects of primitivism, surrealism, cubism, where these allow for a broadening of the iconic field of their representations. For perhaps the central concern of sf art is, precisely, to visualize transformations of the human form, and to represent encounters between humans and "alien" beings, whose shapes invariably involve distortions of a basic Homo sapiens anatomy, to include variations in size, hybridization, truncation, or "streamlining" of its form by removing salient details or simplifying others. Where such alienation effects are needed, we find artists using the gaudy colors of a Paul Gauguin or André Derain, the expressionist distortions of Vincent Van Gogh, Henri Matisse's green or purple faces, the flat wallpaper images and pointillist surface of Georges Seurat. The lush jungle landscapes, with skewed perspective and tangles of massive leaves and flowers, of Henri Rousseau appear over and over in fantasy art seeking to depict realms of the Carboniferous, or other deep time vistas. The levitating figures of Marc Chagall, or giant disembodied heads, such as that of Odilon Redon's "The Gnome," are everywhere, moving in zero-gravity space, or rising against vast cosmic vistas. The model for many evolutionary aliens (that is, evolved from the concept of human beings and their "inevitable" development, as are Wells's Martians) are minimalist figures like Joan Miró's "Person Throwing a Stone at a Bird," two connected conic forms ("head" and "body") on a single huge foot, no arms to "throw," but a stone falling down a geometrical arc, toward a "bird" that is a stick intersected by a curving line. Or we have the strange distorted, minimally recognizable, figures of a painting like Picasso's "Night Fishing at Antibes." The list could go on indefinitely.

Yet, the best way to demonstrate what sf and fantasy artists do with these borrowings is to analyze a few covers where techniques of cubist or surrealist art are present. What we discover is a very different relationship between painting and the "story" it tells. What strikes one about a work like "Night Fishing at Antibes" is the distance created between the human activity of the caption, and the visual world of shapes and forms in which this activity is carried out. The purpose of such captions on paintings of this sort is to accuse the distance between everyday "realistic" actions or visions, and the "alienated" images the artist puts before us on canvas. Sf artists also have captions for their paintings, usually the title of the story their picture represents. The text of these stories, however, is often about this very distance between human and alien worlds or states. The paintings then must suggest this "alien encounter," in many instances by using techniques adapted from canonical art. The purpose of sf art is not to widen the distance further, but rather to point to ways "back," to span the gap between alien and human landscapes and visions. For example, take Howard V. Brown's "cubist" cover for the January 1935 issue of *Astounding Stories*. It depicts a man, dressed in a military officer's uniform, breaking up before our eyes into the multi-perspectival planes common to cubist paintings. One is immediately reminded of Juan Gris's "Portrait of Picasso" (1911)—the same buttoned shirt-uniform, a similar leftward tilt of the multifaced cubes that comprise body and face. But at once apparent are the differences. Picasso's face is obscured by the facets; visual emphasis shifts to the mass of strong planes that form both body and background, rendering the boundaries between human figure and decor irrelevant. The purpose seems to be to efface the "being" of the artist, in terms of ability to act as "Picasso." The "caption" of Brown's painting, however, reveals a different connection between image and story. It illustrates a story by Frank K. Kelly, "Star Ship Invincible." With this title, without reading further, we understand why, in direct contrast to Gris's figure, this many-dimensional man's face is not fragmented, only the body. The decor that surrounds him, strange machinery from which the multidimensionality appears to emerge as by "rays" or sheets of form-bending light, is part of the invincible starship of which this man, with his dominating hand on chest *and* his unbroken smirking face, is captain. "Invincibility" clearly comes from the power to manipulate, at will, the cubist machine, to render one's physical being master of the relativist universe cubist painters revealed. But now the function of cubist art is reversed: it acts, in situations where multidimensional existence has literally become part of the story, to reinstate the human form, not abolish it.

Another two examples are notable. First the Alex Schomberg cover for the June 1961 cover of *Fantastic Stories of Imagination*, illustrating a story called "The Face in the Mask." The "mask" in question appears the place at which unidimensional reality breaks down. Radiating out from its eye is a sort of band or Moebius strip, creating a vaguely five-sided motif that echoes behind the head into fragmented planes of reality—jumbled lines and geometries that suggest a landscape of desolation. The mask itself, a face of ugly, distorted features, is melting like a Dali watch. What becomes interesting here, however, in contrast to the mask and its violence, is the possibility of a face behind it. The story "caption" points in this direction, not in the direction of multidimensionality, in which death lies. What we see, above the mask, is blond hair, a solid-shaped head, holding firm against the decomposing "tilt" of the mask. Below the round collar and white uniform of the classic "Lensman" of sf space opera, or that of a reassuring steward on a cosmic pleasure cruise. Implied in the iconography of this cover is a kind of axiology of styles. The way of cubist art is that of fragmentation of personality, disruption of reality by the misdirecting of human agency—as with the title of the magazine, the way of the fantastic. The way of classic sf space art, in contrast, points to clarity of direction, step-by-step "advancement," again in the literal sense. In his painting, by means of a contrast of styles that favors the human icon rather than its cubist deconstruction, Schomberg reverses the Jekyll-Hyde relationship. The evil twin is no longer the inner being; it is the mask, one in the process of melting away on its own.

Another cover, one that reinterprets futurist and surrealist vistas, is Emsh's (Edmund Emshwiller's) painting for Algis Budrys's "Lower than Angels," on the October 1956 issue of *Infinity Science Fiction*. The checkered foreground of this painting (reminiscent of Giorgio de Chirico landscapes, or more precisely of the checkerboard floors of Paul Delvaux's Brussels murals or his painting "L'Echo") is a giant chessboard. The left foreground is occupied by a naked woman, mounted on a pedestal composed of gleaming metal spikes that surround her body, impel its curve upward to two upheld hands, wrists encased in spikes, hands brandishing two daggers, pointed at a black cosmic landscape, from which (upper left corner) a giant black hand reaches down in menace. Below the hand, another "chesspiece" in this game of cosmic conquest or alien encounter is a needle-sharp spaceship, itself pointed toward the hand and the stars. Rushing toward the woman from the lower right zone—an orange rather than black "sky"—and knocking down conventional chesspieces, is a living "knight," a conventional spaceman, flag on helmet, holding raygun and space sword.

Once again, in the Emsh cover, the sterile geometries and empty planes and vistas of futurist and surrealist art witness their reawakening as cosmic drama. The hieratic statuary of surrealism begins to move, to break the spell of dream. Knocked over by renewed human activity, these chesspieces can no longer be reduced to symbolic "games," to a geometry of destiny, in which humans have become "moves" or permutations. On the contrary, the "queen" sheds symbolic form for a resplendent, defiant body, whose defiance momentarily pushes away the dark hand of the cosmic game player. Instead of symbols (for the surrealists the part of a broken vessel for which there is no corresponding half), we have a landscape of icons, whose presence summon deeper mythic activity and significance. Stepping from his pedestal into action is the knight become iconic spaceman, fusing the images of heraldry with those of high-technology weaponry. The queen awakens as amazon woman, whose bodily thrust causes the metal spikes that contained her to swirl in elegant curves to match those of her naked but metallic flesh. The giant hand, repulsed from the chessboard into a landscape of intergalactic suns, becomes a synecdoche for the menace and challenge of space, the abstraction of symbol now a concretizing trope, the physical part that stands for a physical whole. If the figures on the board are "lower than angels," this comparative reveals them aspiring upward, part of a new revolt of humans against the gods, in which conventional color symbols are replaced by iconic relationships. Black and white no longer designate devils and angels. The spaceman is a "black angel," who partakes of the same darkness of space as the hand, whose color, emerging from the void, may be simply that of flesh, all too human. Indeed, this painting, seen in contrast to the art techniques and forms it invokes, shows us a new way to interpret its images, this time as fundamentally human forms. These have again shattered the unconscious barriers to action set by surrealist dreams, defying by making literal the deep symbols of the oneiric state, replacing these with variations on the consciously striving, unadorned human form, reactivating dreamscapes as terrains of the human will.

Finally, let us look at an example of the most surrealist-seeming of sf art, the Richard M. Powers Ballantine cover for Arthur C. Clarke's *Expedition to Earth*. Clute has this to say of Powers's work: "He never illustrated a story directly; his Ballantine covers—looked at end from end—are an autonomous suite of images. They tell the dream of SF, in their own terms, indelibly."[5] Indeed, Powers's figures, in a general way, remind one of the abstract shapes of an Yves Tanguy. In this particular cover, however, which Clute chooses to illustrate the earlier statement, a connection with the Clarke narrative is visible, if we place that connection on the level of a general iconography, to fit the title *Expedition to Earth*—which sounds so generic we almost let it pass, till we are struck by the irony it bears. For are not we, the Earth people, the ones making "expeditions," to the moon, planets, stars? If we are dealing here with an alien invasion, or a superior civilization coming for first contact, then how can this narrative so easily and comfortably slide into their point of view? Indeed, the Powers painting is situated on alien ground, a flat plane of closed complex curves, like terrain lines on a map. Yet for a place so strange, it is at the same time very close, for the Earth is seen in this world's sky, with continents recognizable. The left foreground is dominated by a large abstract sculpture in the Henry Moore vein—a vaguely humanoid shape whose volumes suggest a "head," "arms," a base upon which it "stands" erect. In front of this "idol" (the viewer is invited to find such humanoid analogies) in the mid-right extreme foreground, we see a shape that suggests an animal, with seal-like head and body volumes. On the viewer's right, mid-cover, there is a parabolic thing, suggesting an antenna, a "listening device," in any case a machine-like entity. Already, in the eye of its human observer, seeing Earth from a new point of view, the landscape becomes less alien the more we look. What is more, between the "idol" and the "machine," we notice a small figure that is definitely that of a human being. However small, this figure casts a long, compensating shadow back across alien space all the way into the right lower corner of the composition. The shapes pointed Earthward cast no shadows in either direction. The human figure is receiving "Earthlight"—why else the shadow? Powers's painting indeed does tell a story, the iconic story all such covers, in one style or another, tell—that of reinsertion of the human icon at the center of new or alien landscapes, "alien" here signified by the presence of canonical art forms.

Toward an Iconology of Sf/Fantasy Art

To study these forms of art, produced by the widest diversity of artists for a number of formats or venues, yet all concurring to represent the "new" or alternate worlds summoned into being by the advances of science and technology, calls for the creation of a new system of analysis. The canonical art of this century is studied in terms of individual artists or "authors," and in terms of schools, movements—terms that designate collective "styles" as aggregate of individual ones. Value is placed on "genius"—the idiosyncratic or "original"—rather than the normative or collaborative vision. It is no longer what is painted that counts—landscapes, animals, and finally the human subject altogether dissolves under the analytical eye of the painter—but *how* it is painted. Sf/fantasy art is often touted, in contrast, as depicting or presenting *new landscapes and "worlds" in and for themselves*, things and places never before seen. In actuality, however, its force comes from its ability to substitute old worlds for new—to reconnect the visually new but devitalized images of modern art the collective myth that unites all ages of human endeavor, to bring forth the basic icons of human visual experience from the formal debris of cubism, surrealism, and other schools of art. Like all mythic forms of art, it calls for an iconic approach, if we are to understand its function and purpose.

Sf and fantasy art restores the anthropocentric vision; the human form remains its central presence, its determining icon. In the Powers cover, the small human figure and its shadow reinstate the measure of man in an otherwise alien landscape, by providing the form by which our eye begins to "decode" the strange shapes of the other figures in terms of a human iconology. It reenacts the trick first used by Pascal when he posited mankind as "thinking reed" at a median point between the infinitely large and the infinitely small, the terrifying vistas opened by modern science otherwise destined to engulf the human.[6] Pascal's reed, in terms of physical size and force, is crushed by a drop of water in this extended universe. At the same time, not denying this physical immensity, it seeks a form of parity with the infinite by claiming that if this world crushes us, it does not know it does so, while we, though annihilated, *know* we are crushed. A small consolation, yet it is from a similar gambit that the human icon is resurrected in thousands upon thousands of examples of sf/fantasy art.

The major sf icons then represent, in mythic fashion, the components of Pascal's new scientific world. First of all, the human form divides into multiple functions or physical stages or "roles": we have male figures, female figures, both young and old; we have children—figures as varied as Ray Bradbury's "small assassin" or Jerome Bixby's Little Anthony in "It's a *Good* Life," iconically summarized by Stanley Kubrick's "star child," an embryo's body but looking at us with the knowing eyes of myriad generations of fallen humanity. Male figures embody the broad sweep of human activity—from godlike figures to cringing victims of experiments gone wrong, of machines in revolt. Perhaps its central iconic representation is Hubert Rogers's painting of the Grey Lensman for the October 1939 cover of *Astounding Science-Fiction*. Here we face sf man in full frontal view, emerging from a metal space capsule, muscular body taut, hands clenched on hips in "fighting posture." Here is man surrounded by metal, yet the muscular creases of his gray uniform seem of harder metal yet. The gray form entirely dominates this cover, with boots posed defiantly on the metal ramp that runs to bottom center, and face and head (strong lines, strong color of flesh) rise to pierce the letters ASTOUNDING that define the top of the composition.

Female figures as well appear in multiple roles: goddess, seducer, witch, victim. sf and fantasy art runs the gamut here. There are innumerable scenes of cosmic rape, women beset by all forms of monstrous attackers, from repulsive aliens to degenerate humanoids, beaten and chained, ultimately rescued by a handsome male figure, either with ray gun or with sword, in deep space or some dark elsewhen, place and weapon are completely interchangeable. The female figure also serves as foil, as on the fascinating F. Anderson cover for November 1951 *Planet Stories*, which illustrates the Stanley Mullen story, "The Pit of Nymphthons." In this composition, the foreground is occupied by a woman (the largest figure in the painting) screaming and ducking in fear of the terrifying spectacle behind her. She is also beset by a leech-like creature latching on to her body. Behind her back, a man without shirt, pistol strapped to waist, charges a "bug-eyed" monster, hurling a World War II grenade at it. Arching above this low-tech scene is a vast horseshoe-like structure, from which another female figure, naked and hieratically frontal, is being "conceived" in a crackle of electric fire. It seems that, over and over, the female figure fails, and is reconceived, yet born not of man and woman, but from some machine. The specter of the Fall, and the primacy of the first cause, the generation of man from woman, plays itself out in this iconic drama.

Reinforcing this "goddess" position, many female figures on covers are oversized. In Rogers's Grey Lensman painting, although the male figure dominated the cover, it remained in proportion with objects surrounding it. Male god figures, in contrast, are often truncated, male heads in huge proportion. Giant female heads are rarer. An example is Walter Popp's cover for the December 1952 issue of *Thrilling Wonder Stories*. Depicted here are giant male and female heads, overseeing the apparently scientific activities of tiny humans, themselves engaged in pondering symbols on a three-sided checkerboard structure. Around the upper reaches of the composition is an aura of fiery energy, that encompasses the male head in an aura. This head, in intense concentration on the humans and their activities, wears a device of "wisdom" on his forehead, and is apparently the guiding force for all he surveys. The woman, in contrast, exists outside the aura, and her face is awestruck, amazed at the goings-on, but clearly not controlling them. And yet, in opposition to a figure like Grey Lensman, most goddess females are full-length figures, not disembodied heads (which no doubt suggests that the essence of male godhood is reason). One of the most striking of these female goddesses appears in the Earle Bergey cover for the March 1951 issue of *Startling Stories*, illustrating Leigh Brackett's "The Starmen of Llyrdis." Against a backdrop of stars and planets, a long gray (no doubt phallic) spaceship moves right to left, mid-cover to bottom, across the cover, plunging into a "sun" on the lower-left. Rising above this sun, occupying the entire left side of the composition is a huge female figure, whole from head to waist. Her head touches the title "STARTLING." Her shoulders are bare, and she wears an evening dress of resplendent material. Her head glitters with stars, and her face is that of a 1950s "sophisticate," lipstick and all. One white-gloved hand (elegant mid-length evening gloves) rests on her hip, the other raises a glass of celestial champagne in toast. Here is a figure coaxing, provoking, toasting male feats of technological prowess: a bitch goddess of the spaceways, modern incarnation of the fickle goddesses of Olympus. There are many such full-length female figures on sf/fantasy covers. Far from Vivian Sobchack's "virgins," these are creatures of power, in the sense that they are "makers" of men, in all manners literal and figurative. Their champagne cup itself has an iconic life of its own, in association with feats of male technology. For example, on Solonevich's cover for the September 1962 issue of *Analog*, illustrating James Blish's *A Life for the Stars*, part of his Cities in Flight series, we find the flying city encased in a spherical "force field," the bottom of which (in homage perhaps to Bergey's woman) looks like the stem of a giant champagne cup, in which the city itself sits.

The other major icons of sf/fantasy art are extensions of the central presence of the human form. Closest to the human is the group animal/insect/"creatures," forms that harken back (moving through the brief period of "animal art" in the late eighteenth century, and medieval bestiaries) to ancient totemic art. Then, moving from the organic to inorganic forms, we have machines. Finally, there are the cities and habitats, forms that make the farthest reach (along with inhabitable machines, such as space stations and generational starships) into the non-human realms of space, void, "hostile" nature. With the animal/insect forms, "recapture" of the human form occurs in a fashion that merely inverts the degradation of that form in medieval sculptural ensembles, such as adorned the entrances to Romanesque churches. Here, the bestialized forms of the damned, and the grotesque animal-human hybrids of the devils who herd their souls, stand in iconic contrast to the pure forms of the elect, and in their center Christ in majesty. Sf and fantasy art, again using Pascal's inverse proportionality, will represent aliens as beings superior to humans in terms of sheer force (as denoted by their physical size in the composition). At the same time, however, they will recapture them by giving them human characteristics, traits befitting our upright position, even where the logic of their own anatomy would prohibit this. The giant insect on Paul's cover for the October 1926 issue of *Amazing Stories*, for instance, occupies the entire right side of the composition, its antennae bending to avoid the large letters "AMAZING" that curve right to left. Given its position of iconic prominence however, the figure is forced, in the viewer's eye, to take on human traits. Thus we see it, despite its many terrifying "arms," reaching out and gently touching the smaller ragged human figure (obviously shipwrecked on this insect planet), as if seeking to communicate rather than destroy.

A like transformation by virtue of position occurs on the famous cover of the July 1939 issue of *Astounding Science-Fiction* by Graves Gladney. Here, occupying the entire left half of the painting is the huge black mass of a satanic-looking feline figure, fangs bared, orange eyes the same color as the lurid sky of its planet. Yet despite such signs of hostility, this "black destroyer" is not ready to pounce on the unsuspecting human spaceship in the lower left. Instead it crouches, tail curled like a large domestic cat, more a tutelary figure than a destroyer for the human charges it oversees. Alien menace is thus domesticated. The same is true for the otherwise visually menacing figures by artist John Schoenherr found on the covers of *Analog* for Anne McCaffrey's Dragonrider stories. In the October 1967 cover for "Weyr Search," a looming dragon figure—massive body and long powerful neck—dominates the left side of a skyline aswarm with flying dragons, tiny humans on their backs—dwarfing the humans in the foreground. More striking yet, intercrossed wings and curved necks of giant dragons dominate the December 1967 cover. In this painting, however, it is clear that, if the humans are tiny by contrast, they are clearly the pattern masters of their elegant flight, seen here in the graceful forms of the creatures as they land.

On sf covers, encounters with animal "monsters" are not depictions of alien menace and destruction so much as reenactments of the human technomyth implicit in mankind's mastery of leviathan, behemoth, and dragon, whereby the evermetamorphosing forces of nature these creatures represent is controlled, turned into an object of aesthetic contemplation. This is clear on the Robert Gibson Jones cover for the January, 1949 issue of *Fantastic Adventures*, illustrating "The Return of Sinbad." In its anachronistic mix of images, the cover depicts "hostile" spaceships blasting away at a giant roc, whose form dominates the left side of the composition, and whose flowing feathers cover its entire lower edge. On the bird's back, in flowing cape and turban, sits Sinbad, the image of humankind's early mastery of natural power, once more pitting that mastery against abuses of such control—the inorganic machine forms that rush in from the inhuman void of deep space to attack.

The machine icon (as more than Frankenstein) represents a more problematic extension of human science and technology, because its form is less easy to reclaim by hybridization, or to reposition in relation to the human form, even when ostensibly created in its image. Behind this icon is not the logic of the dragon, but that of Cartesian *res extensa*, where all that is not human, hence rational, is a machine. Indeed, in sf covers from the beginning, machines appear as a far more menacing, ultimately dehumanizing, presence. Paul's unforgettable cover for the August 1927 issue of *Amazing*, illustrating Wells's *The War of the Worlds*, shows giant striding machines, left top to bottom right in positions of iconic authority, routing hordes of tiny humans. The Wesso cover for the August 1930 issue of *Amazing*, illustrating E. E. "Doc" Smith's *Skylark Three*, depicts a huge spaceship sectioned by a meteor-like "force" that carries away a portion of its engine room, gears and rotors exposed. In this battle of non-human forms, human figures are so tiny as to be almost unnoticeable, indistinguishable from the cogs and wheels of the giant machine. Such landscapes are common in the 1950s covers for *The Magazine of Fantasy and Science Fiction*, where no human forms appear, simply machines, "exploring" dead surfaces of planets, against the backdrop of empty space.

Sf art imposes one other icon between human and non-human: the city, itself in most cases a larger version of the walking machines (robots) and flying machines. On covers depicting them, cities tend also to demand iconic predominance. One thinks of the Leo Morey covers for *Amazing*, notably the March 1935 cover, which depicts a massive, machine-like city stretching as far as the eye can see, over which a lone capsule containing two humans flies. Or, the architectural visions of Paul: the December 1932 *Wonder Stories* cover, depicting a huge yellow arcology, itself projecting a sphere-like habitat, a "hive" around which swarm tiny human "bees"; or the famous *Amazing* backcovers, especially the "City of the Future" painting (April 1942) which, like pistons in some giant machine, offers rows of like spires and domes, parallel causeways on which human ants move in orderly rows. In these paintings, cities become the cruelest extensions of the human form. For in order for them to house us, they cannot (like the robot, or the spaceship) take our form, but we must take theirs, the form of machine efficiency. Our fate then is to leave them behind (the William Timmins cover for the October 1946 issue of *Astounding Science-Fiction*), or worse, to discover, like Lem's astronauts in *The Invincible*, that distant aliens have done what we apparently cannot—abandoned the "city" for other forms of habitation and existence, while we are doomed to see cities everywhere.

From Iconology to Iconography

One can analyze sf/fantasy art in terms of its historical development—as an art form responding to successive "periods" of cultural change. Or one can discuss it as a series of talented artists, each artist shaping the form from within, often in contrast to reigning models of taste, decorum, social "meaning." Yet, if one examines paintings from the Gernsback period to today, one is aware of the iconic constancy beneath surface changes. We see in sf art what seems a parade of different "styles" and formats, new and evermore sophisticated technologies. Its metanarrative appears to follow the relentless march from J. D. Bernal's "world," to "flesh" (machine-bio-organism-human transformations), to "devil," ultimate abandonment of human brain and thought patterns altogether. And yet, if there is a story told by sf art, it remains (despite these changes) the story of the human form itself, menaced, extended, resilient. The covers of early issues of *Amazing Stories* show humans beset by giant creatures, insects, machines. The later covers of Morey and Paul offer titanic cityscapes; the bleak vistas of space art in the 1950s further reduce the human to machine surrogates—small spacecraft circling dead planets against a backdrop of blackest void. Cyberpunk covers of the *Omni* school offer abstractions of circuitry, fractal geometry, heavy metal surfaces. And yet, as with Pascal's reed, a human presence abides in each of these alienated landscapes, if only as implicit presence, the norm by which we measure the exaggerated size, the outlandish importance of forms that usurp its centrality. In the March 1935 Morey cover, the focal point of the vast cityscape is the small, human space capsule, yellow against black, that sits at its center. In Paul's cities on Mars and elsewhere, the rows of sleek, machine-like buildings are ironically inhabited by animal forms, or flying ray-like creatures, "lower" life forms, which point to a necessity for the eye to re-position the human norm between icons of evolution and devolution. Or take Frank Kelly Freas's famous March 1954 *Astounding Science-Fiction* cover, depicting the giant robot holding a frail, wounded human in his metal hand. The blood on the robot's finger, matching that on the human's chest, is a move beyond Pascal. For if an inadvertent poke of the machine crushes the human, now the machine knows that it crushes, and grieves. Beasts, cities, machines—all are re-humanized. As is space itself. The Emsh cover for the April 1954 issue of *The Magazine of Fantasy and Science Fiction* is an example. At first glance, the iconic distribution seems typical—tiny human, monolithic metal spaceship, void of blackest space. But in this painting a blowup happens, the massive ship is about to topple after a failed takeoff, humans are on the run. The comic irony of this painting is that these humans, effaced by their machine creations when they are successful, recover their humanity by making an error. Even cyberpunk art, for all its pretensions, remains an art of recovery. Richard Berry's typical cover for William Gibson's *Burning Chrome* offers a cyber "construct," a pixillated shimmer, suggesting multiple planes of circuitry, chrome, strobelights, being no longer locatable in conventional iconic spacetime. Yet, look again, behind the "electronic" pulsations there are the outlines of a human face.

The iconological dynamic of sf/fantasy art, comprised of a few basic icons in endless permutation according to shape, size, and position around a central human median, is simple, indeed as simple (and central to the question of the rise of a culture of science) as it was in the century of René Descartes and Blaise Pascal. Yet plotting these transformations—creating a spacetime iconography of such forms—is a massive job, one that begins in earnest in this volume. Formerly, this form of art has had little consideration. When such occurred, it either considered its works as mere "illustrations," secondary to the literature it served, or offered a set of paintings, without analysis or connection to the larger field of sf, in coffee table books that we do not seek to compete with, though we list several of them in our comprehensive bibliography as resources. This volume instead offers perhaps the first serious collaborative attempt to examine these art forms in their broadest context. It contains chapters by critics (John Clute, John Grant, Gary Westfahl) who are capable of encyclopedic vision in considering sf/fantasy art in relation to both sf literature and sf culture. There are also chapters by critics (Kathleen Church Plummer, Howard V. Hendrix, Gregory Benford, Samuel H. Vasbinder) able to relate specific areas of its production to the general stock of images—both in painting and architecture—of this century, as well as chapters (by Kirk Hampton and Carol MacKay, Lynne Lundquist and Gary Westfahl, Beatrix Karthaus-Hunt, and David Hinckley) that examine the careers of major authors and/or artists (Richard M. Powers, Margaret Wise Brown and Clement Hurd, J. R. R. Tolkien, Robert E. Howard and Frank Frazetta) as another vector to explore this field.

While inevitably failing to provide complete coverage of the vast and complex realms of sf and fantasy art, these critics, in their collective sense of the richness, importance, and cultural impact of these images, have taken a crucial first step toward realizing an iconography of this art form.

Notes

1. Sam Hunter, *Modern French Painting* (New York: Dell Books, 1956), 120. Later page references in the text are to this edition.

2. Lezlek Kolakowski, "The Two Eyes of Spinoza," in *Spinoza: A Collection of Critical Essays,* edited by Marjorie Grene (Notre Dame, IN: University of Notre Dame Press, 1979), 287-88.

3. Blaise Pascal, *Pensées,* #72, in Pascal, *Pensées and the Provincial Letters,* translated by W. F. Trotter (New York: Random House, 1941), 26.

4. Pascal, *Pensées,* # 420, in Pascal, *Pensées and the Provincial Letters,* 232.

5. John Clute, *Science Fiction: The Illustrated Encyclopedia* (New York: Dorling Kindersley, 1995), 241.

6. Pascal, *Pensées,* #347, in Pascal, *Pensées and the Provincial Letters,* 116.

Part I

Approaches to
Science Fiction Art

2

Artists in Wonderland:
Toward a True History of
Science Fiction Art

Gary Westfahl

While there have been several books about science fiction art, none of them, from the perspective of a literary scholar, seem to be well organized in the manner of a true history, which would divide the field into different eras, explain the principles and philosophies that guided artists in each era, and describe how artists of following eras either built upon or rejected the approaches of their predecessors. Instead, books on science fiction art tend either to proceed mechanically in chronological order or to group artworks by subject matter, with chapters on aliens, women, spacecraft, and so on.[1] Surely, one might argue, we need a more systematic framework for such discussions.

There are two basis hypotheses we might employ as a premise for a history of science fiction art. First, we could assume that science fiction art is an essentially autonomous tradition that has developed and evolved entirely according to its own internal dynamics, or perhaps in parallel to the general history of high art or commercial art. But the assumption is intuitively implausible; after all, the vast majority of science fiction artworks were based on and published with specific science fiction stories, and in a few cases, science fiction artworks have inspired original stories. Science fiction literature and art were supervised by the same editors and publishers and presented to the same readers; and both writers and artists were accepted as members of the same science fiction community. (In fact, the Guest of Honor at the first World Science Fiction Convention in 1939 was artist Frank R. Paul.) While some later artworks do display a certain autonomy from the stories they accompany—Brian W. Aldiss argues that "[t]oday, their relationship to text is often generic rather than specific"[2]—it is difficult to argue that there has been no relationship at all between science fiction literature and science fiction art.

If we turn to the alternative hypothesis—that the history of science fiction art is closely connected to the history of science fiction literature—we must decide how to characterize the history of science fiction. According to one argument, science fiction is one current in Western literature that first emerged as a distinctive form in Mary Shelley's *Frankenstein* and was later best represented by writers like Jules Verne, H. G. Wells, Olaf Stapledon, Philip K. Dick, Stanislaw Lem, Ursula K. Le Guin, and William Gibson. To produce a history of science fiction art following this model, we would seek out the texts of these great writers, observe the art that accompanied those texts, and deduce a tradition to place that art in a coherent pattern of development and evolution. By another argument, which I favor, science fiction is best regarded as those texts that emerged from an understanding of the *idea* of science fiction, so that the genre was born in 1926 with Hugo Gernsback's *Amazing Stories* and its central texts are the works published in the magazines and paperbacks that were inspired by Gernsback's ideas and written for the science fiction community he established. To produce a history of science fiction art following this model, we would begin with the art in *Amazing Stories* and continue to observe the art of magazines and paperbacks, relating that art to major developments in the literature of that tradition.

Evidence that this later approach would be superior ironically comes from a critic who vigorously promoted the first approach to science fiction literature—Brian Aldiss. Having maintained in *Billion Year Spree: The True History of Science Fiction* (expanded as *Trillion Year Spree: The History of Science Fiction*) that science fiction is a form of Gothic literature first seen in *Frankenstein*, he must maintain that science fiction art is a form of Gothic art first seen in the company of *Frankenstein*; thus, his "Introduction" to *Science Fiction Art* begins by reproducing the Frontispiece from the 1831 edition of *Frankenstein* and asserting that "sf [literature] and Gothic are inseparably intertwined. The same holds true for sf illustration." However, he admits that the *Frankenstein* picture "is not an outstanding piece of work,"[3] and after discussing two nineteenth-century Gothic artists, he abandons any attempt to parallel *Billion Year Spree*, instead drifting into a general discussion of science fiction art in the magazines and arranging his book by artists and topics. He even says elsewhere that "Before the SF magazines, there is little that can be regarded as pure generic sf illustration."[4] Aldiss thus acknowledges that his framework for a study of science fiction literature will not serve as a framework for a study of science fiction art.

I propose, then, to employ the history of science fiction literature, as I characterize it, to provisionally construct a history of science fiction art. To summarize a standard view of the genre's history: first, in the 1920s, Gernsback championed and elicited a form of science fiction that juxtaposed narrative with explanations of scientific fact and detailed descriptions of proposed inventions; call this Gernsbackian science fiction. In the 1930s, writers moved to a form of science fiction that reduced science to jargon and nonsense and emphasized exciting adventures, at times mixed with adolescent eroticism; Edmund Hamilton was its most energetic practitioner, and we now call it space opera. In the 1940s, reacting against both Gernsback's didacticism and the immaturity of space opera, John W. Campbell, Jr.'s *Astounding Science-Fiction* supported a form of science fiction that grew out of careful scientific extrapolation and logic; in the hands of later writers, this became what we call hard science fiction. In the 1950s, editor H. L. Gold of *Galaxy* and others inspired a form of science fiction that again deemphasized science, not for exciting adventure but for humor, satire, and improved writing; call this, for lack of a better term, 1950s science fiction. In the 1960s, Michael Moorcock and Harlan Ellison promoted a form of science fiction dedicated to literary quality and stylistic experiments, known as New Wave science fiction. The 1970s, engendering no new form of science fiction, were a decade of breath-catching, consolidation, and nostalgia that combined the lingering New Wave, a new interest in hard science fiction, and a resurgence of space opera (*Star Trek, Star Wars*, and so on). The 1980s and 1990s, however, brought another form of science fiction, cyberpunk, that juxtaposed a fascination with technology, hard-nosed cynicism, and flashy style; William Gibson's *Neuromancer* was its exemplary text and Bruce Sterling its major spokesperson.

Of course, caveats must be attached to any potted history of this kind. First, despite advocates' claims, each new form of science fiction was not a complete departure from tradition, but rather acknowledged and reflected to varying extents the influence of previous forms. Thus a concern for minimal scientific accuracy—Gernsback's priority—has persisted through each changing of the guard in science fiction, and cyberpunk can been viewed as an effort to simultaneously fulfill Campbell's scientific agenda and the New Wave's aesthetic agenda. Second, each type of science fiction, despite changing attitudes, has persisted in its pure form, though its texts may become small in number or relegated to the sidelines. The proof of this is in any modern bookstore, where you can still find examples of Gernsbackian science fiction—though you may have to look in the juvenile section—along with space opera, hard science fiction, satire, New Wave science fiction, and cyberpunk. Finally, though models of this kind should be generally accurate, there will always be a few writers who refuse to fit in the pigeonholes; for example, while Cordwainer Smith might be described as a writer who produced New Wave science fiction before the New Wave, he more accurately seems *sui generis*, a writer dedicated to producing science fiction of his own unique variety, oblivious to any trends, past, present, or future.

If science fiction art is closely linked to science fiction literature, we should be able to construct a history of science fiction art along these lines. There should be six eras of science fiction art, corresponding chronologically and thematically to the eras of science fiction literature; there should probably, but not necessarily, be one artist in each era to usefully represent its character, just as figures like Gernsback, Campbell, Gold, and Sterling usefully represent their literary eras; each new era should in part incorporate or reflect the priorities of previous eras; each form of science fiction art should be found to endure in its pure form to the present day; and there should be a few exceptional artists who fail to conform to these patterns.

As is usually the case when critics assign tasks to themselves, I find that it is in fact possible to sketch such a history of science fiction art.

To identify the first form of science fiction art, recall that Gernsback defined science fiction as a mixture of narrative, scientific fact, and prediction, designed to provide entertainment for the masses, education for young readers, and stimulating ideas for working scientists;[5] what form of art might achieve these goals? First the art must be realistic or representational; some forms of abstraction—like charts or schematic diagrams—might be useful for scientists, but not the general public or youngsters. To be entertaining, the art must be colorful and imaginative; but to offer scientific education or ideas, it must be painstakingly accurate and precisely designed. Gernsback was fortunate to have an artist who produced exactly this sort of art: Frank R. Paul.

To see why Paul is justly regarded as the first and greatest science fiction artist, consider his cover painting for the August 1927 issue of *Amazing Stories* depicting H. G. Wells's *The War of the Worlds*. For entertainment, the colors are striking and well-chosen: against the background of a jarringly serene blue sky, the Martian war machines shine with reflected light from the bright red fires of the burning city; and the ingenious detail of a man fleeing from the Martians *on horseback* graphically contrasts the advanced Martians with the primitive humans. For educational purposes, the machines are drafted with engineering precision, right down to their flexible knee joints, and Paul adds one feature not mentioned by Wells—gripping claws on the feet of the machines—perhaps to explain why such apparently unstable machines would not easily topple over, and perhaps to provide a helpful suggestion for an inventor planning to build such machines.[6]

Trained as an architect, Paul skillfully depicted gigantic future cities—a visual trope that he perfected. Consider his cover of Hamilton's "Cities in the Air" for the November 1929 issue of Gernsback's *Air Wonder Stories*. Highlighted by an incongruous pink background, Paul's flying New York is magnificent in its exact circularity, its multitude of yellow buildings, and tiny cylindrical airships and the Earth below to suggest its immensity. Yet Paul's triumphs are not entirely architectural; in painting "Serenis, Water City of Callisto" for the December 1941 issue of *Amazing Stories*, he offered not only arrays of white columned buildings surrounding a huge fountain, but the spectacle of nearby Jupiter filling the sky, boats on a canal of green water, and four-armed, blue-skinned aliens, including the nice image of an alien woman in the foreground tenderly feeding her iguana-like pets. Here is an alien world of evocative detail beyond the ability of most contemporary writers.

However, this painting—for editor Ray Palmer—reveals a side of Paul that did not interest Gernsback, who primarily viewed him as an adjunct to his didactic and predictive agenda. In every Gernsback magazine, the table of contents page briefly described the cover—in part, no doubt, to prove that the covers were honest advertisements for stories in his magazines, but also to emphasize their educational and scientific value. In the July 1926 issue of *Amazing*, the caption noted that the giant insect was "the Tse-tse fly";[7] the caption describing the cover of the July 1929 issue of *Science Wonder Stories* said, "Mr. Paul, our artist, has shown how, under certain conditions, it is possible for a single man to lift the 60,000 ton steamship *Leviathan* without straining his muscles";[8] and the caption on the cover of the July 1929 issue of *Air Wonder Stories* maintained that

Mr. Paul, has cleverly portrayed in his inimitable style what one of these future aerial islands will look like. . . . science will conquer gravitation sooner or later, and when that moment comes . . . we will have islands like these, floating freely, suspended above our cities and important aerial crossings. They will be used not only for the regulation of air traffic, but for making emergency stops and to allow passengers to change from local to express lines without ever descending to the surface of the earth.[9]

According to other captions the cover of the August 1929 issue of *Science Wonder Stories* "illustrated Captain Noordung's [space station]. . . . the space house proper . . . has a total diameter of about 150 feet. The wide curved surfaces are the reflectors which collect and concentrate the sun's heat. Attached to the space house by means of flexible cables, at the left is shown the observatory and at the upper right the engine house. All three objects remain fixed in space, there being no gravity to dislodge them";[10] an aerial battle on the cover of the August 1929 issue of *Air Wonder Stories* "demonstrates the tremendous power of atomic rays once they have been developed, as they surely will";[11] the cover of the October 1929 issue of *Science Wonder Stories* is "a graphic as well as vivid picturization by our inimitable artist Paul, of what happens when scientists of the future will make it possible for us to get a sort of television picturization of our sub-conscious memories";[12] the cover of the October 1929 issue of *Air Wonder Stories* shows "how the special air car moves at the rate of over one thousand miles an hour, through the artificially created vacuum in the air tunnel. By electrical means the inside of the air tunnel becomes a vacuum in which the onrushing car moves free of friction";[13] and the cover of the January 1930 issue of *Air Wonder Stories* shows "'The Thunderer' drying up one of our lakes by decomposing the water into its elements. With his airship held stationary in the air he lets down two electric cables. A spark passing between them decomposes the water."[14] Just as Gernsback's editorials taught readers how to read science fiction, these comments were teaching readers how to read science fiction art—not only explaining the literal meaning of the pictures, by also pointing out that they depict scientific facts—involving gravity, the properties of a vacuum, or electrolysis—and plausible future developments—like flying cities, space stations, visualized memories, or atomic rays.

It should be noted that, from Gernsback's perspective, Paul's most frequently cited flaw—flat or awkward people—was not really a liability. Gernsback's theory of science fiction never mentioned a need for realistic or complex characterization; an entertaining narrative to serve as a framework for scientific education and prophecy could be achieved just as well with stock characters. Indeed, well-drawn characters, in both fiction and art, might inappropriately distract readers from the important lessons and ideas in science fiction. Thus, in both his strengths and weaknesses, Paul perfectly reflected Gernsback's priorities.

We might call Paul's style of painting *futurist science fiction art*, to acknowledge its kinship to the futurist movement in art and architecture of the early twentieth century that Gibson pays tribute to in "The Gernsback Continuum" and is most easily seen by modern readers in the sets of the films *Metropolis* (1926) and *Things to Come* (1936). Paul did not necessarily share the futurists' technophilia and optimism—the Wells cover reminds us that massive constructs may be sinister as well as inspirational—but there was in both futurist art and Paul an excitement about future possibilities, images of gigantic buildings laid out with stark geometry, and a sense that future developments would both dwarf individual humans and embody human desires. And the influence of Paul is visible in later science fiction art, most notably in Hubert Rogers, whose 1940s covers for *Astounding Science-Fiction* were only more somber versions of Paul's visions.

While Paul remained active and popular in the 1930s, science fiction art began to change, reflecting changes in science fiction literature. While Gernsback had resisted making his magazines true pulp magazines, using a different size and different quality of paper, his and other magazines were reduced by the Depression to true pulp status, and their contents began to reflect the contents of pulp magazines: writers increasingly paid little attention to scientific accuracy or logic and emphasized exciting adventures involving space travel, other planets, and aliens. Several artists might be chosen to represent the new style of art that emerged; but it seems fitting to discuss the artist known as the "inventor of the brass brassière," Earle K. Bergey.[15] True, as Peter Nicholls and John Grant note, he "was by no means restricted to the subject matter that made him famous,"[16] and his cover for the February 1941 issue of *Thrilling Wonder Stories*, for example, is reminiscent of Paul in its cosmic perspective and stiff figures—though Gernsback would have rejected the scientific absurdity of sending a message to space by means of a huge illuminated sign across the face of the United States. However, his covers for the Winter 1946 and September 1948 issues of *Startling Stories* reveal that he did indeed often feature that singular garment. Here we quickly see departures from Paul's style: while Paul's people were often small in relation to their surroundings, Bergey's people are large and foregrounded; Bergey's people look more realistic and natural than Paul's; Bergey's art tends to be less faithful to the stories depicted—I recall no scene of a woman in a brass brassière fleeing through space in Fredric Brown's *What Mad Universe*; and there is clearly little concern for scientific accuracy—Bergey surely knew that a woman flying through space would have to wear more than a space helmet and brassière. We also see in these two covers the three archetypal images of space opera, immortalized by one reader as "the guy, the girl, and the goon": handsome hero, scantily-clad heroine, and hideous monster. This might be termed true *pulp science fiction art*, since it clearly derives from the style of other pulp magazine illustrations.

Much of this art invites or demands little critical comment, especially when artists seem to compete to get away with exposing the greatest expanse of female flesh or to envision the most loathsome aliens. However, when the Vargas girls are omitted and a story provides an interesting idea, the results can be striking. Consider Howard V. Brown, who produced a famous cover for the November 1939 issue of *Startling Stories*.[17] While it is unlikely that efforts to save Earth's animal life from disaster would so exactly mimic the iconic imagery of Noah's Ark, we can still admire this cover, with its huge spaceship in bold primary colors, pairs of exotic creatures marching up the ramp, and guards holding back angry mobs.

Another Brown cover, for the April 1934 issue of *Astounding Stories*, features the familiar space opera triangle—handsome hero and beautiful woman threatened by bizarre alien—but the image of an immense staring eye on a box protruding from a spaceship and emitting a strange gas (or sound?) is unusually evocative. I recall this cover because when I showed some books of science fiction art to my son when he was five years old, he was especially fascinated by this picture. In the best of pulp art, then, abandoning concerns for scientific accuracy or geometric precision can generate a novel juxtaposition of the familiar and the bizarre that is, at least at first, a primary attraction of science fiction; capturing the imagination of a five-year-old, one might argue, is what the "sense of wonder" is all about.

However, Brown is more important for his role in launching the third era of science fiction art, though the instigator of the change was Campbell, who assumed control of *Astounding* in 1938. To please Campbell, the style of science fiction had to be modified: Gernsback was happy to see science fiction as entertainment for the masses, and that was certainly the guiding philosophy behind space opera, but Campbell believed science fiction should appeal only to an educated elite—"no average mind can either understand or enjoy science-fiction"[18]—and its serious purposes were to sharpen the thought processes of budding scientists and guide policymakers in their important decisions regarding future technology.[19] To create art that would appropriately accompany such science fiction, the gaudy colors of Paul and the heroic posturings of pulp art would have to go. Campbell's priorities might be served simply by a more subdued version of Paul's art, which as noted is essentially what was provided by Rogers, the usual cover artist for *Astounding* in the 1940s; Campbell celebrated a toning-down in science fiction art as early as October 1938, when he said, "Already, *Astounding* has taken the word *garish* from the description vocabulary of its covers." But Campbell first desired a particular kind of serious science fiction art—one which, he went on to say, "will add even more of the factor *reality*"[20]—and he chose Brown to create it.

The first example of this new style of art appeared on the cover of the February 1938 issue of *Astounding Stories*, and Campbell unusually devoted most of his editorial to describing it:

The cover is the first of a series—a new *mutant* field opened to science fiction. . . . Howard Brown and I worked over this cover, I trying to get the astronomy accurate; Brown, helping in the more difficult work of interpretation of fact to human understanding. . . . the Sun? It's much too large, really. . . . But that is where Brown's knowledge of the psychology and mechanism of human vision played its part. If he had painted that Sun as it would appear to a camera . . . on Mercury—the color-plate would not have given an accurate representation of *what you would see if you were there*. Human vision is not purely a physical process; it involves physics, but is subjected to the modifying effect of psychology. . . . Brown has off-set that human failing of the eyes. The Sun is disproportionately large, but accurately disproportionate. And as in this first *mutant* cover, our astronomical color-plate covers will be as accurate an impression as astronomical science and knowledge of human reaction can make them.[21]

This is the first manifesto on behalf of what we now call *space art*: realistic pictures of outer space or other worlds as they would appear to a human observer on the scene. Note how carefully Campbell describes the *process* of creating such art; Campbell later asserted that the science in science fiction should be more than a presentation of facts, but a detailed, logical *extrapolation* from the known to the unknown, and he discussed how Robert A. Heinlein employed that technique in his Future History stories. Here, he anticipates the principle in describing the need for careful preparation and thought in creating science fiction art.[22]

The cover itself is not impressive, but the contrast between this and previous science fiction art is dramatic enough to justify Campbell's hyperbole. In a way, we have moved away from the focus on human figures in pulp art back to Paul's epic vision, yet the immensities are not human constructs but natural wonders; and the intense black sky dominating the scene, brightened only by a stark yellow sun, conveys a sense of solemnity that Paul neither aspired to nor achieved. Brown did a better cover for the November 1938 issue of *Astounding*: the picture of a huge, partially eclipsed Jupiter dominating the Ganymedean sky, watched by tiny spacesuited figures, vividly depicts frail human beings striving to master a forbidding environment—and provokes emotions that had never before been stirred by science fiction art. Again Campbell devoted an editorial to the cover, which he had previously called "one of the best science-fiction covers ever published."[23]

As it happens, the *Astounding* covers of the 1940s by Brown and others were not predominantly of this type—I suspect that issues with such covers did not sell especially well—but as painted by artists like the American Chesley Bonestell and the British Gerald Quinn, space art became, in the 1950s, common in both science fiction and nonfiction books about future space exploration. In particular, such art was associated with writers like Arthur C. Clarke and Hal Clement, who produced what we now call hard science fiction. Indeed, embedded in the concept of space art is a key insight of that subgenre: that science fiction can be fruitfully directed not only at creating new mechanisms but also at envisioning and developing fantastic new natural environments. It is the difference, one might say, between Fritz Lang's Metropolis and Hal Clement's Mesklin. And, when the object being considered is both artificial and huge enough to be regarded as a natural world, the resulting art can fuse the styles of Paul's futurist art and space art—as seen, for example, in the original paperback cover of Larry Niven's *Ringworld*, which combines gleaming geometry and the forbidding vastness of space.

The 1950s brought expansion and diversity to science fiction, but its key innovation is summarized in the title of H. L. Gold's first editorial for *Galaxy*, "For Adults Only." He proclaimed that

Science fiction . . . has finally come of age. . . . *GALAXY Science Fiction* proposes to carry the maturity of this type of literature into the science fiction magazine field, where it is now . . . hard to find. It establishes a compound break with both the lurid and the stodgy traditions of s-f magazine publishing. From cover design to advertising selections, *GALAXY Science Fiction* intends to be a mature magazine for mature readers.[24]

A focus on an adult audience, among other things, allowed science fiction to move towards improved literary values—as in *The Magazine of Fantasy and Science Fiction*—or toward humor and social satire—as in Gold's *Galaxy*. And, like the stories, the artists would have to move away from "lurid" (pulp) art and "stodgy" (futurist or space) art to become more polished and versatile. Though Frank Kelly Freas would be a logical choice, the other major artist who emerged at this time, Edmund Emshwiller or "Emsh," can be examined to show how science fiction art changed in the 1950s.[25]

While Aldiss aptly called Emsh "the great all-arounder of sf art,"[26] his work is noteworthy not only for its variety but for its *ambiguity*. Previous science fiction art clearly dictated certain emotional reactions: in futurist or space art, readers are supposed to be awed by massive constructs or astronomical vistas; in pulp art, presumably male readers are supposed to identify with the handsome hero, lust after the brass-brassièred woman, and despise the repulsive alien; but we are not always sure how to react to Emshwiller's art. In his cover for the January 1953 issue of *Galaxy*, the American insignia on the spacecraft implies that we should sympathize with its occupants; but the robots emerging from the ship look strange and menacing. Are these robots our allies or our enemies? Consider the three foregrounded figures in a force field on the cover of the December 1963 issue of *The Magazine of Fantasy and Science Fiction*: the human male seems handsome and admirable; the green-skinned alien man holding a machine seems sinister; but the standing alien woman seems more troubled than threatening. Are these beings heroes, villains, or victims? Each figure suggests a different answer. And his interior illustration for Eric Frank Russell's "Design for Great-Day" in the January 1953 issue of *Planet Stories* is in many ways a standard scene from pulp art—a man emerges from a spaceship to confront reptilian aliens brandishing weapons—yet the man is not handsome, but fat and balding, which mitigates against our standard reaction of support for the human. Is this man a worthy fellow who will emerge as an unlikely hero? A fool, who will make us laugh at his ridiculous mistakes? Or a pompous, arrogant man, like a latter-day Nero, who will make us root for the aliens as they resist his evil plans? Overall, life in outer space or the future seems more complex than it used to be in Emshwiller's art, mirroring the greater complexity of the written science fiction of the 1950s.

As such art resists easy interpretation, it also resists easy nomenclature; but one descriptive term may be useful. Accompanying the pulp magazines were their more respectable cousins, the slick magazines, so named for both their higher quality paper and their greater sophistication. And the science fiction art of the 1950s resembled the art of the slicks more than the art of the pulps; except for its outré subject matter, Emshwiller's interior drawing seems similar to the art then appearing in *The Saturday Evening Post*. Therefore, I suggest that we call the style of art pioneered by Emshwiller and Freas *slick science fiction art*.[27]

According to Grant and Nicholls, "The gritty realism of [Freas's] and Ed Emshwiller's work in the 1950s redefined sf art during that period";[28] and these artists did continue and intensify a tradition of realism of science fiction art (but I would quarrel with the word "gritty," since much of their art was humorous in nature). However, even in the 1950s, there were harbingers of change. Richard M. Powers, who started painting book covers at this time, is the artistic equivalent of Cordwainer Smith, both an anticipation of later styles and an idiosyncratic individual creator; his covers were bold abstractions, with elongated stylized figures amidst ellipses of color and spiraling linear designs. I mention Powers because he was the first science fiction artist I noticed: even as a twelve-year-old browsing in bookstores, I could recognize his distinctive covers for books like Kingsley Amis's *New Maps of Hell* and Leo Margulies's *Get Out of My Sky*; and without knowing his name, I knew these were drawn by one unique artist.[29]

But the links between science fiction art and realism would be firmly and widely broken only during the New Wave period of the 1960s. All previous theories of science fiction at least paid lip service to the notion that science fiction should be scientifically accurate and logical, and this commitment to—or pretense of—science seemingly demanded representational portrayals of imagined wonders. But the major voices of the New Wave, Michael Moorcock and Harlan Ellison, insisted that science should not be an issue in science fiction; by promoting the alternative term "speculative fiction," they even sought to banish the word from discourse. Instead, writers were urged to be wildly imaginative in both their ideas and their writing styles, since the abandonment of science also meant that the clear descriptive prose of much earlier science fiction was no longer necessary. And as writers responded to these calls in part by imitating the innovative styles of early twentieth century writers like John Dos Passos and James Joyce, it was only appropriate that artists would imitate the artistic styles of the early twentieth century, the first great era of abstract art. After all, with no need to provide scientific education or logical scientific predictions, why should artists have to be realistic?

To represent this new era of *abstract science fiction art*,[30] several artists might be chosen; but in America, the New Wave was most strongly associated with Harlan Ellison, and the artists most strongly associated with Ellison were Leo and Diane Dillon.[31] Again, the choice is influenced by personal reasons: while Powers was the first artist I recognized, the Dillons were the first artists I collected. When I saw their covers for the Ace Science Fiction Specials, I was so taken by their appearance—a monochromatic background, with a box of geometric designs above the title and a box of abstract art below it—that I purchased every book in the series, even those by authors I otherwise ignored.[32]

Looking at few Dillon covers from the 1960s, we can see the double freedom that this type of science fiction art offered. Yes, the Dillons did not draw in a realistic manner and freely distorted the figures and objects they painted; but they also at times made no effort to represent the exact contents of the works they illustrated. For example, their cover for *From the Land of Fear* obviously does not depict any event in Ellison's stories; rather, the mingled faces, hands, claws, animals, and objects collectively represent the essence of fear itself, or of everything that humans fear. We also note in this cover a complete absence of any reference to science or machinery; this is true Gothic art to validate Aldiss's thesis, recalling Hieronymus Bosch more than Frank R. Paul, art sprung from human nightmares instead of scientific logic. In other Dillon paintings, the relationship between picture and text is distant and allusive: in their cover for Clifford D. Simak's *Why Call Them Back from Heaven?* we see an image of a prone body (perhaps a corpse), overshadowed by a standing human image (perhaps a ghost, a being still living after death), both connected by tentacles to some kind of gear (perhaps some type of machine keeping the corpse alive). From such clues, we might rightly guess that the novel involves cryonics, freezing dead bodies for possible future revival, which would also account for the emphasis on pale blue colors, suggesting ice; but the painting is clearly focused on conveying the emotional impact of the novel, not its contents. The cover for Bob Shaw's *The Palace of Eternity* shows another prone body with two heads (perhaps dead, perhaps alive) beneath a colorful outburst of flowery petals and a godlike face looking down on, and perhaps caressing, the body; but it would take a prodigious imagination to deduce that the novel describes a space war with aliens that leads to the revelation that all humans are connected to a sort of group-mind that can effectively provide immortality. Again, the cover is best defended as a symbolic representation of the novel's mood: generally violent and gloomy (the predominant dark blues and violets) with an unexpected and joyous conclusion (the bright colors in the middle).

Given the power and beauty of the Dillons' work, and given the virtually unlimited freedom that this style offered artists, one might expect abstract art to become the most common form of science fiction art. However, coincidentally around the time that the Dillons largely abandoned science fiction illustration— 1972—we see most science fiction art turning back to realism. Perhaps, to paraphrase C. S. Lewis, readers found strange worlds depicted in a strange manner represented one strangeness too many; perhaps, just as many writers raised in the liberating atmosphere of the New Wave found that they preferred the rigor of hard science fiction, many artists of the time found that they preferred the rigor of realism; perhaps, from a marketing standpoint, abstract art was too esoteric to attract the mass audience that science fiction publishers increasingly craved.[33] By the 1980s, though, a distinctive new style of abstract art would become popular in science fiction.

In this period, one could say, the science fiction genre came full circle. In the 1920s, the field was dominated by one magazine, *Amazing Stories*, then the only one exclusively devoted to science fiction; in the 1980s, the field was again dominated by one magazine, *Omni*, whose circulation was larger than all other science fiction magazines combined. With Paul's covers, *Amazing* vigorously promoted one distinctive form of science fiction art; with its own covers—produced by various artists but all seemingly produced by the same hand—*Omni* similarly promoted a distinctive form of science fiction art.[34] And just as Gernsback provided explanatory captions on his table of contents page to describe his covers, *Omni* also offered explanatory captions on the table of contents page to describe its covers— though the magazine was training its readers to appreciate an entirely different kind of science fiction art.

To understand the art of *Omni*, we recall that, as described by Howard V. Hendrix,[35] the magazine brought together three different types of material: science fiction and fantasy stories, often highly literary and not especially scientific; articles on present-day and predicted science, frequently emphasizing hard sciences like astronomy and physics like the articles in Campbell's *Astounding*, now called *Analog: Science Fiction/Science Fact*; and articles on forms of pseudoscience or mysticism, like psychic powers, ghosts, or UFOs. This combination of diverse materials seemed parallel to the agenda of cyberpunk fiction; for as Sterling observed, "what cyberpunk represents is an integration of New Wave and Hard SF."[36] In terms of the artistic correspondences I have proposed, such contradictory concerns would seem to demand a form of art that was simultaneously realistic and abstract; and there is in fact a form of art that meets that description: surrealism, defined as "a modern type of art or literature in which the painter, writer, etc., connects unrelated images and objects in a strange dream-like way."[37] In such art, "images and objects" may be depicted realistically, but the ways they are brought together may be highly unrealistic—an apt summary of the *Omni* style.

Taking the *Omni* covers collectively as a final representative artist, consider a typical example, the cover of the August 1983 issue. A realistic human head is cut off at the bottom by a extended geometric plane, which in the background meets a mountain range; the top of the head is also cut off and surrounded by floating globes that resemble planets. The table of contents page says "Michel Tcherevkoff presents a visual interpretation of the ideational process" and speaks of "His striking, surreal images."[38] The cover of the November 1984 issue juxtaposes two hands playing a string game, Egyptian bas-relief figures, an ocean, floating polygons, and the Earth in the sky. According to the table of contents page, "Archetypes pervade Dickran Palulian's painting. . . . Hands emerge from the stones of ancient Egypt, rise above the primordial sea, and reach toward space. The cat's cradle presents a modern riddle: Will technology strip us of all individuality?"[39] Such covers both describe and embody the dilemma at the heart of both cyberpunk and its mainstream cousin, "postmodern" literature: we are coming to live in a world that combines bits of the past and bits of the future, but these are not smoothly integrated, but jarringly juxtaposed in a manner suggesting that all conventional categories are breaking down and can no longer be relied on; so the world indeed becomes a gigantic puzzle. Faces appear, but they are arbitrarily cut off; ancient art is next to a modern view of Earth from space. Literary critics of postmodern literature speak of its writers' use of "collage," roughly combining chunks of raw material from various sources; so it is appropriate that its characteristic art often takes the form of a surrealistic collage.

In two other *Omni* covers, we see the aspect of dichotomized modernity that is most central to science fiction: the combination of humanity and technology—as in the cyborg, or the human consciousness "downloaded" into a computer—and the consequent blurring of the lines between the two. The cover of the December 1988 issue features another woman's head, this time overlaid with various pieces of machinery; "She represents the 'Venus of the future,'" says the table of contents page, "an expression of technology, humanity, and nature—with a dimension of mystery."[40] And the cover of the June 1988 issue shows a woman attached to a spaceship flying through space, not even bothering to wear a brass brassière. Superficially, the cover harkens back to the eroticism of pulp art; but despite her nudity, the woman, colored cold blue, with light beaming from her eyes and metal bands on her shoulders and breasts, fails to be alluring—the touches of unreality make her seem machine-like and unappealing. The simultaneous exposure and suppression of sexuality, of course, is another aspect of the postmodern that can excite critics to rhetorical excess.

Though the word is problematic in its several meanings, I call this style of art *surreal science fiction art*,[41] but "Omni science fiction art" might do just as well, to indicate both its source and its omnivorous appetite, drawing in and combining aspects of all previous science fiction art. *Omni* covers may offer at times the massive artificial constructs of Paul, the attractive human figures of pulp art, the imposing astronomical landscapes of space art, the sophisticated realism of slick art, and the unrealistic images of abstract art. The novelty here is the way these elements are starkly juxtaposed, a bringing together of opposites that is, critics say, one key characteristic of the postmodern.

Overall, I have shown that we can indeed outline a history of science fiction art to correspond to the history of written science fiction. However, to justify such an exercise, I must explain why a history of this kind might be useful. Briefly, I wish to suggest show how this view of science fiction art might help in the study of science fiction literature.

First, if this model is accurate (as summarized in Table 1, we should find a preponderance of certain styles of art at certain times, even if those styles do not suit particular writers. It is not surprising that in the 1960s, my era of abstract art, Signet Books replaced the slick realistic covers on its Heinlein novels with gaudy semi-abstract designs, or that Clarke's "documentary" novel about space flight, *Prelude to Space*, was retitled *The Space Dreamers* and provided with a colorful abstract cover, no doubt to attract the chemically-altered fans of the "trip" sequence in *2001: A Space Odyssey*. Generally, however, we should find that a certain type of writer is accompanied by one appropriate style of art: most Heinlein covers should be slick art, and most Clarke covers should be space art.[42] Thus, examining the styles of cover art could provide data to help us classify problematic writers.

As a pilot project, I surveyed the cover art of three writers to evaluate David G. Hartwell's claim, made throughout his and Kathryn Cramer's anthology *The Ascent of Wonder: The Evolution of Hard Science Fiction*, that J. G. Ballard is a hard science fiction writer. I chose two writers—Hal Clement and Larry Niven—who are universally known as hard science fiction writers and looked at and classified the art on every cover of their books in the J. Lloyd Eaton Collection of Science Fiction and Fantasy Literature, excluding duplicates; I did the same for Ballard's books, excluding his mainstream novels. Granted, the books in the Eaton Collection may not be complete or representative and some classifications may have been hasty or

Table 1
A Proposed True History of Science Fiction Art

Era	Style	Description	Representative Artist(s)	Associated Literature
1920s	futurist sf art	huge buildings, cities, geometric symmetries	Frank R. Paul	Gernsbackian sf
1930s	pulp sf art	focus on humans, heroes, sexy women, monsters	Earle Bergey	space opera
1940s	space art	scenes of space, other worlds, alien landscapes	Howard Brown, Chesley Bonestell	hard sf
1950s	slick sf art	realism, variety in subject matter, ambiguity	Ed Emshwiller Frank Kelly Freas	1950s sf
1960s	abstract sf art	semi-abstract or abstract images; no machinery	Richard Powers, Leo and Diane Dillon	New Wave sf
1980s	surreal sf art	surrealism; real objects combined in unreal manner	various *Omni* artists	cyberpunk sf

or questionable; however, even allowing for experimental error, my results (see Tables 2 and 3) reveal a clear pattern. Both Clement and Niven attracted a large number of space art covers, exactly what we would expect for hard science fiction writers, and Ballard attracted only one such cover. If someone protests that this is simply because Ballard rarely deals with space travel in his works, there is a second pattern: the large majority of the Clement and Niven covers were realistic, displaying the various styles of art common to science fiction before 1960 (futurist art, pulp art, space art, slick art); the large majority of Ballard covers were nonrealistic, displaying the styles of art common to science fiction after 1960 (abstract art, surreal art). So the usual classification of Ballard as a New Wave author is confirmed by his characteristic art; and these data do not represent the judgments of commentators with possible axes to grind, but rather a large number of individual decisions by artists and publishers who were solely interested in presenting covers that would most appropriately reflect and advertise Ballard's books. To be truly meaningful, such research would have to be more thorough and could never be relied on exclusively; but it would provide useful supplementary information of a sort not otherwise available.

We may also gain by viewing science fiction art not only as an effect of, but also an influence on, the literature it accompanied. In the 1920s, Paul at times provided grand and impressive covers for petty and prosaic stories; but his persistent grandiosity may have inspired the "Thought-Variant" stories published in the 1930s by *Astounding* editor F. Orlon Tremaine, where writers wrestled, however ineptly, with issues more vast than marvelous new inventions or space pirates. The eroticism of pulp art at times seemed incongruous next to the pristine stories they depicted; but the continuing images of all that female flesh may have prodded writers to produce more frank sexual stories, as in Philip José Farmer's *The Lovers* (1952). Arguably, innovative science fiction art consistently precedes innovative science fiction literature; in my view, the space art of the late 1930s and 1940s predated by a decade the true emergence of hard science fiction,[43] and Powers was popularizing experimental art well before most writers produced experimental stories. Rather than regarding new literature simply as an outgrowth of or reaction to earlier literature, then, we might improve our understanding by including art in the picture and seeing art and literature engaged in interactive evolution.

As a final benefit of this project, consider a predictable objection: that I am overly simplifying, even distorting, the history of science fiction art. How can I call the 1940s the era of space art, when most 1940s art was firmly in the pulp tradition? How can I call the 1980s an era of surreal art when most 1980s art was realistic? And some may complain of excluded artists: where are Hannes Bok, Virgil Finlay, Vincent DiFate, or Michael Whelan, to name only a few major artists who are neither represented in nor congruent with this scheme? Were they omitted because they inconveniently did not fit my categories? These were exactly my own misgivings as I created this model;[44] thus, my projected history of science fiction art serves to reveal the inadequacies of our histories of science fiction literature.

For parallel objections can be made to the literary history I used as a structuring

Table 2
Categories of Cover Art for
Three Science Fiction Writers
(Raw numbers, followed by percentages in parentheses;
percentages do not always total 100 due to rounding off)

Writer	Futurist	Pulp	Space	Slick	Abstract	Surreal	Total
Hal Clement	1 (3)	11 (35)	11 (35)	3 (10)	5 (16)	0 (0)	31 (99)
Larry Niven	4 (7)	12 (20)	17 (28)	4 (7)	21 (34)	3 (5)	61 (101)
J. G. Ballard	0 (0)	1 (2)	1 (2)	9 (20)	30 (65)	5 (11)	46 (100)

Table 3
Realistc and Nonrealistic Cover Art
for Three Science Fiction Writers
(Raw numbers, followed by percentages in parentheses)

Writer	Total Realistic Art (Futurist, Pulp, Space, Slick)	Total Nonrealistic Art (Abstract, Surreal)
Hal Clement	26 (84)	5 (16)
Larry Niven	37 (61)	24 (39)
J. G. Ballard	11 (24)	35 (76)

device. It is wrong to epitomize the 1940s as an era of hard science fiction; even Campbell's *Astounding* published writers like A. E. van Vogt who were not particularly scientific, and other major magazines—*Amazing Stories, Thrilling Wonder Stories, Startling Stories,* and *Planet Stories*—emphasized space opera. And it is wrong to describe the 1980s as a cyberpunk era, since the vast majority of new writers who emerged at that time were not of the cyberpunk school. Yet critics keep mouthing glib generalizations and limiting their research with restrictive parameters, lavishing attention, for example, on 1980s writers like Gibson and Sterling and ignoring writers like C. J. Cherryh, Dan Simmons, and Michael Swanwick. Grafting this potted history onto science fiction art exposes its weaknesses only because histories of science fiction art have generally been more eclectic and diverse in their loosely organized surveys. My subtitle, then, allows this entire chapter to be interpreted as a satire, designed to expose the stupidity of histories of written science fiction by absurdly imposing their patterns on science fiction art.

Perhaps I would not go that far; but I now feel inspired to imagine a project precisely opposite to my original goal: How might we construct a history of science fiction literature that would be similar to most histories of science fiction art? As it happens, there already exists an example: Paul Carter's *The Creation of Tomorrow: Fifty Years of Magazine Science Fiction.*[45] Like historians of science fiction art, Carter does not insist upon a rigid structure for his survey; he groups discussions of stories by their topics—robots, aliens, and so on; and he does not limit himself to a few selected masterpieces, but ranges freely over the entire field, examining both major and very minor works. If Carter's book has not been influential, that may be because he does not impose a tidy framework on his research and seems instead to be rambling and disorganized; yet one can argue that is exactly the kind of study that is needed to truly reflect what is often, on examination, a unmanageably diverse genre.

As an ameliorative conclusion, I suggest that both science fiction literature and art in fact require two types of history. At times, no doubt, we need to establish structures, so that different eras are clearly delineated and represented by a few examples, as a good working summary and stimulus for thought. But at other times we must be reminded that our fields of study are more inchoate and variegated than such simplified structures can convey. I began by implying that scholars of science fiction art might benefit by imitating the well-organized scholars of science fiction literature, but I conclude by suggesting that scholars of science fiction literature might also benefit by imitating the disorganized scholars of science fiction art.

Notes

1. Of recent books on science fiction art, the best available is undoubtedly Vincent DiFate's *Infinite Worlds: The Fantastic Visions of Science Fiction Art* (New York: Penguin Studio: Wonderland Press, 1997). Other worthwhile studies include Anthony Frewin's *One Hundred Years of Science Fiction Illustration* (New York: Pyramid Books, 1975; first

published 1974), though its coverage is limited to science fiction art from 1840 to 1940. Jacques Sadoul's *2000 A.D.: Illustrations from the Golden Age of Science Fiction Pulps* (Chicago: Henry Regnery, 1975; first published 1973) and Brian W. Aldiss's *Science Fiction Art* (New York: Bounty Books, 1975) both have good selections of illustrations, though they largely rely on thematic organization (Aldiss adds a "Gallery" of noteworthy artists); and Lester del Rey's *Fantastic Science Fiction Art 1926-1954* (New York: Ballantine Books, 1975) presents excellent reproductions of many magazine covers in chronological order.

2. Aldiss, "Illustration (From the Beginning to 1978)," in *The Encyclopedia of Science Fiction*, edited by John Clute and Peter Nicholls (New York: St. Martin's Press, 1993), 611.

3. Aldiss, "Introduction," in *Science Fiction Art*, 3.

4. Aldiss, "Illustration," 611.

5. For more information on Gernsback's theories, see my *The Mechanics of Wonder: The Creation of the Idea of Science Fiction* (Liverpool: Liverpool University Press, 1998).

6. Frewin points out this detail, 55.

7. "Our Cover," *Amazing Stories*, 1 (July, 1926), 289. This and the captions listed in notes 7-13 were unsigned and were presumably written by Gernsback or one of his editors.

8. "On the Cover," *Science Wonder Stories*, 1 (July, 1929), 99.

9. "On the Cover," *Air Wonder Stories*, 1 (July, 1929), 1.

10. "On the Cover," *Science Wonder Stories*, 1 (August, 1929), 195.

11. "On the Cover," *Air Wonder Stories*, 1 (August, 1929), 99.

12. "On the Cover," *Science Wonder Stories*, 1 (October, 1929), 387.

13. "On the Cover This Month," *Air Wonder Stories*, 1 (October, 1929), 291.

14. "On the Cover This Month," *Air Wonder Stories*, 1 (January, 1930), 579.

15. Nicholls and John Grant, "Earle K. Bergey," in *The Encyclopedia of Science Fiction*, 111.

16. Nicholls and Grant, "Earle K. Bergey," 111.

17. Aldiss (*Science Fiction Art*, 68) attributes the cover to Brown; Frewin (111) says it "may well be" by Brown; but del Rey ([58]) attributes the cover to Bergey. Here, I trust the judgment of Aldiss and Frewin more than del Rey's.

18. John W. Campbell, Jr., "Science-Fiction," *Astounding Science-Fiction*, 21 (March, 1938), 37.

19. For more information on Campbell's theories, see *The Mechanics of Wonder*.

20. Campbell, "In Times to Come," *Astounding Science-Fiction*, 22 (October, 1938), 11.

21. Campbell, "Mercury," *Astounding Stories*, 20 (February, 1938), 97.

22. For science fiction scholars, it is indeed fascinating that Campbell explained and achieved a new style of science fiction art well before he explained and achieved a new style of science fiction literature. This apparent reversal of priorities suggests that illustration in fact has been very important in the history of science fiction, which makes its relative neglect a major problem in our understanding of the genre.

23. Campbell, "In Times to Come," *Astounding Science-Fiction*, 22 (October, 1938), 6. Interestingly, just as Gernsback once made a story with a scientific error, Geoffrey Hewelke's "Ten Million Miles Sunward," "educational" by announcing a contest for readers to spot the error, Campbell similarly capitalized on an error in Brown's cover: "Jupiter" announced that "There is an error in the picturization. . . . I decided to let it go through as is for the interest of the reader. . . . The nature of the error—and why it is such—will be shown next month, in the Analytical Laboratory. I'll try to publish the names of those who spot the error correctly in the Brass Tacks column in the January issue. So go to it!" ("Jupiter," *Astounding Science-Fiction*, 22 [November, 1938)], 6). He later explained that the shadow cast on Jupiter was incorrectly shaped ("The Analytical Laboratory," *Astounding*

Science-Fiction, 22 [December, 1938], 154). Like his science fiction stories, Campbell's art could thus provide useful practice in scientific thinking.

24. H. L. Gold, "For Adults Only," *Galaxy*, 1 (October, 1950), 2.

25. The choice was dictated entirely by circumstance: my first public discussion of the subject was at a conference that also featured a presentation by Frank Kelly Freas, so that extended discussion of Freas's art seemed superfluous.

26. Aldiss, *Science Fiction Art*, 43.

27. Although, as pointed out by R. D. Mullen ("From Standard Magazines to Big Slicks: A Note on the History of US General and Fiction Magazines," *Science-Fiction Studies*, 22 [March, 1995), 144-156), this common terminology is not accurate.

28. Grant and Nicholls, "Frank Kelly Freas," in *The Encyclopedia of Science Fiction*, 452.

29. Another 1950s artist who produced "semi-abstract covers," Brian Lewis, is discussed in Aldiss, *Science Fiction Art*, 45.

30. I use the term "abstract" in its broadest sense to refer to all art which moves beyond the representational; the term also applies to nonobjective art, where the art has no referent in the real or an imagined world, but I note in passing that true nonobjective art seems rare in the science fiction field.

31. In the 1960s, Harlan Ellison hired the Dillons to work on virtually all of his books; his fondness for their work is best shown by the fact that his landmark anthology *Dangerous Visions* (1967) was dedicated "with love, respect, and admiration" to them (*Dangerous Visions #1* [New York: Berkley Books, 1969], 4).

32. Unusually for the time, the series was promoted using the DIllons' names: for example, the back-page advertisement for future Ace Science Fiction Specials in the first book of the series, Clifford D. Simak's *Why Call Them Back from Heaven?* (New York: Ace Books, 1967) said that these "major new novels" would be "presented with distinctive covers by Leo & Diane Dillon" (192).

33. Though some abstract art, as already implied, was commercially successful; Grant and Nicholls argue that "Powers was one of the first to show that semi-abstract images of some sophistication could sell sf; the Dillons went on to prove the point incontrovertibly" ("Leo and Diane Dillon," in *The Encyclopedia of Science Fiction*, 334).

34. What is surprising about this apparent uniformity of style is that, as was pointed out to me in conversation, *Omni* never commissioned cover art, but employed only "found art"; the magazine thus managed to promote a distinctive style of art entirely by careful selection, not by directly instructing or influencing artists.

35. Howard V. Hendrix, "Making the Pulpmonster Safe for Demography: *Omni* Magazine and the Gentrification of Science Fiction," in *Science Fiction and Market Realities*, edited by Gary Westfahl, George Slusser, and Eric S. Rabkin (Athens: University of Georgia Press, 1996).

36. Bruce Sterling, Interview with Takayuki Tatsumi, *Science Fiction Eye*, No. 1 (Winter, 1987), 27.

37. *Longmans Dictionary of Contemporary English* (London: Longmans, 1987), 1065.

38. Untitled and unattributed caption, table of contents page, *Omni*, 5 (August, 1983), 4. The next two notes similarly refer to untitled and unattributed captions.

39. Table of contents page, *Omni*, 7 (November, 1984), 4.

40. Table of contents page, *Omni*, 11 (December, 1988), 2.

41. The problem is that the term "surreal," commonly used in a variety of ways, may also apply to styles of art I am grouping together as "abstract"; thus, Nicholls and Grant refer to Powers's "Surrealist style" ("Richard M. Powers," in *The Encyclopedia of Science Fiction*,

952). In my terminology, supported by several glossaries of art that I examined, "abstract" can properly refer to any art where objects are distorted beyond the representational; but I am using "surreal" more narrowly to refer to art which may depict objects representationally but combines or juxtaposes them in an unrealistic manner.

42. And we should expect this to be true even if the particular Clarke work in question is not hard science fiction. As one spectacular example, Ballantine Books in 1969 reprinted *Tales from the White Hart* with a cover depicting a detailed space station—although, of course, no space travel of any kind occurred in Clarke's atypically playful stories in the collection.

43. I argue at length that hard science fiction emerged during the 1950s in my *Cosmic Engineers: A Study of Hard Science Fiction* (Westport, CT: Greenwood Press, 1996).

44. In addition to the issues of oversimplification and omitted artists, there are two other large areas neglected by my model. First, there is fantasy art, which arguably began as a modern, self-conscious genre in the pages of Farnworth Wright's *Weird Tales* magazine, not *Amazing Stories*, and which, in its early stages, clearly reflected the influence of Gothic art far more than did science fiction art, as seen, for example, in Hannes Bok's work. Later, fantasy art often combined Gothic imagery with a kind of prettified pastoral realism, Frank Frazetta being one obvious representative. At times, fantasy art has been closely intertwined with science fiction art; at other times—particularly today—it seems an entirely separate field, which is why this volume deals with fantasy art in a separate section. Another neglected area is comic book art, which initially, in the late 1930s and 1940s, employed a cartoonish style derived from comic strips that was never featured in the science fiction magazines. As the genre emerged, however, its art grew more sophisticated, roughly paralleling the evolution of science fiction art (though generally behind by about a decade); thus, it could be argued, one can find pulp art in 1950s comic books, slick art in 1960s comic books, and abstract and surreal art in 1970s and 1980s comic books. Overall, though it is possible to see fantasy art and comic book art as offshoots or relatives of science fiction art, I suspect that experts in these areas would prefer, with some justice, to develop their own explanatory models to characterize these fields.

45. Paul Carter, *The Creation of Tomorrow: Fifty Years of Magazine Science Fiction* (New York: Columbia University Press, 1977).

3

The Northrop Continuum:
Science Fiction Illustration and
the Flying Wing Aircraft

Howard V. Hendrix

In William Gibson's 1981 story "The Gernsback Continuum," the image that opens the photographer-narrator's episode of temporary semiotic insanity is the vision of a flying wing:

And one day, on the outskirts of Bolinas, when I was setting up to shoot a particularly lavish example of Ming's martial architecture, I penetrated a fine membrane, a membrane of probability. . . .
Ever so gently, I went over the Edge—
And looked up to see a twelve-engined thing like a bloated boomerang, all wing, thrumming its way east with an elephantine grace, so low that I could count the rivets in its dull silver skin and hear—maybe—the echo of jazz.[1]

Similarly, the episode which closes the narrator's episode of alternate probability is also the image of "a flying wing over Castro Street," though this flying wing is described as "almost translucent" (23) and "tenuous . . . as though it were only half there" (35).

The most frequently occurring "evidence" of the existence of this alternative or "Gernsback" continuum in the story is, in fact, the image of a flying wing aircraft—occurring five times altogether. Though one of those five is the twice-mentioned Castro Street sighting, this type of aircraft is clearly the flying signifier of the story's lineage between and among the constellation of ideas that make up the "Gernsback continuum": namely, Gernsbackian scientifiction, populism, technophilia, futurism, and Nazism. Gibson describes the dreamworld of the Gernsback continuum as possessing "all the sinister fruitiness of Hitler Youth propaganda" (33). Then again, Gibson also describes actual "American Streamlined Moderne" (24) factory buildings of our continuum as possessing "a kind of sinister totalitarian dignity, like the stadiums Albert Speer built for Hitler" (26).

In Gibson's story, the 1930s are said to have produced "a generation of completely uninhibited technophiles" (24)—as well as the greatest popular success of fascism and Nazism. The industrial designers of the 1930s, says Gibson, "were populists, you see; they were trying to give the public what it wanted, and what the public wanted was the future." (26) Mussolini put it only slightly differently when he said that "Democracy has deprived the life of the people of 'style': that is, a line of conduct, the color, the strength, the picturesque, the unexpected, the mystical; in sum, all that counts in the soul of the masses. We [Fascists] play the lyre on all its strings: from violence to religion, from art to politics"[2] (cited in Nolte 333).

Gibson's story suggests, however, an arc of inevitability, a gravity's rainbow leading from *futurismo* to *fascismo*: "The rockets on the covers of the Gernsback pulps had fallen on London in the dead of night, screaming" (27). The story presents us with a historic choice: either the Nazi shimmer of Frank R. Paul's "spray-paint pulp utopias" (25) or "the human near-dystopia we live in" (35). Curiously, in Gibson's story, "really bad media" of our continuum "can exorcise your semiotic ghosts" (33). Plugging into the current Mass Dream (particularly through television, or through pornography like *Nazi Love Motels*) can drive out those images of alternate realities previously built by the human mind, the still-surviving Fragments of an earlier Mass Dream.

At the very time that Gibson was writing "The Gernsback Continuum" and emblematizing that lost technophile/technofascist 1930s universe through repeated iterations of the flying wing image, however, that vision of the flying wing was proving to be more persistent in our consensus reality than Gibson or his narrator might have guessed. It had been thirty years since the last great Northrop flying wings, the B-35s and B-49s, had flown. (You may remember the B-49 as the flying wing jet bomber that drops an atomic bomb on the Martians in George Pal's 1953 film *The War of the Worlds*.) Yet thirty years after the old Northrop flying wings had disappeared, those 1930s-rooted dreams of all-wing flight were about to come true—again. The Phoenix rising from the ashes of the Northrop B-35 and B-49 flying wings would not be seen publicly until several years after Gibson's story appeared, but that Phoenix was already undergoing secret flight tests at the time of the story's writing. That Phoenix goes by the name of the Northrop B-2 Stealth Bomber.

The B-2 debuted during the Reagan presidency with an initial price tag of half a billion dollars each. (By 1995, they cost more than one billion dollars each.) The B-2 is the fullest realization of that dream of 1930s designers like John Northrop in the United States, G. T. R. Hill in Britain, and the Horten brothers in Germany: namely, the high-lift, low drag, pure wing aircraft. The B-2, also—perhaps not so coincidentally, given the persistence of vision —shares the exact same wingspan dimension, 172 feet, as the Northrop B-49 of thirty years earlier.

The linkage of flying wing aircraft-futurism with Nazism, however, neither begins nor ends with Gibson's story. In popular culture one finds Indiana Jones (in *Raiders of the Lost Ark* [1981]) battling a big German bad guy on and over a Nazi flying wing aircraft with anhedral dropped wingtips. In the movie *Philadelphia Experiment II* (1993)—a fine example of "really bad media"—the Germans won

World War II because, in our 1993, U.S. Air Force scientists attempting to "temporarily stealth" an F-117 Stealth fighter accidentally send that nuclear-armed, radar invisible fighter to Germany in 1943. In that other timeline, that Stealth fighter eventually nukes New York, so that Deutschland really is *uber alles*. (The F-117 is an all-wing aircraft—it has no vertical tail section—but is not a *pure* wing aircraft because it does have two angular fins at the back.) In *Independence Day*, the highly successful 1996 reworking of *The War of the Worlds*, a scene from the George Pal film is almost exactly recreated: in the 1950s version, a flying wing drops a nuclear bomb on the invaders; in the 1990s version, a B-2 drops the bomb.

The flying wing aircraft has, in fact, been linked with the future in the popular imagination generally, and with science fiction specifically, since the dawn of the age of flight. John William Dunne, the Englishman who was the first designer to create a practical tailless airplane, was obsessed with the notion of an inherently stable aircraft. The source of this obsession, Dunne claimed, was his reading of a Jules Verne story when he was thirteen—a story that inspired Dunne in his lifelong dedication to the dream of a "flying machine that needed no steering, that would right itself regardless of wind and weather."[3] As a result of this obsession, Dunne became familiar with the *Zanonia* seed and its amazing flying qualities. He did not become seriously involved in the problems of flight until 1901, however. As an army lieutenant home on sick leave from the Boer War, he was encouraged in his planning, sketching, and modeling of aircraft by none other than H. G. Wells, with whom Dunne corresponded. Wells urged Dunne to concentrate on the problems of control and balance, reinforcing Dunne's obsession with tailless craft.

Dunne's influence on later flying wing designers was profound. The great flying wing designers of the 1920s, 1930s, and 1940s, particularly Hill, Northrop, and the Horten brothers, often referred to Dunne's work when discussing the problems of stability and control. Wells too helped to keep the ideal of the inherently stable, flying wing aircraft alive in the popular culture, both through his fictions (many of which were reprinted in the early Gernsback magazines) and through the films based on his fictions—particularly the 1936 *Things to Come* (based on his novel *The Shape of Things to Come*), notable for both its giant flying wing aircraft and for Wells's very personal involvement in the film's production. For both Wells and the popular imagination generally during the 1930s, the literal "shape of things to come" was the chevron or boomerang shape of the Flying Wing.

As Michael Korda has noted, *Things to Come* "became gospel for both sides in the dispute over armaments and foreign policy, and contributed greatly to the idea that air raids would destroy the enemy's will and plunge him back into the Stone Age. When Hitler saw the movie he was deeply impressed, and ordered Göring to screen the picture, as an indication of what the *Luftwaffe* must be prepared to do, while British Prime Minister Neville Chamberlain thought [the film] a powerful argument for peace." The appeasers took the film's "picture of London in ruins as an accurate portrayal of what would happen if Hitler were provoked to use the *Luftwaffe*," but the film also "sustain[ed] the belief of the Air Ministry and Winston Churchill in the efficacy of the heavy bomber."[4]

Not so very long after Wells's death, the film *The War of the Worlds* updated Wells's other novel in an especially Wellsian fashion: namely, through the joint use of two Wells-predicted technologies that had "come true" as a result of World War II—flying wing bombers and nuclear weapons. On aesthetic grounds, the filmmakers chose the flying wing B-49 as the aircraft elected to deliver against the Martians a nuclear weapon, humanity's last great technological hope against the invaders from space. Never mind that the B-49 was in fact not designed for nor capable of delivering nuclear weapons, and that the B-49 was itself being consigned to the slag-heap of history before *The War of the Worlds* was out of the theaters. However, the filmmakers finally got it right with *Independence Day*, in which a truly nuclear capable and active-service flying wing, the B-2, again attempts to nuke the aliens.

That the older Northrop flying wings lasted longer in art than in life is particularly appropriate. Phrases like "ideal" and "on aesthetic grounds" can't be avoided here. Aviation and space pioneer Dr. Theodore von Karman, speaking of the demise of the B-35 and B-49, wrote, "I have always thought it a shame that Northrop's Wing failed. [Northrop] believed that if something is beautiful it is right. Visionaries with daring and imagination should succeed."[5] "Style," "grace," and "beauty," "an extraordinary quality that caught the fancy and imagination of the public"—these are the sorts of terms and phrases that occur again and again in the literature about Northrop's flying wing aircraft. Northrop publicly may have spoken and written about high lift and low drag, "improved efficiency of the airplane" and "all the functions of a satisfactory flying machine disposed and accommodated within the outline of the main supporting airfoil," but his more private communications reveal that his motivations were deeply aesthetic in nature. It was not the "fancy and imagination of the public" alone was caught by "an extraordinary quality" of flying wing aircraft.[6]

What, though, is the nature of this appeal? If we agree with Ernst Nolte in *Three Faces of Fascism* that "the era of the world wars is identical with the era of fascism,"[7] and that this historical epoch reached its zenith during the 1930s, then we cannot deny that, historically, futurism is a major component of a fascist aesthetic. That this aesthetic was conscious can be seen in the reminiscences of Michael Korda, whose father Vincent helped brother Alexander Korda bring Wells's *Things to Come* to the screen. During the making of the film, we are told, Vincent Korda was "busily ransacking the libraries for avant-garde furniture designs, architectural fantasies, helicopters and autogyros, monorails and electric bubble cars, television sets and space vehicles." The nursery of the younger Korda in Hampstead "became a repository for [Vincent Korda's] rejected design models, and while other children were playing with trains and toy soldiers, I was playing with rocket ships, ray guns and flying wings."[8] If, as Gibson's story suggests, the designers of the 1930s were populists giving the public what it wanted, and if what it wanted was the future, then what about the future was appealing?

A perusal of Gernsbackiana quickly shows that pulp futurism was in many ways the Idea of Progress—bigger, better, faster, more—metastasized into a "style." The popularity of streamlining is a case in point. As Gibson's narrator notes,

The Thirties had seen the first generation of American industrial designers; until the Thirties, all pencil sharpeners had looked like pencil sharpeners—your basic Victorian mechanism, perhaps with a curlicue of decorative trim. After the advent of the designers, some pencil sharpeners looked as though they'd been put together in wind tunnels. For the most part, the change was only skin-deep; under the streamlined chrome shell, you'd find the same Victorian mechanism. Which made a certain kind of sense, because the most successful American designers had been recruited from the ranks of Broadway theatre designers. It was all a stage set, a set of elaborate props for playing at living in the future. (25)

Streamlining, then, gave the impression of windblown speed even to objects (like pencil sharpeners) that were stationary. Such effusive stylistic proclamations of "Speed!" and "Energy!" suggest an impatience with the present—that if we can just go fast enough the future will erupt in our midst. Certainly there were aspects of 1930s life—worldwide depression for one, buildup toward a new war, for another— that might have led people to become impatient and frustrated with their present, seeking solace in a play-acted future, in style as displacement and psychological coping mechanism.

The flying wing was in many ways the ultimate embodiment of this fascination with streamlining. It really was designed in a wind tunnel. In the air it was a pure form, all wing, no clunky vertical surfaces to distract from the clean, flying horizontal line. It didn't matter that the flying wing didn't actually go faster than more conventional airframes (and often went slower); the point was that it looked like it *should* go faster. Its lines fulfilled a psychological need for an almost archetypal aesthetic purity—a need that the futurists recognized as the need for the future *now*.

Nowhere is this clearer than in the pictures of Northrop's N-1M flying wing, parked on the desert floor of Muroc Dry Lake beside media cameramen filming it with their kludgy cameras from atop their late 1930s automobiles. In those photos, juxtaposed with the hulking cars, the N-1M is an apparition, a bit of the Gernsback continuum made flesh, as much an irruption of the future into the present as a flying saucer would be. Curiously, in the late 1940s, the military in fact claimed that a disc-shaped all-wing aircraft—the V-173 Zimmer Skimmer or "Flying Pancake" and its fighter experimental prototype, the XF5U-1—was responsible for many of the UFO discs sighted at that time. Flights of the Northrop B-49 flying wing were also supposed to have engendered a number of the reported UFO sightings of the time.

With the mention of UFOs, we have now reached the point where "style" pushes toward "collective unconscious." In "The Gernsback Continuum," Gibson's photographer-narrator visits Mervyn Kihn, "free-lance journalist with an extensive line in Texas pterodactyls, redneck UFO contactees, bush-league Loch Ness Monsters, and the Top Ten conspiracy theories in the loonier reaches of the American mass-mind." Kihn's explanation for the UFO problem and for what the narrator saw is that

People see these things. Nothing's there, but people see them anyway. Because they need to, probably. You've read Jung, you should know the score. . . . Everything normal, and then there's the monster, the mandala, the neon cigar. In your case, a giant Tom Swift airplane . . . . I'd say you saw a semiotic ghost . . . semiotic phantoms, bits of deep cultural imagery that have split off and taken on a life of their own, like the Jules Verne airships that those old Kansas farmers were always seeing. . . . That plane was part of the mass unconscious, once. You picked up on that somehow. (28-30)

The mention of the mandala here is of interest, because it provides us with a link between flying wings, flying cities, and the unconscious. In the late 1940s, when Northrop realized that his flying wings might find a civilian use even if they didn't find a military one, his corporation made a publicity film depicting a cross-continental flight aboard a flying wing aircraft, spacious as a cruise ship, passengers all housed within the ample wing, able to stare straight forward into the space they were flying through, on an equal footing with the pilot, seeing the world when and how he saw it—an egalitarianism sadly lacking in the cigar-shaped bomber buses-with-wings of our continuum's airfleet.

We encounter something even more spectacular in "The Gernsback Continuum" when the narrator tells us, "I hesitated over one sketch of a particularly grandiose prop-driven airliner, all wing, like a fat symmetrical boomerang with wings in unlikely places. Labelled arrows indicated the location of the grand ballroom and two squash courts. . . . New York to London in less than two days, first class dining rooms, sun decks, dancing to jazz in the evenings" (25-26). With such an image, we are already a long way toward the "flying oil refineries" of James Blish's Cities in Flight series, Edmond Hamilton's "Cities in the Air," Jonathan Swift's Flying Island of Laputa, Hugo Gernsback's "10,000 Years Hence—A Prediction," and the mandala-saucer of the Mother Ship in Steven Spielberg's *Close Encounters of the Third Kind*.

It is difficult at first to see how the traditionally sprawling—and very much dependent—cityscape could be at all like the pure wing aircraft, noted already for its self-containment and aerodynamic self-sufficiency. The mandalic floating city, however, strives for the best of both worlds. In Oriental art and religion, the mandala is a symbol of the universe. For Jung it is the archetypal expression of wholeness, the self, the totality of the individual, conscious and unconscious. The flying city, like the mandala itself, is an image of wholeness, of self-sufficiency—as self-contained as the universe.

In science fiction illustration, these flying cities are often domed in bubbles of force so that they possess the same slickly aerodynamic look as the flying wing. A city as unified, fast, and sufficient unto itself as a flying wing—literally, a "city on the move," so streamlined and progressive that it must break free of the Earth. A flying wing wrapped around the city inside as the aerodynamic shell was wrapped around the pencil sharpener. A mobile "place" free of all the traditional constraints of place.

The danger, of course, occurs when these deep cultural and aesthetic images of autonomy—the pure wing, the mandalic whole —shift from the autonomy of the individual self to the totalizing of social energy needed to make the future *now*, the marshalling of the individual many into the singular whole, the city with all its many inhabitants speeding into the same future, everything and everyone headed swiftly and aerodynamically in the same direction. From there it is only a short step to the oneness of "Ein Volk, Ein Reich, Ein Fuehrer," to the well-controlled body politic, that giant individual—the totalitarian state—created out of the masses of the individual many.

The idea that "if it is beautiful it is right" points out the difficulties that arise when we confuse two traditional branches of philosophy, namely aesthetics and ethics. The "beauty" and "elegance" of Einstein's $E = mc^2$ leads to Hiroshima. The glorious pageant of progress too often leaves a desert in its wake. The aerodynamic sleekness of the B-2 does not change the fact that it is a late-strike nuclear bomber. Cities, for all their shining hurry, seem today more prone to dying than flying.

Perhaps it is appropriate that the last human images Gibson's narrator encounters from the Gernsbackian universe are shining happy people in Lucite sandals—echoes of the futuristic, vaguely Athenian-looking utopias of *Things to Come*. Such an image harkens back to the earliest detailed utopian vision on record—Plato's *Republic*. It is probably wise to remember, however, that Plato's beautiful and logical and orderly city-state is a fascist utopia. Gibson's story leaves us treasuring our "*human* near-dystopia" (emphasis added) by reminding us that the beauty which comes of order is probably antithetical to the autonomy which comes of freedom. The flying wing world of Gernsback and the technophiles is a beautiful dream, a Platonic ideal. Ultimately, however, it must fade because it offers only the marble perfection of the unchanging—and therefore doomed—society. Gibson's story vividly illustrates the idea that a human world must include chaos, and that any beauty based on monocultural order will, in the end, prove too reductive and simplistic—even fatally so. That social orderliness of the world of the flying wing ultimately comes at a cost that outweighs its beauty.

Notes

1. William Gibson, "The Gernsback Continuum," in *Burning Chrome*, by Gibson (1986; New York: Ace Books, 1987), 27-28. Story originally published in 1981. All subsequent page references in the text are to this edition.

2. Benito Mussolini, cited in Ernst Nolte, *Three Faces of Fascism: Action Française, Italian Fascism, National Socialism*, published in German in 1963, translated by Leila Vennewitz (1965; New York: Signet Books, 1969), 333.

3. John William Dunne, cited in Michael Taylor, *The World's Strangest Aircraft: A Collection of Weird and Wonderful Flying Machines* (New York: Regency House, 1996), 64.

4. Michael Korda, *Charmed Lives: A Family Romance* (New York: Random House, 1979), 122.

5. Theodore von Karman, cited in Garry R. Pape and John M. Campbell, *Northrop Flying Wings: A History of Jack Northrop's Visionary Aircraft* (Atglen, PA: Schiffer Military History, 1995), 93.

6. John Northrop, cited in Pape and Campbell, 40.
7. Nolte, 24.
8. Korda, 123.

4

Less Is More:
Empty Space, Invisibility,
and Modern Design

Kathleen Church Plummer

In the early 1930s, Rudolf Schindler (1887-1953), the noted Vienna-born California architect, designed some very sparsely furnished interiors in Los Angeles. It was Schindler's aim, as his work illustrates and his writings document, to reduce the furnishings in the interior to a minimum. Like Frank Lloyd Wright, for whom he went to work in 1918, and other modernists, he favored built-ins, but typically he went a step beyond Wright by attaching his built-ins to the periphery of the wall so as to leave empty space in the middle. "Furnishings," he stated, "lose more and more of the character of convex-plastic individual pieces which clutter up the room. They merge instead with the house, leaving the room free to express its form."[1] What moveable furniture there was should be, in his words, "translucent," that is minimal in mass, or better, foldable, so that it could be put away against the wall when not in use. In one of his interiors, the remodel of Wright's Freeman House, Schindler went so far as to build a slot in the wall so that a large couch could be slid away to provide room for the owner to dance for her friends before the great fireplace.[2]

Here we have it—the ultimate room—free space. As Mies van der Rohe (1886-1969) said, "Less Is More."[3] Nothingness is the ideal. This dematerialization of our physical surroundings (both actual and virtual)—the elimination of furnishings, walls, and indeed, entire buildings—is an important theme running through the history of modern design from the 1850s onward. It also became part and parcel of science fiction imagery, both in word and illustration. In science fiction, with its adherence to Wellsian traditions of the 1880s right up through the 1930s (and even today), the fantasies of crystal buildings and disappearing furniture were perpetuated and still condition our vision of the future world—a world of vast spaces inside and out, dotted with various creatures, including humans in flowing, diaphanous garments. Because this vision still has a hold on our consciousness, it is important to understand where it came from.

First, a few words on the background of this study. I began this work in 1967, studying the so-called "Streamline Moderne" style of the 1930s and its correspondence with science fiction illustration and literary description, notably in the pulp magazines. It became clear at that time that the streamline style embodied many of the ideals of science fiction, and also that the science fiction illustrators (especially Frank R. Paul) and writers recognized the appropriateness of streamline architecture for the future world.[4] By now, I and others have also traced many threads of connection between real world architects and science fiction illustrators and writers.[5] Most recently, for example, an historian working at the Museum of the City of New York unearthed a drawing that Frank R. Paul submitted to the competition for buildings to be built at the New York World's Fair of 1939 (unfortunately, it was rejected), and I have been tracing Frank R. Paul's connections with pioneering modernist artists in Vienna and Berlin, including Professor Bruno Paul,[6] famous modernist designer and head of the Berlin Academy of Arts and Crafts.

Meanwhile, in the past twenty years, I have become more and more aware that the "International Style" of the 1920s and 1930s—the style that crystallized in the 1920s at the famous school of design, the Bauhaus, in Germany, the style that was dubbed the true and correct modern style by the design establishment[7] (in contrast to the Streamline Moderne, which was called "modernistic")—was equally as futuristic and fantastic as streamlining. Older critics (notably Sigfried Giedion) had emphasized the International Style's characteristic fantasy elements,[8] but critics of the last thirty or forty years, with a few exceptions, have tended to see modern design as rational, functional Machine Age design. A Bauhaus chair such as the bent tubular metal chair of 1925 by Marcel Breuer, called the "Wassily" chair, has been seen as masterful chiefly in its exploitation of a new industrial material (bent metal tubing, suggested to Breuer by bicycle design); and glass architecture, represented by Mies van der Rohe's 1922 project for a glass skyscraper, likewise was appreciated mainly for its revolutionary use of a steel skeleton and glass curtain wall construction, also seen in his Barcelona Pavilion of 1929—sometimes considered *the* masterpiece of International Style modernism.

Looking at these designs now, however, we see them very differently: we see the Pavilion as a revolutionary attempt to dematerialize the building, to reduce it, inside and out, to a shimmer of color and light reflections, to eliminate its plasticity to the point that it approximates an invisible building. Taking another example, we examine the glass wall, seen in the glass house (1949) by Mies disciple Philip Johnson: it is not just an exercise in modern machine-age materials; rather, in both aim and effect, it resembles a wonderful illustration of Sir John Tenniel for *Through the Looking Glass*.[9] Something quite fantastic is going on here. For another example: consider a minimalist interior by Marcel Breuer (Berlin, 1929), with its furnishings so insubstantial that they seem to be made of lines drawn in the air. And for another: a chair by Mies (the Brno chair of 1930), "transparent," Breuer would have called it, an approximation of the invisible chair, just a few planes hovering in space. Or note the dissolution of both the building and its contents, even the supporting columns, in the interior of Mies's Tughendhat House of 1930. This is the stuff of fantasy and science fiction, as a comparison with the glass columns of the interior from the science fiction film of the 1930s, *Things to Come*, will confirm![10]

This brings us to the question asked in this chapter: were the modern designers of the 1920s and 1930s really pursuing the idea of the invisible, and if so, where might they have gotten their ideas? In answering these questions, we shall also discover, as a bonus, the sources of much of the imagery of the future world that we see in popular science fiction stories and films.

The ideas of an "invisible" architecture and empty interior space must somehow trace back to nineteenth-century popular stories involving invisibility, from fairy stories to science fiction. The general interest of the nineteenth century in things invisible was illustrated, for instance, in the early stage show called "Phantasmagoria," in which ghosts were materialized, or in later magic shows in which bouquets of flowers, birds, rabbits, people, and even elephants, could be made to disappear with the touch of a wand. These illusions of appearance and disappearance must have had an exhilarating effect on children growing up in the period just prior to and during World War I and in fact on most twentieth-century children (especially in the years before television).[11] The Victorian fascination with the invisible world was also evident in glass and iron architecture, which as science fiction fans well know was used by early writers, notably Edward Bellamy in *Looking Backward* (1887) and H. G. Wells in *When the Sleeper Wakes* (1899) as the architecture of the future world.[12] But of all of the manifestations of the interest in the invisible, perhaps the most important influence on budding designers were the stories and illustrations in children's books, particularly the fairy stories and their illustrations.[13]

In late nineteenth-century science fiction, carrying on the fantasy tradition, objects, architecture, and even people were often invisible. We even have instances of invisible furniture in early Wells: the bed in *When the Sleeper Wakes*, which popped when it was pricked, "like a glass bubble."[14] And then we had invisible humans, giving a scientific spin to earlier nineteenth-century notions of invisible beings. The theme of the invisible being, about whom much has been written,[15] was evident not only in actual stage shows, and in seances, in which spirits were "materialized," but also in the Victorians' general interest in the material and immaterial aspects of the self—body versus soul/spirit/ghost, and also, most importantly, the infatuation with fairies, who could become invisible at will.[16] And the persistence of this tradition of dematerializing the body persists as a theme in science fiction from Fitz-James O'Brien[17] through Wells (*The Invisible Man*, 1897) and into the twentieth century (right up to *Star Trek*'s "Beam me up, Scotty"). In the 1920s and 1930s, the subject of our current study, this interest was indubitably alive and well in popular science fiction literature and film, for example, in the 1929 story of Sir Arthur Conan Doyle, "The Disintegration Machine."[18] And in illustration, wonderful images of crystal cities, glass furnishings, and enormous empty spaces abounded, continuing to hold sway right up through the 1940s.

Let us look now at the work of the European pioneers of modernism, in particular those working in the 1920s at the famous German design school, the Bauhaus, in particular for symptoms of their delight in the invisible, and an explanation of their sources. Interestingly enough, it was in Germany that production of children's books reached a height of technical perfection and mass-distribution in the period of the 1870s through World War I,[19] and the reading of fantastic literature was encouraged (for its moral lessons), and even, in fact, required in the schools.[20] And in Germany, just as in other European countries at the turn of the century, the young modernist designers were sometimes employed as illustrators for books of fantasy.[21] So it is not surprising that images of invisible worlds and objects would enter into the young designers' consciousness or emerge in architecture and design as they envisioned a new world to rise from the devastation of World War I. We can imagine that encouragement to fantasize about restructuring the world was in itself encouraged by such children's literature (and also toys).

Illustrating this process are two of the early figures promoting the aesthetic of the invisible at the Bauhaus—two Hungarians: Marcel Breuer (1902-) and Laszlo Moholy-Nagy (1895-1946). Breuer was the gifted student who later became a Bauhaus teacher, and was chosen to design the furniture and interiors of the new Bauhaus building (including Gropius's office) when it was built at Dessau in 1926, and also houses for several of the masters. He very well may have been exposed to fantastic literature as a child, but if he was not he was soon exposed to others with these enthusiasms in Vienna and Berlin, especially, in the early 1920s, his teacher Moholy-Nagy. Moholy-Nagy was the eager Hungarian who burst in to take over some of the Bauhaus courses in the early 1920s with his commitment to Machine Age aesthetics and practical ways of producing new designs for industry. He had been in Berlin during the final years of World War I, where he and other members of a group of radical designers and thinkers were enthusiasts not only for new glass architecture, but also for fantastic literature (Yevgeny Zamiatin's *We*, for example, with its glass paradise, and the visionary poetry of Paul Scheerbart[22]). Reyner Banham has noted, furthermore, that Moholy was inspired by the color-illustrated magazines he read in his youth, and a statement of Moholy's made in 1928 attests to this influence: "We need," he said, "Utopians of genius, a new Jules Verne."[23] In teaching the preliminary design course at the Bauhaus, he had his students make, as a basic kind of design for the future world, abstract compositions of glass, flat metal planes—sculpture that was mostly open space.[24]

The modernist interior, then, not surprisingly, became an empty interior, an empty space from which, we can imagine, the furniture has vanished! While Schindler's interior took the approach of removing the furniture, interiors by Breuer, in the mid-1920s, took a different tack: the furniture was just barely there. It was reduced to planes floating in space. In Breuer's terminology, "transparency" was, along with mobility, lightness and economy of materials, the aim of these designs. In 1927, Breuer wrote, "the pieces of furniture and even the very walls of a room have ceased to be massive and monumental, apparently immovable, and built for eternity. Instead, they are more opened out, or, so to speak, drawn in space. They hinder neither the movement of the body nor of the eye."[25] To this effect, he made his famous experiments with chrome-plated tubular steel, beginning with the famous Wassily chair of 1925, which gave the sitter the feeling of floating suspended in space. Chairs by Mies and others followed this example: seats cantilevered out into space, with two legs rather than the usual four.

But do we have any real evidence (beyond Breuer's discussion of "transparency") that invisibility, in addition to a sensation of magical suspension, was what these designers were after? Indeed we do, in a Bauhaus publication authored by Moholy-Nagy. Here we see the evolution of furniture, as envisioned by Moholy, culminating in the invisible chair. Writes Moholy, "In the future we will be sitting on a resilient column of compressed air!" The Wassily chair was represented as the nearest approximation to the ideal.[26]

If Breuer was a prince in the kingdom of transparency, Moholy was the king. By nature a practical man (and one with the gee-whiz kind of inventiveness, a knack for turning fantasy into real invention, that we would find in a Hugo Gernsback publication) he showed in his famous design book *Vision in Motion* actual experiments with compressed air.[27] After coming to the United States at the closure of the Bauhaus, he worked with his students in Chicago and with industry to develop transparent lucite furniture—another method of achieving the invisible. He made the first paintings on plexiglass—paintings with the support apparently not there, a culmination of many years of experiments with effects of transparency in his oil paintings. Moholy was a radical pioneer, beginning in the early 1920s with photography, later making the first paintings on plexiglass (a culmination of earlier experiments with effects of transparency in oil on canvas). His inventions also included light-sculpture, sculpture which was made only of light, and sculptures of transparent lucite.[28] Interested in all that was forward-looking, he participated in the creation of the sets for Vincent Korda's film of the 1930s, *Things to Come*. However, his designs were evidently cut from the final film. With lucite cones and towers (resembling Mies's skyscraper project of 1922), his designs for the world of the future were, he complained, too far advanced for the producers of the film to accept.[29] All in all, his work represents the influence of popular science fiction in the pursuit of effects of invisibility.

Along with Breuer and Moholy-Nagy, many of the other pioneering modernists of the 1920s and 1930s were also concerned with the disappearing building and its contents. Schindler, in California, is exemplary. George Fred Keck, another American, is also a good example, with his two Crystal Houses built for the Chicago Century of Progress Exhibition of 1933 indicating his commitment to a world of glass.[30] At the Bauhaus, however, perhaps the best-known exponent of the empty interior and disappearing building was Mies, father of our glass block skyscrapers. In his interiors of the 1920s, Mies created a universal empty space, divided just where necessary by partition walls, made possible by the steel frame/curtain wall construction, and furnished with the absolute minimum of objects. In the Barcelona Pavilion of 1929, he managed to dissolve the interior walls and columns into a shimmer of colored light, the dematerialization of the building enhanced by the play of light upon the colored marble walls by the dancing reflections from the pond outside the glass. It actually approached, in effect, that of the display that Mies and his cohort, Lilly Reich, did the same year for the German silk manufacturers: an empty space, divided by the flimsiest of shimmering colored partitions. Like the silk display, which contained no furniture whatsoever, the Barcelona Pavilion was conceived as empty space, not to be lived in, really, but to be moved through.[31]

Invisible buildings and transparent objects, and large empty spaces also became part and parcel of popular science fiction—from Wells's descriptions of worlds of the future extrapolated from advanced glass and iron architecture of the late nineteenth century to the other masterpieces of science fiction literature from the 1920s to the 1950s and beyond. To cite just two examples here, there are the transparent domiciles of Zamyatin's *We*[32] and Arthur C. Clarke's *The City and the Stars*.[33] There are others too numerous to mention, including many from the stories and illustrations published in the pulp magazines. In these we find crystalline buildings, and transparent objects of all sorts: for example, the transparent coffin, the transparent machines, transparent automobiles and spaceships, alike in spirit to and contemporary with transparent materials being developed in the real world.[34] Science fiction films were excited about transparency as the setting for the future world as well, but the early ones had a bit of difficulty finding materials that could convey the correct effect—curtains of cellophane, a new material of the 1920s, were just not satisfactory, while glass furniture—as made for the sets of *Things to Come* in 1936—worked a bit better.

The real-world interiors and furnishings discussed so far, designed by architects from Austria, Germany, and Hungary, and also many science fiction interiors, all show an infatuation with empty space. We must note that the interiors they created were not just empty interiors for the sake of being empty. They were, in most cases, representations of the out-of-doors brought indoors. The desire to live freely outside, close to nature, was at the root of the modernists' desire to create invisible environments. The idea of outdoors brought indoors had special appeal to Germans at the turn of the century, at which time there was a revival of folk and fairy stories in which people go into the wilderness to seek or by accident to find transformation. There were groups of German young people who acted these ideas out, for instance, those known as the "Wandervögel,"[35] or the radical group of young artists known as "Die Brücke."[36] We see in paintings of members of Die Brücke a few of the young folks frolicking nude at the side of a lake. (Incidentally, it was in this very decade—the first decade of this century—that social nudism was being promoted in Germany, where by the 1930s it had garnered the participation of 30,000 people.[37]).

Architecture providing an outdoor-type space, as it appeared in nineteenth-century science fiction (and on into the twentieth century) and also the interiors of the real world of the 1920s and 1930s, derived directly from the revolutionary glass and iron architecture of the second half of the nineteenth century, most importantly, the Crystal Palace of 1851 built by Joseph Paxton for the Great Exhibition in London, but also including the fabulous Parisian Department stores with their colored glass domes, the impressive market halls and glass-roofed train sheds, and other glass roofed buildings of both small and great (even staggering) proportions built in Europe in the Victorian era.[38] Many turn-of-the-century, glass-domed rooms reveal very clearly a desire for the roof to approximate the sky itself—we find wonderful representations of the sky in glass roofs by Tiffany, and by Vienna architect Joseph Maria Olbrich. (See, for example, Olbrich's Sezession Building of 1897, which renders in bronze a bower of leaves overhead.) Interestingly, it was recognized at the time that these buildings had qualities connecting them with fantasy literature—the Crystal Palace, revolutionary in its effects of insubstantiality and delightful in its dazzling reflections, was described as a building from "fairyland."[39]

The fact that the Crystal Palace was derived from greenhouse architecture points up the fact that the glass and iron buildings were thought of as means of achieving an outdoor space indoors, but specifically an outdoors that achieved perfect climate control. The space inside, like many of the science fiction interiors that it inspired, provided a perpetual summer afternoon, full of light (so important in the years before Thomas Edison's lightbulb) and warmth, one in which one could, if one had a mind, take off one's clothes and run about in flimsy garments. It is not too far-fetched to suggest that these interiors, as they were pictured in twentieth-century science fiction, provided, in a Machine Age version, an afternoon in fairyland.[40]

Sometimes modern interior spaces represented not exactly nature brought indoors, but rather empty spaces infused with color and light, as exemplified in Mies's Barcelona Pavilion.[41] Up through the 1920s the pursuit of a multicolored architecture was a major concern of the modernists (one that historians of the last fifty years have not been particularly aware of due to the unavailability of colored photography in the 1920s). In the writings of the visionary architects in Berlin during World War I, the crystalline architecture of the future was envisioned as multicolored—full of the effects of Tiffany, who had contributed his glass to some of the most enchanting glass and iron interiors of late nineteenth-century Europe. This sort of colored interior is of course part of the literary tradition of science fiction and of fantasy going back to the early nineteenth century, and even earlier. (See, for instance, Samuel Taylor Coleridge's "Kubla Khan," the *Arabian Nights*, and other literary works imbued with Orientalist imagery.[42]) It was undoubtedly given tremendous popularity by the development of chromolithography for illustrating children's books. As mentioned before, it is not surprising that it was in Germany that a polychrome modern architecture developed, given the leadership of the Germans in production of books of fantasy and especially in the printing of wonderful colored illustrations for these books.[43]

How this colored glass interior became a force in the real world architecture of Germany in the 1920s is a story worth telling. It is now well known to architectural historians. The colored glass interior appeared in Berlin at the outset of World War I in the work of Bruno Taut (see the Glass Pavilion built for the Cologne Exhibition of 1914), under the influence of Tiffany and the visions (also influenced by Tiffany) of fantasy/science fiction poet Paul Scheerbart, Taut's close friend. The notion of a polychrome, crystalline architecture spread through members of the radical artists' groups, notably the members of the Glass Chain, a secret society of designers who exchanged drawings and writings about the future world and its architecture from 1919 to 1921.[44] These interests carried into the work of the Bauhaus (Gropius, for instance was a member of the Glass Chain), and we can see the effects in architecture and design through the 1920s. By the 1930s, however, the interest in multicolored environments seems to have waned, although it often persists in the interiors envisioned in popular science fiction.

Thus far, we have noted in the empty spaces of the modern interior a strong whiff of fantasy. The spaces are empty, it seems, because things that ought to be inside have somehow disappeared. They are empty because they are really not indoor spaces at all, but the outside magically brought in, and this indoors/outdoors imbued with a very pretty colored light and the climate of a perfect day. But this is not all—there is more! They, just as much as the interiors of *Things to Come* or of Frank R. Paul's illustrations, were thought of as places for free, unfettered movement of the body—vast spaces, with plenty of room to walk, to run, or to dance. In the real world a few examples may suffice to illustrate this concept.

Schindler wanted, even in his small interiors, the fullest amount of room for movement. Because the occupants would be swiftly moving through the house, Schindler noted that the ceiling decoration in the modern house would be of negligible importance (people would not be sitting down, as in ages past). He wrote: "The ceiling in the modern house has completely disappeared above our line of vision and we no longer lavish our decorative talent on its surface. Our intensity of movement or action has increased the necessity of elbow room. The accepted standing and walking position of the conventional ballet (heels together, toes apart) has given way to the more active one of the toes pointing straight ahead."[45] (We see an example of this new type of dance in the movements of Isadora Duncan, which resembled those of children playing in the out-of-doors, whose freedom the fairies encapsulated.)

Likewise, Mies's interiors were places for moving through, just as were the exhibition displays he designed in the year preceding the design of the Barcelona Pavilion. We can surmise that at some level he conceived of all these interiors as spacious enough for dancing, since at the Bauhaus that same year he had designed similar partitions as sets for one of the Bauhaus "festes," in which the dancers actually danced in and out of the moveable partitions. Le Corbusier at the same time, 1929, was also committed to the idea of the interior as an empty stage for movement, expressed, for instance, in the famous Villa Savoye, with its "promenade" through the building, and in his Parisian houses of the same date.[46]

To stretch a point, we can think of the modernist interior, the domain of such supposedly rational sorts as Breuer, Mies, Schindler, and Le Corbusier, as a realization of fairyland itself—outdoors brought indoors, magically enclosed, providing by imperceptible means a perfect summer afternoon with plenty of room to fly. The new interior of the early 1930s was conceived of as a creation in four dimensions, in Schindler's words, "Space Architecture."[47] While clothed in Machine Age garb, just as Buck Rogers, with his flying belt gives the ideal of fairy flight a science fiction spin, these interiors show the influence of a longstanding literary heritage.

Postscript

At this point the question arises of whether there was an actual connection between the development of "invisible" architecture and furnishings in Europe from the 1880s to 1930 and popular science fiction in the pulp magazines. It is important to bear in mind that both Gernsback (from Luxembourg) and Paul (from Vienna) came from this Germanic cultural milieu, as did other illustrators of the pulps, such as "Wesso" (H. L. Wessolowski), who was trained in Berlin. Germany and Vienna just prior to and during World War I were steeped in the tradition of fantasy literature, seen in children's books and early science fiction, as well as in the advanced architecture of Europe.[48] It is obvious, of course, that they took their cues from the traditional iron-and-glass architecture to which we have already referred. Frank R. Paul most significantly continues the tradition of the glass roof and the representation of an indoor/outdoor space of vast proportions, right up to the 1940s in his marvelous back-cover illustrations for *Amazing Stories*, although he always picked up new ideas along the way (for example, streamlining).[49]

Furthermore, science fiction illustrators, particularly Frank R. Paul, undoubtedly knew the radical architects of Europe in the first two decades of the twentieth century. A study of Paul's earliest drawings for the Gernsback magazines shows distinct similarities to some designs by the Glass Chain and the work of Taut in particular, suggesting he knew Taut's publications. Paul, for example, uses the crystal skyscraper motif (also used by the Bauhaus designers, in fact, as a symbol for the new world) very early, showing his familiarity with Taut's Alpine Architecture (1919). Some of his early alien landscapes are almost direct copies of ideas of Taut's.[50] Given the fact that Paul was an art student in both Vienna and Berlin (and also, evidently, Paris) in the first part of this century it is not surprising that he knew these images of the Glass Chain or that they would continue to inform his vision of the future world long after he immigrated to the United States. Paul's covers often reflect as well the influence of the early illustrations of the famous Professor Bruno Paul, director of the Berlin Academy of Arts and Crafts; could it be that Frank was Bruno Paul's son, or nephew?

The situation was undoubtedly similar for other immigrants who became illustrators for the science fiction pulps, carrying early European ideas over to America and perpetuating them in the world of popular science fiction. That designs for "invisible" architecture and objects represented a Germanic vision of the future world with which Hugo Gernsback was familiar probably accounts for the fact that Gernsback was so supportive of and also so dependent upon Paul as his illustrator.

With their roots in Europe, Paul and others (notably Wesso) perpetuated this vision of glass architecture, invisible furnishings, and even crystalline forms into the 1930s, albeit adding new styles and new ideas as they went along. (It is said that Frank R. Paul kept a file of futuristic designs in his desk.)

And so with this shared heritage, the idea of empty spaces in the interior and the invisible building became, at least for a period in the 1920s and 1930s, a staple of both the real-world architecture of the modern movement and popular science fiction. In science fiction it lasted much longer. And one might argue that it is popular science fiction that has kept that vision of what the world of the future should look like alive today.

Notes

1. R. M. Schindler, "Furniture and the Modern House: A Theory of Interior Design," [part one], *The Architect and Engineer*, 123 (December, 1935), 25. (See also part two in volume 124 [March, 1936], 24-28.) I am grateful to Dr. Robert Winter for his remarks on the radically reductive nature of Schindler's interiors presented at the Schindler Symposium, the University Art Museum, University of California, Santa Barbara, 1996.

2. Jeffrey Chusid, lecture given at the Schindler symposium. See also the chapter by David and Patricia Gebhard in *The Furniture of R. M. Schindler*, edited by Marla Burn (Santa Barbara: University Art Museum, University of California, 1997).

3. See Werner Blaser, *Mies van der Rohe: Less Is More* (Zurich: Waser, 1986).

4. Kathleen Church Plummer, "The Streamlined Moderne," *Art in America*, 62, (January/February, 1974), 46-51. See also literature defining the relationship between visionary poet Paul Scheerbart (especially his Glasarchitectur, Berlin, Der Sturm, 1914) and German architects at the turn of the century, beginning with Reyner Banham, "The Glass Paradise," *Architectural Review*, 125 (February, 1959), 87-89; "Paul Scheerbart's Glass World," in *Glass Architecture by Paul Scheerbart and Alpine Architecture by Bruno Taut*, edited by Dennis Sharp (New York, Praeger, 1972); and Rosemary Haag Bletter, "The Interpretation of the Glass Dream: Expressionist Architecture and the Crystal Metaphor," *Journal of the Society of Architectural Historians*, 40 (March, 1981), 20-43.

5. For discussion of science fiction illustration, see Plummer, Views from the Rocket Ship: Machine Imagery in Science Fiction of the Twenties and Thirties (unpublished thesis), Department of Art, University of California, Santa Barbara, 1974.

6. On Bruno Paul, see Alfred Ziffer (Hrsg.), *Bruno Paul: Deutsche Raumkunst und Architektur zwischen Jugendstil und Moderne* (Munich: Klinkhardt and Biermann, 1992; catalog of an exhibition held in 1992 at the Munich Stadtmuseum). See also Gillian Naylor, *The Bauhaus Reassessed* (New York, Dutton, 1985), 23-24, for Paul's influence on the Bauhaus. Bruno Paul was also a famous illustrator, known for his caricatures and cartoons— some under the alias of Kellerman—in the Saturday magazine *Simplicissimus*. (Comparisons of his style with that of Frank R. Paul leave no doubt as to his influence on Frank.) Bruno Paul moved from Munich to Berlin in 1906, becoming the head of the Museum of Industrial and Applied Art and the Academy of Arts. He was also Mies van der Rohe's first employer (1906-8).

7. The style was defined in an influential exhibition held at the Museum of Modern Art in 1932. See Henry-Russell Hitchcock and Philip Johnson, *The International Style* (New York: Norton, 1932).

8. Sigfried Giedion, *Space, Time, and Architecture* (Cambridge: Harvard University Press, 1954), passim. From lectures given in 1938-39.

9. Lewis Carroll, *Through the Looking Glass and What Alice Found There*, illustrated by Sir John Tenniel (London: Macmillan, 1871). *Alice's Adventures in Wonderland*, also with Tenniel illustrations, had been published in London and New York by Macmillan in 1865, and was translated into French in 1869.

10. *Things to Come*, a film by Alexander Korda, with sets by William Cameron Menzies, 1936. For Wells's instructions to the makers of this film, see H. G. Wells, *Things to Come: A Film by H. G. Wells* (New York: Macmillan, 1935). It was based on his novel *The Shape of Things to Come*.

11. For a discussion of these stage shows, see Melbourne Christopher, *Magic: A Picture History* (New York: Dover, 1991). First published by Dover in 1962 as *Panorama of Magic*.

12. See Esther McCoy, "A Vast Hall Full of Light: The Bradbury Building: 1893," *Arts and Architecture* (April, 1953), 20-21, 42-43, and Plummer, "The Streamlined Moderne," for discussion of this influence.

13. On late nineteenth-century children's books, see *Victorian Children's Books: A Brief Survey*, edited by Joyce Whalley (London: Victoria and Albert Museum, 1973), particularly the chapter entitled "Tales of Fantasy and Imagination." The first translation of the Grimms's *Fairy Tales* appeared in England in 1820, and in the 1840s Herbert Cole began the revival of interest in traditional tales. Hans Christian Andersen's stories, the first to make the transition from folk tale to modern tale of fancy, were first published in England in 1846, illustrated by A. L. Gaskin, according to Whalley, who states that with the success of *Alice's Adventures in Wonderland* the right for children to read for pleasure was firmly established, so that "by the end of the century it might be possible to find children who had never read an 'improving' book of the old sort, but who would probably be well-versed in fairy tales, school stories, and adventures of every kind" (14). Whalley suggests that fairy stories provided a shared international experience for nineteenth-century children, from their appearance in the translations of French stories by the Countess D'Aubnoy and by Charles Perrault, which were often reissued for children with special illustrations (58).

14. H. G. Wells, *When the Sleeper Wakes*, in *Three Prophetic Novels of H. G. Wells*, edited by E. F. Bleiler (New York: Dover, 1960). For more information on glass in science fiction, see Plummer, Views from the Rocket Ship. As for glass in fairy stories, one of the earliest and most popular examples is of course, *Cinderella and the Glass Slipper*, edited and illustrated by George Cruikshank (London: D. Bogue, 1853), and there are many other examples in the late nineteenth century.

15. On invisibility as a literary theme, see Brooks Landon, "Styles of Invisibility: Sustaining the Transparent in Contemporary Prose Semblances," in *Styles of Creation: Aesthetic Technique and the Creation of Fictional Worlds*, edited by George Slusser and Eric S. Rabkin (Athens: University of Georgia Press, 1992), 245-59.

16. On fairies, see especially, Colin White, "Fairies," in *The World of the Nursery* (New York: Dutton, 1984), 105-17.

17. A character in a Fitz-James O'Brien story of 1851 is cited by Isaac Asimov as the first invisible man in science fiction (as opposed to fantasy) literature in *Isaac Asimov Presents the Best Science Fiction Firsts*, edited by Asimov, Charles G. Waugh, and Martin H. Greenberg (New York: Beaufort Books, 1984). H. G. Wells's *The Invisible Man* appeared in 1897.

18. Sir Arthur Conan Doyle, "The Disintegration Machine," in *The Best Science Fiction Stories of Arthur Conan Doyle*, edited by Charles G. Waugh and Martin H. Greenberg with an introduction by George E. Slusser (Carbondale: Southern Illinois University Press, 1981).

Note that Doyle was a relative of Richard Doyle, the famous illustrator and illustrator of one of the first picture books about fairyland, *In Fairyland: A Series of Pictures from the Elfworld* (London: Longmans Green, 1870), with color illustrations printed by Edmund Evans, so it is not surprising that Sir Arthur took up this theme. The early science fiction films of Georges Méliès are filled with people who transform themselves or simply disappear (thanks to the use of the stop-action camera), according to Albert J. LaValley, "Traditions of Trickery" in *Shadows of the Magic Lamp*, edited by George Slusser and Eric S. Rabkin (Carbondale: Southern Illinois University Press, 1985).

19. For detailed discussion, and many colored illustrations, see *Die Bilderwelt im Kinderbuch: Kinder-und Jugenbucher aus funf Jahrhunderten*; catalog of a 1988 exhibition of the Kunst und Museumbibliothek und des Rheinischen Bildarchiv der Stadt Koln, herausgegeben von Albert Schug.

20. See Ulrike Bastien, "Die 'Kinder-und Hausmarchen' der Bruder Grimm," in *Der Literaturpadagogischen Diskussion*, 19 and 20 (Jahrhunderts: Geissen, Haag und Herchen, 1981), cited in Jack Zipes, "The German Obsession with Fairy Tales," in *The Brothers Grimm: From the Enchanted Forests to the Modern World* (New York: Routledge and Kegan Paul, 1988).

21. Illustrators of fairy tales in Germany include, for instance, Paul Gösch (1885-1940), member of the Gläserne Kette, whose work is illustrated in Timothy Benson, *Expressionist Utopias: Paradise, Metropolis, Architectural Fantasy* (Los Angeles: Los Angeles County Museum of Art, 1993; catalog of an exhibition), 188-89. In England, they include Ruskin and the Preraphaelites and famous arts and crafts designers, significantly Walter Crane and C. A. Voysey, and in Scotland, in the early twentieth century, members of the Glasgow School, C. R. Mackintosh and his wife Margaret Macdonald.

22. Yevgeny Zamiatin, *We*, translated by Mirra Ginsberg (New York: Viking, 1972); first published in English, New York: Dutton, 1924). It was written in 1920-1921—just the same years Moholy claims to have discovered transparency—and not admitted to publication by the Soviets.

23. Quoted in Reyner Banham, *Theory and Design in the First Machine Age* (London: Architectural Press, 1960; Cambridge: MIT Press, 1980), 217.

24. Illustrated and discussed in Hans M. Wingler, *The Bauhaus* (Cambridge: MIT Press, 1969); first published as *Das Bauhaus* (Cologne: Verlag Gebr. Rasch and Co. and M. DuMont Schauberg, 1962). Moholy was influenced by the Russian constructivists, Gabo and Pevsner.

25. Text of advertisement for Breuer's furniture, 1928, quoted in Christopher Wilk, *Marcel Breuer: Furniture and Interiors* (London: Architectural Press, 1981; New York: Museum of Modern Art, 1981), 67.

26. Moholy-Nagy, caption accompanying photographs of Marcel Breuer's chairs in *The Bauhaus Journal*, no. 1 (1926), reproduced in Gillian Naylor, *The Bauhaus Reassessed* (New York: Dutton, 1985), 106: "Everyday we are getting better and better . . . in the end we will sit on resilient air columns."

27. Moholy-Nagy, *Vision in Motion* (Chicago: Paul Theobald, 1947) illustrates Moholy's experiments with compressed air.

28. Lucite furniture is illustrated in *Vision and Motion*.

29. Moholy-Nagy, *Vision in Motion*, 267. According to Moholy, "This same set with revolving cones, photographed with a multiplying prism, produced so rich a visual effect that the editor of the film did not dare to use it." Richard Kostelanetz in *Moholy-Nagy* (New York: Praeger, 1970, 5-6) attributes the cut to "personal preferences."

30. See George Fred Keck's crystal houses for the 1933 Century of Progress in Brian

Horrigan, "The Home of Tomorrow," in *Imagining Tomorrow: History, Technology, and the American Future*, edited by Joseph Corn (Cambridge: MIT Press, 1986), 137-63.

31. Matilda McQuaid, *Lilly Reich, Designer and Architect* (New York: The Museum of Modern Art, 1996; catalog of an exhibition at the museum, 1997).

32. *We*, 7.

33. Arthur C. Clarke, *The City and the Stars* (1956; New York: Bantam, 1984).

34. For illustrations from pulp magazines, see Anthony Frewin, *One Hundred Years of Science Fiction Illustration* (London: Jupiter, 1974), and for discussion, see Plummer, Views from the Rocket Ship.

35. On the Wandervögel, see Christopher Laue, *Der Bund der Wandervögel und Pfadfinder: Tradition und Politik in der Jugenbewegung der Weimarer Republik* (Heidenheim: Sudmarkverlag, Fritsch, 1987).

36. On Die Brücke, see Reinhold Heller, "Bridge to Utopia: The Brücke as Utopian Experiment" in *Expressionist Utopias*, edited by Timothy Benson, 62-83. Erich Heckel's "Scene in the Woods" (1910) is on page 69, Ernst L. Kirchner's "Bathers Tossing Reeds" (1910) on page 70, and Max Pechstein's "Dancers and Bathers at a forest Pond" on page 73.

37. On social nudism, see Fred Ilfeld and Roger Lauer, *Social Nudism in America* (New Haven: College and University Press, 1964).

38. Giedion, 227-39.

39. Giedion quotes a visitor (Luther Bucher) writing of the Crystal Palace in 1851 as follows: "It is a sober economy of language if I call the spectacle (of the interior) incomparable and fairylike. It is *Midsummer Night's Dream* seen in the clear light of midday" (251-52).

40. It was in the 1920s and 1930s that both Europeans and Americans made great advances in artificial lighting (with the end of achieving a steady perfect lighting level) and also artificial heating and cooling, to the point that it was noted that windows were no longer needed in our buildings. Some science fiction writers picked up on this theme, including Wells, in his instructions to the makers of the film *Things to Come*. For more complete discussion, see Plummer, Views From the Rocket Ship and "The Streamlined Moderne."

41. For a description of coloristic effects in Mies's work, see Jean Louis Cohen, *Mies van der Rohe* (London: SPON), 1996, 26-27.

42. On fantasy illustration. see Brigid Peppin, *Fantasy Book Illustration 1860-1920* (London: Studio Vista, 1975), which contains biographies of many famous illustrators, especially in England.

43. Colored illustrations were thought at first to be an addition especially to attract children (fancy colored books were often given as gifts). Interestingly Hans Christian Andersen once complained that he thought the publishers of one of his later editions had gone overboard in making such fancy colored illustrations.

44. On the Gläserne Kette, see *The Crystal Chain Letters: Architectural Fantasies by Bruno Taut and His Circle*, edited and translated by Iain Boyd Whyte (Cambridge: MIT Press, 1985). On the Glashaus and Taut, see Whyte, "The Expressionist Sublime," in *Expressionist Utopias*, 118-37. For a biography of Taut, see Whyte, *Bruno Taut and the Architecture of Activism* (Cambridge: Cambridge University Press, 1982). On Tiffany's influence in Europe, see Herwin Schaefer, "Tiffany's Fame in Europe," in *Art Bulletin*, 44 (December, 1962), 309-28.

45. Schindler, "Furniture and the Modern House," 26.

46. Le Corbusier's concept of "promenade," seen in his interiors of the 1920s, was influenced by his admiration for promenades on ocean liners, as illustrated in his *Towards a New Architecture* (London: Architectural Press, 1946), 92-95; first published in English

in 1927, and originally published as *Vers Une Arquitecture* (Paris: Editions Crøs, 1923).

47. Schindler, "Space Architecture," in *Dune Forum* (February, 1934), 44-46.

48 See Plummer, Views from the Rocket Ship, for full discussion.

49. Some of Paul's early illustrations, such as "The Infinite Vision" and "Station X" of 1926, suggest he may have read Taut's *Die Stadtkrone*, published in Jena, 1919. The Stadtkrone (City Crown) "was for Taut a symbolic city building making a bold silhouette against the sky, visible from all over the city, much as an oriental pagoda or minaret or a Gothic spire could be seen to dominate the surrounding buildings," according to Banham, *Theory and Design*, 266. Other Paul illustrations show the influence of contemporary progressive buildings in Vienna, such as the municipal gas works of 1893-96.

50. For example, an illustration of Paul's for "The Second Swarm," in *Amazing Stories Quarterly* (Spring, 1928), 274, shows exactly the same arrangement of buildings in a circle that Taut imagined for a new Folkwang Schule (with a crystal house) in 1919-20, reproduced in Whyte, *The Crystal Chain Letters*, 48.

5

"Getting It Right":
A Reflection on Titans and Technology*

Gregory Benford

In the twentieth century, as others note, the Western world broke the close link between art and science, as prevailing currents flowed away from external nature to internal feelings—a big factor, I believe, in what C. P. Snow argued was a growing divide between "the two cultures." Scientists studied nature, artists studied themselves. They also showed the modernist shattering of consensus reality, rendering experience through abstraction, surrealism and stress on the non-natural ways of seeing (cubism, for example).

Space art can rebuild the bridge between these two cultures, celebrating nature on the broadest canvas, reflecting both scientific and aesthetic values.

My interest in space art was first sparked by the works of Chesley Bonestell, so I was thrilled, in 1969, to visit the artist at his home in Carmel. To recapture that moment, let me begin by reprinting a short essay I wrote as a fan in 1970 after that meeting, titled "The Science in Science Fiction: The View from Titan."[1]

To get to Carmel and avoid the neon jungles that infest the northern and southern California coasts, you must travel on the sheer coastal route, brave the fogs and curves, you must take Route One. Carmel is an appendix to Monterey, an afterthought of summer cottages and organic food stores. There are a lot of writers and artists there and they are to be seen avoiding work in the afternoons, sipping coffee in the Tuck Box or thumbing paperbacks in the small book store.

To reach his house you turn off Route One in the geometrical center of town, the bisection point, and travel but a block up a dead end street. His house is cloaked in pine and wisps of the fog that pursued you down from Santa Cruz. It looks warm and cozy; orange splashes signal to you through the windows. You wonder why reading lamps seen through windows in winter seem to glow with a sunny warmth, kindling meaning, while in the summer they are just reading lamps in the distance.

His rug muffles your inward step. A cat melts away at your entrance. His wife makes coffee in the wide kitchen. You and he sit in deck chairs. Feeling of being a movie producer; look for your name on the back. But he has been there, you have not; he worked for Disney and Pal. Just a chapter in a long life.

There was a portrait of him on the cover of *The Magazine of Fantasy and Science Fiction* in the early 1950s, but you do not remember it until an hour later, finding it in an odd corner of his work room. He has not changed from those days. He is over eighty now and his face carries a weight behind it while still retaining its walnut-brown look. A smile crinkles everything.

Here in the house, sipping tea in green Japanese mugs that warm the hands, you see the work for which he is not known. Oriental prints. Portraits, belying the common judgment that he cannot render the human figure and make you feel with it. Delicate pencil work. Architecture, stress and design, massive stones balanced in a fine grid of lines. "I see the patterns first, then the rest. I was an architect, you know, before the first world war. I designed the ceiling of the San Francisco opera house."

After that? "I travelled. I saw the world. I lived in New York and Paris and London and finally Los Angeles. Designing buildings and then movie work, backdrops, special effects. Disney did a lot of innovation in special effects, but it required someone who could draw and paint with such detail that the film viewer wouldn't catch an error. Things had to be real. I learned much that way. We were very well paid; that was Los Angeles."

There are no astronomicals inside the house. To see them you must go outside, up an exposed wooden staircase, into the study. There they crowd the room in the heady smell of fresh paint, rags, stretched canvas. A congress of infinities.

Does he ever read the things he has illustrated? No, he doesn't like science fiction very much. Not enough solidity, perhaps. He rarely if ever willingly puts a human artifact into his work, a spaceship or a pressure dome, or a space-suited figure. He doesn't have any idea of what the future will bring and feels awkward trying to visualize it. But stars and planets, yes, the astronomer friends he has can give him descriptions of how things must be there and he can see it, too, in some closed mind's eye, so that it comes out right. Most science fiction is quickly outdated, anyway. Look at all the fins on space ships, and the cloudless Earths. Better to stay away from it.

Someone in Palo Alto has made prints of two of his oils. One is of an expedition that has landed on a dry, rust-orange Martian desert and is deploying equipment. It seems oddly out of balance and unconvincing, not his best work. The other is better: Saturn from Titan. His classic signature piece. Wrong, of course, since we now know that the methane atmosphere there blankets everything. But it was right when he painted it, the way any scientific theory is correct as an approximation of the truth which is never fully known, and that is all anybody can ask. He has a few prints left. We should not feel that it is necessary to buy anything, of course. We take Saturn. There is something awesome in the mass of the planet even at this distance, a cold white with a hard curve to it. Looking at it you believe in your soul that planets are gods and men but pawns.

There are stills from motion pictures he has done. George Pal, worlds colliding, rockets, *"The Day The Earth Stood Still,"* a Groucho Marx hanging from a 20th story window against city lights done in oil, but the distant car headlights moving. Stop-motion. Planet-wrecking. It was a lot of fun and a lot of money but his reputation will probably rest on the astronomicals displayed in Boston and New York and San Francisco. Double stars and novae and howling unseen storms in deep atmospheres. A sense of the infinite.

At the center is craft. A view of Saturn at dawn from the Grand Tour probe: it stands dead upright on the easel, half-finished. "Black is very difficult. It is so hard to get the absolute pure black in comparison with the soft color of an atmosphere or a star's envelope. Almost impossible, I think, unless one practices a great deal. I have seen very few painters who can handle it, even in abstracts."

He shows us a few abstracts he has done and they are very good, though none uses very much black. He has tried everything and mastered many techniques, though he has sold very little of it. Most of the good oils he keeps for himself; he can afford to. For a while there was a rush to buy his astronomical oils and he nearly became a factory, turning them out faster than he should have, but that is past. Most sold to aerospace engineers and now they have less extra money and perhaps it is just as well.

He works hard and keeps a regular schedule but he cannot keep up with the load of work. Today arrived an offer from *Playboy* which he will accept for a three page oil, even though it will mean disturbing his schedule. His agent is trying to get him to do another book of the sort he did with Willy Ley, but there is no time. Perhaps next year.

You speak of working together on a book. He thinks *Profiles of the Future* is a good title but you tell him Arthur C. Clarke has already used it. Well, something else, then, but keep in touch.

(Connections: the book doesn't go through because you are too busy to finish the chapters that year, and then you move to the University and there are years of intense physics after that. But he gives you a name of a friend, just a boy who he knows does good work but has had few opportunities—after all he is but eighteen yet, give him time. In a few months you hear from him—Don Davis—and then you sell a novel, *Jupiter Project*, the first one worth a damn and as true to the Jupiter we know as you can get it. Don Davis does two oils to illustrate it. The next year it is published and prompts a letter from Robert Heinlein, which is as much as anybody could ask for. A friend praises it too, exclaiming that you were so lucky to get someone so like Bonestell to do the cover. The whole set of principles is now a tradition and it came mostly out of this one man. Connections.)

The only science fiction person he sees these days is Heinlein, he says, who lives an hour away on the coast. He likes the Heinlein approach; it seems more honest somehow, closer to the tenuous facts of science. And the Heinlein futures have a lived-in feel. "He's the titan of the field," the old man says reflectively, never remarking on his own stature in the landscape he and the writers inhabit.

He does not see many artists. Carmel is a center for them but they are mostly dabblers, amateurs. He does not have much interest in the young: he thinks their technique is poor. They do not see how important it is to *get it right*. The test of learning to draw a cow is not in the fingers but in the eye: you must learn to see the cow. Few do this today. "Once having seen it, you must draw or paint so that others can see it. Not the thing itself, but the way it seems, that is art. What else is there?"

Though we exchanged cards afterward, I never saw Chesley Bonestell again. Soon, however, I became aware of a different style of space art—Soviet space art— which, while often impressive, appeared to display very little interest in "getting it right." However, the stereotypes were shattered when I became acquainted with the works of Soviet painter Andrei Sokolov, who was working in his own way to fulfill Bonestell's agenda.

In general, several features distinguish Soviet space art from the American version. Instead of erecting theoretical frameworks to explain these differences, I prefer a painterly approach, not a critical one. When I think of the many Soviet-era space paintings I have seen, both in the United States and in Soviet galleries, I remember fuzzily painted groups of indistinguishable figures striding toward the unknown. American sf and astronomical art, in contrast, usually featured traditional lone figures against immense landscapes.

In U.S. sf and space art, realism rules. This is part of the hard sf aesthetic, the Bonestellian "rocks and balls" school as some Russian painters have described it. Such reality was the stuff of *Astounding Science-Fiction*. To illustrate its value, William Hartmann, a space scientist at the University of Arizona who has a parallel career as a painter, recalled to me how he had depicted pedestal formations on comets, setting up and painting at a specialist comet meeting. Several astrophysicists, including David Brin, had theorized that rocks on the surface would shield the snow and ice beneath them, so that the rest of the landscape evaporated during close passage to the sun. The comet would then literally "grow" toadstool-like formations. Hartmann drew this, and soon enough, the effect proliferated into NASA brochures. (Yet when the prediction was stated in a paper to a journal, it was rejected. Now it is finally conventional wisdom, based on direct observations.)

In contrast, the USSR's state artists preferred symbolism, with European sf artists often falling somewhere in between these poles. Such moody, symbolic work usually appeared in U.S. sf only in magazine illustrations like those of *Galaxy* magazine, to portray social sf. (Marx spoke of scientific socialism, but the Soviet tradition, even when literal in appearance, invoked social goals, not scientific ones.) Referring to this moody school as "symbolic-fantastic," Sokolov said, "The theory of relativity might yield images that could be shown only in emotional, artistic form. It could be a symbol, a fantasy, a dream."[2] Contrast this with attempts to show the relativistic Doppler effect, as observed from a starship, called by Frederik Pohl the "starbow."

"Portraits of courageous pioneers of space," as Sokolov put it (160), were sanctioned by the Soviet space program, so realistic work did have a place. Cosmonaut portraits were in great demand for offices, regional galleries, public buildings.

As someone keenly aware of the value of such representational art, Sokolov was an oddity in Russian space art, a realistic worker with direct access to astronauts. He could remark from inference, "Landscapes seen from an airplane are vague and colorless, because we observe them from inside the atmosphere with the light scattered from all around. Cosmonauts are not impeded by the scattered light; they see the Earth in all its magnificence" (158).

He had an immense advantage. Necessarily, Americans did not, since even today no professional artist has flown in space—though several astronauts have turned to art later. So Americans concentrated on photographs. Soviet cosmonauts studied Earth with color-sample atlases and color-measuring viewers, confirming that perceived colors are remarkably more vivid than views from aircraft. Our eyes discern details twenty times finer than a typical camera and two hundred times better than a TV image. We also have far more subtle color perception. For the first time, an artist with the Soviet-era readings could compare nighttime clouds lit by city lights, by lightning, and by moonlight. Peculiarities emerged: no up or down, no atmospheric perspective, sharp contrasts of light and dark, arriving suddenly.

Sokolov had cosmonauts compare his sketch with the real scene as it passed below, writing comments on the sketch about color, form and lighting. (Alexei Leonov, the first space walker, has done primarily realistic paintings and sketches, using his own experience and Sokolov's data.) Using frequent interviews with cosmonauts, he gave this vivid description:

It is especially nice to observe . . . at the terminator, when valleys sink into darkness and a chain of snowy mountains is shining in the background. Late in the evening, just beyond the terminator, the very high mountains glow red-orange, like live coals. . . . Mountaintops cleave the clouds, leaving a wake like that of a ship. Tropical thunderheads, lit by lightning flashes at night, recall the blooming buds of white roses. . . . The shining constellations of cities at night, enmeshed by a glittering web of highways is also very lovely. One's heart fills with pride at our accomplishments when one recognizes from orbit artificial seas and water basins, and cultivated fields, particularly in virgin lands. (158-59)

In this passage we see how much of Soviet society retained the pride common in nineteenth-century America about the domesticating hand of humanity upon the untamed wilderness.

Not all decisions on either side of the cultural divide came from aesthetic ideas. The Soviet Artists' Union was ordered from above to produce art heralding the great space achievements, so there was work to be had. Landscape painters migrated in, symbolists found ready employment. ("Most of it looks like Russian music sounds," American Jon Lomberg remarked to me.) Even the most highly regarded "space artists" cared little for the facts of their subject. On a rare junket to the West, at Voyager's Neptune encounter, as a body they skipped the Jet Propulsion Laboratory tour prepared for them, in order to go to Disneyland!

(Sokolov apologized for them.)

Contrast this with Bonestell, the father of the American school. He painted his classic "View from Titan" in 1944, soon after Kuiper's measurement of methane in the atmosphere of Saturn's major moon, Titan. Saturn hangs clear and cold above a frosted landscape. But by the 1970s further work showed that Titan's atmosphere was very thick, so that at its surface the pressure was even higher than one Earth atmosphere. Saturn would be forever shrouded by the opaque methane clouds. So Bonestell painted later views, accounting for this. He did not scrap the earlier work, just updated his views to those of the scientists. In honor of this, astronomers began in the 1980s to call the blue-sky layer above the methane haze, where perhaps one could peer out at Saturn, not the Titan Stratosphere, but the Bonestellosphere.

I think this contrast of aesthetics, the presence or absence of that hard-sf commitment to "getting it right," is the principal difference between the American and the European/Russian temperament. No doubt, both schools of space art have their virtues. However, as a hard sf writer who strives for scientific accuracy in my stories, I have a natural fondness for artists who strive for scientific accuracy in their depictions of space. It is such artists—like Bonestell, Hartmann, and the idiosyncratic Sokolov—whom I most admire.

Notes

1. Gregory Benford, "The Science in Science Fiction: The View from Titan," *Amazing Stories*, 50 (June, 1976).

2. Andrei Sokolov, "To Infinity and Beyond," in *In the Stream of Stars: The Soviet/American Space Art Book*, edited by William K. Hartmann, Andrew Sokolov, Ron Miller, and Vitaly Myagkov (New York: Workman, 1990), 160, 163. Later page references are to this edition.

6

The Vision of Space:
The Artist's View

Samuel H. Vasbinder

Science fiction art, from its earliest expressions, began to explore the possibilities of the depiction of space. The covers of Hugo Gernsback's magazines were famous for this, as were earlier paintings and drawings from the Verne era of the nineteenth century.[1] Since space in the Western tradition is literally nothingness, and a blank page could hardly excite the reader looking at a magazine or book, imagery needed to be supplied that could bring the idea of the presentation of a point in space far removed from this Earth clearly and forcefully to the reader. Three main strategies were almost immediately used and have, with variations, been in use ever since. These are: Pure Space (images in a star field), Near Space (planetary images superimposed on space), and Implied Space (images that strongly suggest space).

Within this set of strategies, there are several icons that constantly reoccur; perhaps the strongest is the Ship, which remains the primary icon for space. In using the deep space theme, one is made aware of the ships that can go there, the ships that have been there, or the ships that are there. Sometimes this icon is joined with the Woman in Space, usually a head or head and torso. Jael's powerful image "The Dream Lives," a tribute to Christa McAuliffe, shows such a Woman, hanging in space against a background of stars and places, images within an emptiness that the images define in a surreal way that creates its own excitement of place. This illustrates perfectly what G. K. Chesterton meant when he observed that the dignity of the artist lies in keeping awake the sense of wonder in the world.[2] Consequently, such a sense of wonder and echoes of a place are created in the imaginary star field coupled with floating surreal images that blend the near-world concept with the hint of exploration of interstellar distances. The Space Battle is another popular icon used that conveys the sense of space. In Janny Wurts's "Under Fire" or "Attack on Pel Station," the viewer is plunged into the heart of an action in the deepest space, a place unavailable physically, but capable of finding a powerful reality within the mind. As Desmond McCarthy observed, "the whole of art is an appeal to a reality which is not without us, but in our minds" (17). The art of space, regardless of how or where it occurs, is an expression of this idea since the reality of space is one that, for the time being at least, exists wholly in our minds. No one has actually been there to see and perceive, yet this art demands a strong sense of reality to make itself felt. It is our imaginary view of this totally imagined reality that gives it force and interest. All of these products of the brush help the viewer imagine the places of the story more powerfully, although it is the artist's own view of things. But it is the Ship in all of its mutations, against a field of stars or planetary landfall, that primarily excites the imagination.

Pure Space

In order to define nothingness, something must be in it, something that can be seen as an intrusion, as a special artifact that the mind can evaluate. The idea of space in Western art is nothingness, emptiness; but in Chinese art, for example, emptiness is organic, potential, capable of producing something out of itself, a fertile presence that brings forth shape, the pregnancy of the cosmos out of which all is born. One might see this same philosophy in the art of Pure Space, where emptiness is regarded as pure potential waiting to be filled with an image intruding into that space, growing not only in it but out of it. Paintings of planets exchanging electrical forces or caught in the same webs of energy show this concept clearly at work. Oldenburg believed that "art is a technique of communication [in which] the image is the most complete technique of communication" (25). In space art, the image is the only means of communication. Strong and alien feelings are present in the work of Pamela Lee, but there are other qualities that must be present as well. One of these is the image that evokes vast distances, either the distances between the stars or within a planetary system. The *Star Trek* view-plate aboard the *Enterprise* presents a three-dimensional star-field that seems to be moving past the ship as it forges ahead in space. But this is short-term and one would soon tire of it because it lacks detail and creative choice. It is merely white points of fire moving past us in a viewing plate. Joel Hagen solves this problem with his "Orion Nebula" and his "Triffid Nebula." The wonderful color of the painting, highlighting the burning gasses and incendiary pockets of this interstellar artifact, thrills the viewer by seeming to take him there. Space itself, empty and immense, is defined with an object that is encompassable by the human eye and mind, spectacularly colored, light years long; yet as we view the painting, we seem to be present, taken incalculable distances from Earth into the interstellar vastness and given a godlike place to stand and witness the phenomenon of an exploding, expanding patch of hot gasses. But this alone does not give the sense of scale, the drama of deep space that planetary presences do. In Kim Poor's "Saturn from Tethys," one sees the superimposed images of planets small and large, the eccentric point of view from a planetary moon where we see the rings of Saturn edge-on with the planet half-risen beyond it, all drawn to a scale that implies the immense size of the planet and the diminutive place where we stand to witness. Thus, Pure Space is given a point from which we can view it: the Place Without a Center is given a locality in which to have its being and persuade the viewer that it is real. One of Lee's astronomical paintings, again, works in a similar manner as we view a galactic core that seems to be exploding with the force of a million suns. In this painting, we are made to stand on a platform above the planet behind which can be seen the immensity of emptiness that also has its own presence. Even blackness assumes a substantial presence here, further amplified by the tiny humans in space gear in front of us: tiny, lonely, Lilliputians in a universe of unknowable size. The minuteness of the figures against the enormous fields of space create the sense of distance and immensity that Pure Space conveys. Poor's "Supernova" is a case in point. It is interesting that many of these paintings have been used not only for science fiction illustration, but have appeared in hard science astronomy publications as well.

Near Space

Near Space uses a similar design to convey the sense of space itself, but it uses a different set of perspectives. Near Space is one of the most popular methods of handling the depiction of space. One might have in this figures at work on a planet surface with stars clearly seen in the background, not seen as they are from this Earth, but from some alien surface that is obviously in closer contact with the stars. One of its outstanding properties is its ability to take us more directly to a place where, instead of being placed at some theoretical point in space, the viewer has a tangible place to sit or stand. The humans with whom the viewer identifies are placed in a specific location, that is, on board a spaceship or on an asteroid surface. In the technique of Near Space presentation, ships or people are seen hovering in space above a world or on the surface of an alien planet with space in the background, obviously in an airless place or some other situation where space is clearly and readily a major part of the depiction. A painting by Frank Kelly Freas from *Planet Stories* shows the artist using the old impressionist technique of The View Through the Keyhole to show an exciting moment taking place somewhere in space. Magazine covers depicting space often presented such a space setting, where the viewer can identify strongly with people or aliens in the scene. Identification with place, the ability of the human mind to accept a new environment existing entirely within the imagination, has worked well for the depiction of space and readies the reader for the stories within the covers of the book or magazine. Thus, the painted image has been an important part of the science fiction scene. Artists were employed from the earliest times to aid in the identification of the unfamiliar. Verne's *Twenty Thousand Leagues under the Sea* is a case in point: the original French edition had numerous illustrations to help the reader visualize an undersea boat that had as yet been seen only in the imagination.

In the Near Space mode, the human figures are large and are seen against a dominant planetary landscape, as in Richard Hescox's painting "The Pacifist," where the human figure is clearly seen on a platform high over the Earth. Over the Earth, one feels that one is in space, hovering or floating above a planetary surface. Thomas Kidd's "Outposter" is in a similar situation; the human is clearly identified in a confined space that looks out on a planetary landscape above which a battle is in progress. In "Lord of the Skies," ships hover above a distant planetary surface. Here, Vincent DiFate uses just a section of a giant ship to convey the sense of size. Michael Whelan, in a painting done for himself while he was in art school called "Outward Bound," depicts the length of the ship seen against an asteroid and not only places us in distant space, but gives us a sense of having travelled to some distant location far from this world we inhabit. Even more extreme is the fragment of a space tug by Don Maitz completely isolated in a non-specified area of space itself. Movement, distance, the idea of being far removed from our local place and time are all present here. John Berkey's imaginary ship exhibits all these traits, but in addition shows the fantastic convolutions that many modern spaceships have evolved into. It stands in stark contrast to the smooth-bodied, fin-carrying ships from the Gernsback era. DiFate also exhibits his ability to place the viewer in an alien setting suggesting distant space and advanced technology. Such works limit us in our viewpoint, but imply light-year distances and allow us to be present in a place that, were it not for the imagination of the artist, we could never be. These images can be serious, as in Whelan's painting, or they can be comical, as James Christensen visualizes for us, a creation out of odds and ends flying through some far-distant space. Observing Bob Eggleton's "Baroque Space Ship," all science fiction aficionados understand the messages it sends, even if those messages may differ from person to person. By means of these techniques, one becomes aware of the ship that can go there, or the ship that is there, mysterious, alone, above some unnamed asteroid, on an adventure that could be written about it in a thousand ways. But the power of the ship's image, the strength of the perspective, its power conveys a sense not only of deep space itself, but of an expedition or an adventure.

Near Space allows the viewer to be a direct participant in a very special way, an organic growth in sheer emptiness that is filled with exciting images. While planets, stars, and star fields are done with an eye to astronomical accuracy, the spaceships, the hardware, the spacesuits, and the weaponry are all products of the artist's imagination. It is this accuracy that gives us the heightened realism that is the hallmark of the Near space concept as seen in Ron Miller's paintings. Coupled with the astronomical accuracy of the planets or stars, they all make the realism of the scene more intense. It is realism that creates the strongest sense in the viewer of the creation of place. It was this very thing that Josef Albers spoke of when he postulated that the concern of the artist is the discrepancy between physical fact and psychic effect, since space art to the greatest degree makes use of the facts of the physical universe as filtered through the artistic consciousness in such a way that the strongest psychic effects are produced. Albers spoke of an art that was non-representational, an art reduced to a variety of colored squares that evoked on a purely psychic level the messages they contain. His art was the volumetric insistence of Paul Cézanne, the cubist mode of Pablo Picasso and Georges Braque carried to one of its farthest possibilities. His art was not space art, and I imagine Albers would be insulted to have his work coupled with science fiction. But his statement contains an essential truth about art that must not be limited to abstraction alone. Space art also presents its information in at least two ways: first there is a shared community of belief between artist and viewer who have read the stories and have seen the science fiction worlds in operation, which the image reinforces; and there is also the unexpected vision of the individual artist, unique and alone, never in existence until that moment of being painted and then shared with others who will understand the message, even the meaning of the message.

Implied Space

Implied Space has two methods of presentation. The first of these shows a scene in which space travel to distant places is clearly present through alien landscapes or spaceships taking off, landing, crashed or in some other way connected to the stellar deeps. The second is the surrealistic image where one or more figures is seen in a multi-faceted background that could include star fields, planetary images, or futuristic environments.

Janny Wurtz shows us a spacecraft lifting off in "Lift Off," which, coupled with our current perceptions and experiences with NASA craft, strongly implies space. No space landscapes are present, but space hovers in the background as a powerful idea that is conveyed by the image. Similarly, Steve Dodd's "Preparing the Trojan" shows a giant spaceship being readied for interstellar travel. The design of the ship and its strange hangar environment prods the imagination to imagine the possibilities. David Cherry's "Quitting Time at Station Core" takes us inside a giant ship where the vast emptiness in which the figure hovers correlates to the space outside this environment. At the time Cherry painted this, he was fascinated with the cylinder inside the ship in *Star Wars*. He studied the theory of vectors and used other mathematical approaches to art to create his effect for us of a figure floating in a vast but defined space. But, as he acknowledges, if he placed his figure in the right proportion, it would be so tiny as to be unusable and unrecognizable. So he paints the figure against the background in such a way that it dominates this vast space, but reminds us of the exterior of this environment, which is space itself through which the Ship makes its way. Such interior environments have been used multitudes of times to allow the viewer to enjoy an alien environment while imagining where in some far distant place it might exist.

The rusting, wrecked spaceship, with or without a desiccated crew, has been a staple of science fiction space art. Angus McKie depicts a dead figure in a space suit lying in the barren sands before a deteriorated but incredibly huge ship. The same is true of Peter Elson's paintings where we are aboard a wrecked space liner, but are able to look out of it upon alien scenes. The wrecked spaceship is a highly romantic image, which is one of the chief images of the film *Alien* (1979), as well as other spinoffs of this film. Rusting sides, torn metal, strange instrument panels, and unknown equipment from some future culture all combine in these images to imply the presence of space without actually showing it.

The surreal image, often a collage of images, has been a staple of science fiction art's presentation of space. As previously noted, Jael's woman floating in space offers us a vista of stars and a ship as well as an idea of far distances. Virgil Finlay did much the same thing in his floating women among the stars, images done for the pulp fiction market. In his illustrations for "The Star Dice," Finlay gives us an incredibly complicated star field and portrait done in pen and ink alone. A more contemporary view is Judy King Rieniets's "In the Beginning" painting, where a full-length woman floats in a complex romantic star field. John Zeleznik takes the viewer to some far-flung elsewhere for his depiction of a woman in his "Taliz." Maitz again presents his spacesuited, seated figure called Spaced Man with a pillar of light rising from his head, which promises a strange adventure in unknown places. A David Mattingly painting handles the collage concept in a strange way, almost in an anti-science stance, presenting the still body of the spacesuited figure at the enthroned feet of a God whose kingdom seems to be the stars themselves. Often, bookcovers use the collage technique to show humans against a collage of machinery and stars.

Such surreal collages convey a sense of space and space travel, of humans present in this unending night of space sprinkled with stars, adventures, and alien beings fraught with danger and dangerous quests, the Arthurian legends thrust into the future where there are new grails to pursue, new vows to uphold, incredible distances to be crossed to meet the sought-after moment. In one exquisite nude study, Freas offers his version of the floating woman. James Gurney, before *Dinotopia*, depicted a spaceman musing before an incredible ship suggesting distant travels. The artists in the situations they have depicted have been able to make such places come alive, to suggest the incredible distances between the stars, the costumes and weaponry of the participants, and most of all, to take us there, even momentarily.

Conclusion

It should be noted then that all these techniques to depict space as a place reflect one of the most important aspects of science fiction. As noted by the great artist of the Romantics, Caspar David Friederich, it is the artist's great, and possibly greatest, merit to stimulate the viewer spiritually and arouse thoughts, feelings, and sensations (193). The artists of space create in the viewer the greatest spirituality and arouse thoughts, feelings, and sensations of the most dramatic kind. It is these images that speak to us of space and the stars, where the immense emptiness is carved out into beautiful and startling imagery of vast proportions or of delicate spontaneity, an immense emptiness whose promise is of the promise of the future beyond all of us, where space speaks its silent messages between the burning stars.

Notes

1. For a gallery of Gernsback magazine covers, see Lester del Rey, *Fantastic Science Fiction Art 1926-1954* (New York: Ballantine Books, 1975); for examples of Verne illustrations, see Arthur B. Evans, "The Illustrators of Jules Verne's *Voyages Extraordinaires*," *Science-Fiction Studies*, 25 (July, 1998), 241-70.

2. Cited in Michael Whelan, *The Art of Michael Whelan* (New York: Bantam, 1993), 13. All subsequent parenthetical page references in the text are to quotations or statements from this book and this edition.

7

Shapes from the Edge of Time: The Science Fiction Artwork of Richard M. Powers

Kirk Hampton and Carol MacKay

> When we dream, we dream Richard Powers.
> —John Clute[1]

The death of painter and illustrator Richard Powers (1921-1996) marked the loss of an artistic giant whose light has been long obscured from view by the anonymous, mass-market field in which he did most of his work—paperback book illustration. From the point of view of art history, his success was very nearly his undoing. From the point of view of science fiction, he created resonant visual emblems of the genre's inner paradox. Powers's significance—at least within the sphere of commercial illustration—has been well acknowledged, but his status as an American surrealist has been recognized to an entirely inadequate extent. Robert Weinberg's *A Biographical Dictionary of Science Fiction and Fantasy Artists* calls Powers "the most influential science fiction artist of the 1950s," acknowledging that he, "more than any other artist, changed the perception of science fiction from space opera to real literature."[2] Powers's covers for science fiction novels number in the hundreds, and include classics such as H. G. Wells's *The Time Machine*, Isaac Asimov's *The End of Eternity*, and Arthur C. Clarke's *Childhood's End*; in addition, he provided jacket art for poetry, mystery novels, horror collections, magazines, and record albums. Outside the world of illustration, Powers was known and respected—if not famous—as a "surrealist" painter, favorably compared to the likes of Yves Tanguy, Salvador Dali, and Arshile Gorky. He was even featured in a four-man show at the Museum of Modern Art in 1952, and New York's Rehn Gallery has displayed his work and placed several pieces in important collections of modern American art.

If we listen to the words of artists and readers influenced by Powers, we begin to sense the astounding impact his work had—especially when we consider that his paintings were almost invariably viewed as 5" x 7" book covers. For a work of art to have any effect at all under such circumstances—much less a momentous influence on both the minds of science fiction readers and the genre itself—

bespeaks a very special potency indeed. The profound impression these paperback book covers made on consumers of science fiction is evoked by Rick Lieder.[3] Like countless other fans of all ages, Lieder "began to recognize and buy books with his covers" (23), the artwork of the tiny book as often as not utterly outstripping the imagined world between its covers. For Lieder, Powers's artwork was more than a visual attraction or pulpy titillation. The visions he saw on those many covers came to represent to him "the wonderfully *alien*, the different, the unique. It was a way of seeing, as well as a particular style, that influenced me . . . unconsciously—in my own career as an artist." And we agree with Lieder's assessment of Powers's stature, his work setting "a standard which should be used as a highwater mark by all artists both in the field and out of it" (24).

Another eloquent artist, Robert Colby, invokes just how vividly this remarkable illustrator leapt from the bookracks into the viewer's mind, forever altering the genre itself even as it became part of the reader's dreams: "Those abstract, ambiguous but evocative shapes on the cover were telling me not to expect anything obvious from what was inside, that wild ideas were at work, that these were important books, a vital part of our modern culture" (22). Yet another appreciator, Mark Rich, says simply that Powers's work "was my world, and Powers's paintings weren't a part that I questioned" (24). For Rich, Powers's illustrations utterly transcended their commercial task. They "reflected a philosophic point of view! They showed a mind at work; they showed that the fiction inside the covers might well reflect endeavors of a fully human nature," giving this young form of fiction a cachet far beyond anything it had known before. Powers's career and influence represent an unprecedented confluence of two separate artforms in the history of our culture.

Given his busy and market-driven career, Powers's art is linked ineluctably to the genre whose vision he defined. His work embodies essential, yet disturbing, qualities inherent in science fiction itself—qualities that textual science fiction is reluctant or unable to fulfill, simply because to do so would obviate the possibility of storytelling. As appreciators like Rick Lieder and Robert Colby have indicated, Powers's vision, like science fiction itself, reaches toward a supernal fusion of flesh and technology—a point where intelligence and matter merge, where creatures, machines, buildings, and landscapes have coalesced, and where all things are connected, all things are possible. This furthest conceivable extrapolation of the future is the place toward which science fiction tales point but cannot reach, for it represents a world without distinctions or chronology, where no stories are possible.

Powers's classic 1957 cover for H. G. Wells's *The Time Machine* epitomizes the new dimension of art that he brought to the genre.[4] It was also an appropriate one for Powers, because in a sense all science fiction stories are "about" time travel, usually taking us at least a little into the future—and once this projection into time has begun, its implications reach precisely toward worlds like the ones Powers drew for us. The figure of the Time Traveller seems both human and alien, at once monumental and lost, as if the extraordinary environment itself made him something other than human. The machine he reaches back toward with a long, tapering arm is itself a tiny spatial paradox, a confection of curvilinear shapes and of sparkling, purest light.

What is that landscape he looks out at, its images so potently evocative that the viewer, too, finds himself transposed into it? And over to the right—what is that monster (or machine) rising on clouds of grayish light, or perhaps emerging in blue spray from a burgundy ocean? What bleak, yet beautiful blending of night and day is represented by the brown sky with its tattered crimson rainbow, filled with the dry streaks of clouds (or dust) and black, unknown forms floating in the sky? The illustration—tiny as it is—affects us like some hypnogogic vision that follows one into wakefulness, too vivid to stay behind. The very force of this cover highlights the features of Powers's art that are potently disruptive of the genre itself. We find a verbal analogue to this disturbing quality in the text of Wells's novel itself, in the scene depicted on that very cover, when the Time Traveller moves briefly forward to the twilight of the Earth—to a time when there is no distinction between daylight and night, to where living creatures seem more like encrustations of rock, and to where "all the sounds of man, the bleating of sheep, the cries of birds, the hum of insects—all that was over" (88-89).

This visit to the edge of time is unbearable to the Time Traveller: "A horror of this great darkness came on me. The cold, that smote to my marrow, and the pain I felt in breathing, overcame me. I shivered, and a deadly nausea seized me." For purposes of our thesis we might view these sentiments as those of the storyteller confronting the world of Powers's paintings. And what must the response of the timebound storyteller be to such a vivid world--albeit a world he reaches toward? Wells describes it accordingly: "Then I felt I was fainting. But a terrible dread of lying helpless in that remote and awful twilight sustained me while I clambered upon the saddle." From a metaphysical point of view, the Time Traveller has been approaching the imminent destruction of all storytelling: "I cannot convey the sense of abominable desolation that hung over the world. The red eastern sky, the northward blackness, the salt Dead Sea, the stony beach crawling with these foul, slow-stirring monsters, the uniform poisonous-looking green of the lichenous plants, the thin air that hurts one's lungs: all contributed to all appalling effect" (87). In time-travel stories, the anagogical tends to become part of the story itself; but fiction, being based on distinctions, must remain timebound and must work with distinctions. Small wonder Wells's hero shuns a world where time is about to end and where opposites have all but merged.

This artistic masterpiece—appearing multiply and in such an absurdly tiny form—is typical of how Powers quietly reshaped the genre. Breaking away from their pulp pedigree, his covers incessantly slip away from representationalism into new forms of abstraction—most notably, one in which the illusion of depth seems to be maintained, even into the far reaches of what would normally be called abstract art. The alleged mass-market illustrator was in fact a covert artistic operative, exploring the intersection between the representational and the non-representational.

A case in point is Powers's masterful cover for the 1956 Ballantine edition of

Arthur C. Clarke's *Reach for Tomorrow*.[5] Here again, the artist experienced the good fortune (a bit rare in his busy career) to illustrate a book worthy of his own brilliance. This remarkable cover was printed in landscape orientation—all but unheard-of for mass-market paperbacks of the day—and he presents us with another indelible vision fusion, melding the representational with the abstract. In this tiny work, a broad cityscape of some kind is rendered in smooth gradations of tan and brown, so far beyond our world that the buildings (or machines or rocks or entities) have the wildness of a desert landscape set against clouds, or distant dust, in a spatial field gorgeously empty and infinite. In the foreground, houses (or craft) silently disregard the laws of gravity, casting pristine shadows on the rose-tinged ground. The lone, tiny figure we see adds a sense of vast scale and of isolate strangeness—some sort of sentry in red standing on the platform of some sort of tower. And to the left, one of those mysterious floating objects has fallen and lies awkwardly on its side—for this is not a newly minted world but one possessing great age, looking backward endlessly, forward to nothing.

Though we cannot say that the cover of *Reach for Tomorrow* is based on a story or passage from the book, we can still find a character in one of the stories worrying aloud about the horrific impossibility of the end of time: "Have you ever wondered, Jack, what the human race will do when science has discovered everything, when there are no more worlds to be explored, when all the stars have given up their secrets?" (72). This query is from a story called "The Parasite," in which a sublimely decadent creature from the future feeds off the more vital emotions of the distant past. Once again, characters shudder at the world that all science fiction stories point toward, but cannot touch, and the language evokes fear and the genre's horrifying, fascinating fusion of infinity and nothingness. Working in a pop-culture milieu, with all the anonymity of a medieval artisan, Powers virtually created a new form within the domain of painting—one in which the artist's ability to maintain illusory space is stretched past its limit, as it fills with increasingly incomprehensible shapes. The viewer has the illusion of perfect impersonality, the visual imagination of the end of time.

The fast-paced, anonymous sweatshop of paperback illustration turned out to be one in which an artist of the first rank could channel his infinite visions. Powers had no time to consider the specific content of his books—but this circumstance merely expanded his potent vision. His challenge was to create some sort of generic, cosmic vision of this most far-reaching type of fiction, true to the spirit of the books he was illuminating, but generally detached from the restrictions of identifiable characters or even physical forms. Thus, when he was hired to depict the wholly invisible creatures of Murray Leinster's 1958 novel, *War with the Gizmos*, the result was a breathtaking *tour de force*, seemingly abstract and filled with tortured forms and overstretched lines reminiscent of Gorky, yet still mysteriously "representational"—in the sense that the forms seem to float in an illusory three-dimensional space.[6]

To complement Leinster's yarn, Powers creates a universe of floating abstractions that yet seem human, organic, metamachine-like, and landscape-like—a world in which all stories seem capable of happening at once. It is a universe both quintessentially science-fictional and beyond the pale of textual science fiction. Powers's outrageously inspired cover for this novel gives us a subtle example of the infinite that lies behind the future-reaching storyteller's art. And once again we can peer into the texts to find at least a touch of the ineffable, the anagogical far end that gives science fiction its punch—but too much of which would render it storyless. Leinster is a straightforward writer, not given to stylistic tricks. Yet observe how, in the prologue to *War with the Gizmos*, he gives us at once the flesh and the emptiness, how even his workmanlike prose combines the concrete and physical with the ineffable:

There is no point, now, in reviewing the controversy about the Gizmos' origin. Some still insist that they came from outer space. This is hard to believe, because a spaceship under Gizmo control is almost impossible to imagine. . . . [T]he legends of fiends and *djinns* and *efrits* and *ghuls*, and of eerie inhabitants of remote, are singularly convincing when one considers them in connection with Gizmos. . . . They had the enormous advantage of being totally unreasonable. (6)

Since the reader has no idea what a Gizmo is, Leinster is in effect "painting" an illusory space and filling it with incomprehensible objects—just as Powers stretches his forms beyond recognizability.

Once again, we experience in the text the fear and infinite nothingness that lie at the very edge of science fiction. The Gizmos are "unreasonable," just as the end of time was unreasonable for Wells's Time Traveller or the infinitely evolved mind-parasite of Clarke's short story: they afflict the minds of the characters. Leinster's storytelling craft in this prologue to the novel makes this a compelling opener, for the reader doesn't even know the basis for these brief, but sublimely negative, speculations. The author uses inexplicability as a device to intrigue the reader even as his narrator struggles with it (or dismisses it) as the aftermath of some unknown, terrifying adventure. The statement that the Gizmos "had the . . . advantage of being totally unreasonable" is just a touch of the storyteller's discomfiture at confronting the mind-boggling limit toward which even mainstream, non-visionary science fiction points, and from which dangerous source it gets its power.

Science fiction book covers might seem an unlikely venue for such a development, with time constraints and almost microscopic manner of display, yet fellow illustrator Paul Lehr emphasizes the strange artistic freedom in the field: "In the old days at Berkley Publishing [for whom Powers did hundreds of covers], they let me do pretty much what I wanted, and as a result, the covers were very personal" (Weinberg, 177). And Powers's innovative vision perfectly paralleled that of the fictional genre itself: to tell stories of the increasingly untenable, to extrapolate known reality toward something timeless and unknown. The titles of the books he was called upon to illustrate alone betray science fiction's intentions: *Beyond Infinity, No Boundaries, The End of Eternity.*

Powers was not utterly lost in the paperback world he helped to recreate, even as he helped shape the evolution of an entire genre of fiction through his puissant visions. He is recognized as a surrealist painter, most notably compared with the French surrealist Yves Tanguy (1900-1955). The two artists' biomorphic imagery and three-dimensional, dreamworld illusionism are indeed strikingly similar, and Simon Wilson's reference to Tanguy's "landscapes of the mind" recalls much of the commentary on Powers's work.[7] Powers especially distinguishes himself from his artistic cousin by his career-long exploration of the boundary between representation and abstraction. Some of the shapes floating in Powers's more radical covers recall those of Gorky, Jean Arp, and Joan Miro—and yet one always senses that Powers's forms float in some sort of paradoxical landscape, constantly approaching an impossible visual representation of a non-Euclidean universe.

Science fiction writers themselves work with dichotomies parallel to those of Powers's art, but as we might expect, the storytellers are by force of their craft and/or their own dispositions obliged to work more heavily in the areas we have termed "fleshy" and "timebound." These authors, too, like to bring the reader in contact with the infinitely ineffable—but in the texts themselves it must remain only a brief contact, very often taking the form of an inexplicable emotional struggle, almost always involving fear and the evocation of infinity/nothingness.

If Powers seemed always to grasp the essence of the genre, sometimes succeeding in profiling the essence of even the most complex of science fiction classics, his 1961 cover for A. E. van Vogt's novel *Slan* is an inspired case in point.[8] Here, author and illustrator approach the threatening strangeness inherent to the genre from perspectives opposite yet complementary to one another. Powers's cover is a strangely informative *inverse* to van Vogt's text, yet they intertwine marvelously. *Slan* is told from the viewpoint of the embodiments of the fearful unknown—the genetically superior beings known as *slan*. In this story, the ordinary human characters recoil from the mysterious mutants just as Wells's Time Traveller recoiled from the anagogical future he confronts, or Clarke's parasitic host from the superior, yet degenerate, creature occupying his mind, or even the people in *War with the Gizmos* from the "unreasonableness" of the invaders.

Van Vogt lets us see in from the ineffable edge of science fiction. With his customary brilliance, however, he employs the slans' telepathic abilities so that they feel what the humans feel, placing us inside the mind of a young, still-undeveloped slan. Thus, van Vogt the storyteller has it both ways. To Jommy, the boy-slan, it is men's fearful thoughts that are threatening:

The steady wave of vagueness that washed from the crowds all around grew into a swirl of mind clamor. . . . The men . . . were crossing the street, their faces dark with an expression of an unpleasant duty that had to be done. The thought of that unpleasantness, the hatred that went with it, was a shadow in their minds that leaped out at Jommy. It puzzled him even in this moment when lie was concentrating on escape. (5-6)

To complement this approach through contrast, evoking the inevitable dual qualities of fear and infinite nothingness, Powers's cover seems to present the slan as they might look in the deepest unconscious of the fearful humans of the novel. We see a coiling, smokey creature vaguely resembling a squid or an octopus, and the monstrous, half-formed mouth of a screaming creature (prescient of H. R. Giger's *Alien*) with its tendrils hanging—truly a monster defying all our distinctions and laws as it sags down menacingly from a white nothingness. *That's* how the humans in this novel feel! And of course, given visual art's capacity for ambiguity, it may be that Powers's cover depicts the human psyche as perceived by the telepathic, hunted slan. It may be fear painted from both sides at once.

Some science fiction writers are well aware of how the thrust of the science fiction imagination moves toward an annihilation of the possibility of storytelling. In his "Afterthoughts" to the collection *Tales of Known Space*, Larry Niven describes two dilemmas resulting from his own inventiveness. His Known Space series "ends" with *Ringworld*:

Though I've written stories in the series since *Ringworld*, writing that novel made me realize how tangled and complex my basic assumptions had become. There were too many unlikely miracles left over from individual stories. For example, from *World of Ptavvs* came a stasis field so useful that every story set later in time must be examined for reasons why a stasis field would not solve the problem.[9]

The practicing author—faced with the need to project forward in time, where fewer and fewer story possibilities occur—must continually invent and reinvent the concepts that will ultimately bring him to the edge of time. As he describes some further complications in the Known Space series, Niven's reaction is a lighter version of Wells's Time Traveller, seen as the storyteller reacting to a Powers landscape: "But the story was already too complex; I couldn't open that can of worms too!" As for the eradication of distinctions, Niven acknowledges this as well, when he tells the reader, "If you want more stories in the series you can make them up yourself" (223). Just as Powers's figures meld into the landscape, so Niven allows the boundary between reader and writer to disappear, as he invites the reader to step into the void of fear and infinite nothingness that is the essence of creativity for this genre.

If Powers's art does depict an alluring edge toward which science fiction stories are drawn, then we might seek out at least a few verbal depictions that seem like analogues to Powers's illustrations. In Stanislaw Lem's *Solaris*, the vision of the protean, enigmatic planet seems indeed to reverse our *modus operandi* so far, and verbally evoke something Powers might draw. Here, the narrator describes some of the mysterious formations of this possibly sentient world:

The mind-bending architecture of this central pillar is held in place by vertical shafts of a gelatinous, almost liquid consistency, constantly gushing upwards out of wild crevasses. Meanwhile, the entire trunk is surrounded by a belt of snow foam, seething with great bubbles of gas. From the center toward the periphery, powerful buttresses spin out and are coated with streams of ductile matter rising out of the ocean depths. Simultaneously the gelatinous geysers are converted into mobile columns that proceed to extrude tendrils that reach out in clusters. . . . [T]hey call to mind the gills of an embryo, except that they ooze trickles of pinkish "blood" and a dark green secretion.[10]

The formation being described is spoken of as "illustrating" or "sometimes contradicting, various laws of physics"—much like Powers's structures—and Lem might be describing other, machinelike images seen frequently in Powers's painting—except, as Lem says, "they resemble no machine which it is within the power of mankind to build." Lem is capable of linguistic feats that virtually parallel Powers's visual illusions. He speaks of the planet's formations as solid entities, intimately if problematically involved with three-dimensional space and the laws of physics. At the same time (and note the passage's almost prissy concern with matters of sequential ordering) Lem evokes a disturbing sentience within the complex interactions of the structures, all confounded by his insistent use of the passive voice.

And what does the artist himself have to say? We normally expect silence from artists—especially as to the sort of parallel between the visual and the textual we have been tracing here—but in his 1983 portfolio called *Spacetimewarp*, Powers collected sixteen of his paintings, mostly illustrations of science fiction novels, and wrote neologistic, fantastic, funny, science fiction-sounding captions for each painting, riffing fragments of his own mythology, giving us a piquant taste of what sort of language his own paintings might inspire, if they were to come before the stories.[11] Powers's world of *fFlar* seems to be situated appropriately at some phenomenally distant future, and/or in a parallel universe. (Plate 2 apparently occurs "on a day the artist designates as the $\alpha\varphi\pi$ 21-θth of $\Delta\gamma$, 17,700,426 A.D.") What is going on here? Well, explanations of the hypertechnology of a near-infinite future—inasmuch as they are even ventured—become themselves fantastic, even poetic; the two halves of science fiction's dichotomy become, from our perspective back here in the abysmal past, intertwined. After all, in the unimaginably distant future, if we extrapolate science as advancing continually, science itself moves beyond our ken and becomes a creature of the imagination.

Powers's blurbs for *Spacetimewarp* are rife with orthographical fun, puns, soundgames, and often self-mocking parody—a use of language that has all the qualities to take us, snickering, to the edge of time. One remarkable painting is captioned as follows: "Gog-fFlar, Quasarquark of fFlar, Gog of Magog, God of Goads, Goad of Goats, Guard of Groans, Groan of Groins, Gert of Frobes, Frobe of Forces." The shapes in that painting (originally the cover for the novel *Wine of the Dreamers*) are quintessential Powers figures—entities (or objects, or both) that seem to have been deconstructed and reconfigured so many times, in so many impossibly convoluted ways, that they exist as ur-forms, floating between abstraction and tangibility, obeying physical laws which themselves have become subjugated to the powers of mind. Fitting, then, that the words of the caption should echo and meld until language itself becomes a Joycean, aleatory music. In general, our use of proper names seems intended to solidify the object being named, and Powers's comedic verbal echoes of the sort of formal reading of titles for potentates we all have heard undo the very sense of massification such strings of names seem intended to achieve.

It is also significant, of course, that Powers is not in the position of the actual science fiction storyteller. He is free to bounce crazily from one thought to another, playing games, without the responsibility of making connections or stringing things together. His "scientific" explanations are parodies of science fiction exposition, as with the inner jacket of the portfolio sleeve: "The destabilization of the concept of Time as a function of Space, which the astralguru/physicist G* first introduced into the Metamanual of Infraquasarian Zen, has led to the isolation of Spacetimewarp as the underlying function of Simultaneous/Alternate Universe Projection." The central notion in this passage of surreal science is that of melting ("destabilization," "Spacetimewarp," the concept of simultaneous/alternate universes). Thus, Powers does playfully with language what he does forcefully with art. In this case, he echoes "science talk"—that fast-paced rattling off of concepts and theories that seems ironically to overwhelm rather than enlighten the intellect—while his hellbent melding of morphemes takes us to the fearful, funny edge where nothingness meets infinity.

The edge-of-time quality we have been discussing in Powers's illustrations is indeed one of the key elements in many—possibly all—classic works of science fiction. In different ways, the canonical works of the genre push us toward that impossible realm where distinctions disappear, time stops—and storytelling itself must end. It is the genre's unbelievable good fortune to have stumbled and then seized upon Richard Powers as its definitive visual conjurer—the artistic genius who painted these visions for decades, till they became our dreams.

Notes

1. John Clute, "Great Illustrators," in *Science Fiction: The Illustrated Encyclopedia*, by Clute (New York: Dorling Kindersley, 1995), 241.

2. Robert Weinberg, *A Biographical Dictionary of Science Fiction and Fantasy Artists* (Westport, CT: Greenwood Press, 1988), 20. Besides providing an excellent historical overview of science fiction art, Weinberg has written a detailed account of Powers's life and influence, including a lengthy (but still partial) list of the artist's published work (see 217-22). We are especially indebted to Willie Siros, longtime cataloger of the L. W. Currey Science Fiction and Fantasy Collection at the Harry Ransom Humanities Research Center at the University of Texas at Austin, for his full perspective on Powers's life and art. Siros supplied us with bibliographic printouts of Powers's cover art, as well as putting us in touch with John Anderson, who has been compiling his own checklist of Powers's artwork (last copyrighted 1988). We are also grateful to the Eaton Collection for permission to consult the extensive Powers holdings at the University of California at Riverside. The best recent resource for the interested student of the Powers canon is Jane Frank's *The Art of Richard Powers* (London: Paper Tiger, 2001).

3. Rick Lieder (with Kathe Koja), "A Richard Powers Appreciation," *ReaderCon 5* (Cambridge, MA: privately printed, 1992), 23. All other quotations from Lieder, as well as those from Robert Colby and Mark Rich, are taken from this souvenir book, which features Powers's artwork and includes another partial bibliography (26-29), excerpted from Anderson. Seven years earlier, Powers was also the featured artist for "The First Occasional Lone Star Sci Fi Convention and Chili Cookoff" (Austin, Texas, 1985).

4. Powers produced two covers of *The Time Machine* for Berkley, in 1957 and 1963,

which differ only slightly in coloring and sharpness of outline; we are referring to the earlier one and citing its pagination in the quotations that follow. Although we suspect Powers always signed his cover artwork, his signature does not necessarily appear on the final product.

5. Ballantine Books published Powers's cover illustration for *Reach for Tomorrow* in two formats—one a full-length landscape turned to the horizontal, the other a partial reproduction of the same painting cut to vertical. Our references here are to the fuller version.

6. All Leinster citations are to this edition of *War with the Gizmos* (Greenwich, CT: Fawcett, 1958).

7. Simon Wilson, *Surrealist Painting* (London: Phaidon Press, 1991), 78. Wilson is here studying the school of "oneiric" painters, whose work seems "dream-inspired."

8. All van Vogt citations are to this edition of *Slan* (New York: Ballantine Books, 1961), whose cover illustration is especially reminiscent of Powers's studies in horror—yet another of his specialties in cover art.

9. Larry Niven, *Tales of Known Space* (New York: Ballantine Books, 1975), 222.

10. Stanislaw Lem, *Solaris* (New York: Berkley, 1971), 127.

11. The collection, published by Doubleday, is self-described as "sixteen full-color paintings of fFlar and fFlarians suitable for framing." Most of the reproductions are about 10" x 12", all on slick paper.

Part II

Approaches to Fantasy Art

8

Notes on the Geography of Bad—
and Good—Fantasy Art

John Clute

> The essence of visual rapture is metamorphosis.
> —David Denby[1]

This chapter is about the location of badness. It suggests some reasons for the unfitness of most fantasy illustrations to the texts they purport to illuminate, all of which boil down to one premise: that fantasy illustrations focus on the wrong parts of the worlds of fantasy. It comes as something of a relief to be able to say this. In the absence of a principle of explanation—whether or not the arguments sustaining it ultimately convince—one is left with nothing but cultural broadsides: that fantasy illustrators are simply incompetent (which is manifestly false); that the inherent nature of fantasy texts *requires* illustrators to focus on Art Nouveau landscapes, elves, broads in bras, peplum-begirded matrons, crones in fuligin, Paris Metro portals, dragons, brandished swords, haloes of lightning circumambiating edifices and magi and bowls, big clouds with more than a chance of rain (all of which is also manifestly false); that written texts are incompossible with a visual illumination of those texts (an argument we will not take up here). So it is a relief even to be wrong about the reasons for the badness of fantasy art. It is better than despair.

By a geography of fantasy we do not mean to describe fantasy texts in terms of the landscapes they are set in, or the medievalized villages and towns and edifices that normally speckle these landscapes, or the Rorschach maps that commonly precede the beginning of the written word part of the experience. A geography of fantasy is properly a body English of Story. This iteration deliberately reflects the truism that landscape in the Romance is a metaphysical pathos of the emotions and events occurring in the telling; but suggests further that the actual physical shape and order of the fantasy world, over and above the affects that might transfigure the Matterhorn in a non-fantasy Romance, manifests the nature of the Story being told.

Great Stories—which are ultimately not subject to paraphrase, which are dangerous, which *turn* like serpents in the mind's eye—occasion geographies that are themselves motile, that hover at the edge of change, that *reveal* themselves as the Story unfolds. It might be impossible in the twenty-first century to find competent fantasy readers who are still unfamiliar with the geography that is unfolded in J. R. R. Tolkien's *The Lord of the Rings* (1954-1955); but those readers, if they existed, would find on their first reading that landscape unfolding in a fashion dangerously new, dangerously open to meanings that had not yet been meant. For those readers, Middle-Earth is a true fantasy landscape.

The catch is that a fantasy Story, once told, like Tolkien's, is almost certain to be twice-told, reduced to a template other writers exploit. This process became almost unavoidable during the latter years of the twentieth century, a time when the nostalgia for fixed environments became acute. After a Story has become templated, the geography that clothed the original suffers a sea-change from latency into finished setting, from imago into fossil, from meniscus into Fantasyland. The inherent verb at the heart of the sentence of the fantasy Story, which is *to loosen* (Tolkien might have said "escape"), turns into the bondage of the preterit. The taste of belatedness in conventional template fantasy does not derive from settings sunk deep in time but from a grammar of Story that lacks forward urgency, lacks the threat of transformation that can only come from something happening *next*. Conventional fantasy is preteritic: it squats in the tedium of *is*; it does not *do*. Its transformations are sheddings.

We are able to approach our hypothesis. It is that fantasy illustrations are bad in direct proportion to their distance from the action of genuine fantasy, which is generally metamorphic, and always a threat. The further they are from the action, the more restraining the bondage that keeps them from where that action is. The logical extreme of this argument of distance would be to suggest that those fantasy illustrations (they comprise a great majority of those published) which are taken from publishers' stocks, without reference to the text they purport to illustrate, are those most profoundly exiled into the bondage of the hinterlands, that they manifest most extremely the action (or, more properly, the absence of genuine action) characteristic of Thinning (discussed later). Other specific forms of bondage (or Thinning) suggested so far have included estrangements in time, ontology and grammar.

As sketched out just now, this description of the badlands of template as the natural focus of that great mass of fantasy illustration which is of no earthly use clearly does not come as a solitary intuition. It is clearly based on a definition of fantasy that excludes most genre fantasy from serious consideration. There is no need here to supply a full recension of the arguments utilized by this writer in developing a pragmatic (though metaphor-ridden) model of the full fantasy Story; a narrative resume, in the first person, may suffice.

In 1992, when John Grant and I began to create the entry structure for what would become *The Encyclopedia of Fantasy* (1997), the task of developing a model of the full fantasy Story, one that would help us weight our entries so as to concentrate on the most significant authors and titles in an essentially undefined "fuzzy field" rather than a self-conscious genre, fell primarily to me. Grant concentrated on other regions, though he contributed entries on Perception and

Reality and Technofantasy to this phase of our joint endeavor. Gradually, in fits and starts (the original talk that inspired the current chapter being one of the fits), a four-part model of fantasy gradually evolved, based on the presumption that fantasy inherently creates/occupies a story-shaped world.

Fantasy, as I suggested in one entry in the finished book, is a way to tell stories about the fantastic. This may sound innocuous enough, but it concentrates a considerable amount of argument as to what regions of the fantastic could not adequately be incorporated into a definition of fantasy whose central texts were works by authors like E. R. Eddison or J. R. R. Tolkien. To say that fantasy is a way to tell stories about the fantastic suggests that surrealism, magic realism, most poetry, much of the postmodernist disassembly project, dream tales, and various other categories circumambiate but do not much help to define fantasy itself. We were left with a definition of fantasy as a story set in a world which is impossible *but which the story believes*.

In the end, we arrived at a fourfold articulation of this definition, a model whose coterminousness with models based on the seasons was essentially a coincidence, though a welcome one. The model can be described in cartoon terms through an annotated iteration of the four terms which define it.

The fantasy story of the model begins or recollects a Land at peace, an Eden, a condition that is interrupted by a *Wrongness*, like the Nazgul who haunt the perimeter of the Shire, or the visitor from Porlock. Eden—the Land—is suddenly ago.

This alarmed condition is succeeded by a succession of movements of *Thinning*. Thinning might almost as well be called Bondage (or Metamorphosis Bound—discussed later), though it does seem useful to use something of a neologism here. Thinning is what happens when Eden is lost: a clangor of action but no direction home. Battles are fought but the war is being lost. It is a state of restriction or imprisonment, literal or metaphorical. It is being immured, through a spell or freezing metamorphosis, into the wrong shape, like Grandfather Trout in John Crowley's *Little, Big*, or Ariel in *The Tempest*; or into stone itself, like the inhabitants of Oz in the greatly underrated film *Return to Oz* (1985), who are transmogrified into statues, and remain in that state until Dorothy returns. It is amnesia, either of the protagonist (who, for instance, might not yet have discovered that he or she is an Ugly Duckling awaiting transformation into a Hidden Monarch who is hidden no longer) or of the Land (whose rulers have forgotten the Words of Power, or which has thinned into a desert because a curse of unknowing has been laid upon it). It is what happens to the Land when the Land becomes Fantasyland. It is the maze that obscures the Threshold. It is being in the wrong time (too late, or not yet). It is the punishment of being who you are, like any mortal person longing for transcendence, or like Prometheus. It is, finally, a reflection of what happens when Story forgets itself: inherent in almost any fully unpacked fantasy tale is a sense that a Story which has been lost, or has lost itself, must be found again. Or the Bondage will be eternal. The way to escape the amnesias of Thinning is to tell the Story again.

The way to begin to tell the Story again is to recognize it. After *Wrongness* and *Thinning*, therefore, comes *Recognition*. The movement from Thinning to Recognition seems to me to lie at the heart of fantasy. If there is one phrase that expresses the central movement of fantasy it might well be: Bondage loosens. The verb of Fantasy is to loosen. It is at this point that Story melts the ice, unlocks the wanweird that binds the world from metamorphosis. The moment of Recognition is often signaled by trompe l'oeil effects in the writing, like the moment in Peter S. Beagle's *The Last Unicorn* (1968) when, locked into human semblance in the desolate thinned edifice of the bad king, the Knight of the Doleful Countenance who refuses to be healed, the heroine can be seen simultaneously as a young amnesia-stricken girl and as a unicorn, shiveringly ominous, auguring change. The scene is observed by Molly Grue, a companion figure who is also metaphorically pregnant with the possibility of flowering.

For Molly Grue, the world hung motionless in that glass moment. As though she were standing on a higher tower than King Haggard's, she looked down on a pale paring of land where a toy man and woman stared with their knitted eyes at a clay bull and a tiny ivory unicorn. Abandoned playthings—there was another doll, too, half-buried; and a sandcastle with a stick king propped up in one tilted turret. The tide would take it all in a moment, and nothing would be left but the flaccid birds of the beach, hopping in circles.[2]

So Recognition is the moment when amnesia lifts, when the protagonist learns or remembers what Story it is that is telling him or her, when statues are suddenly warm, when the Land begins to drink from long-withheld springs, when the Dark Lord turns into yesterday's newspaper, when the masks begin to metamorphose into realer faces, when the Story remembers itself.

After this comes the *Healing*, a term which (taken straight from Tolkien) acknowledges the Christian tenor of much twentieth-century fantasy.

But the central moment, the moment of the loosening of bondage, the moment of rapture, is the moment when Thinning passes into Recognition. What might constitute an adequate fantasy illustration of *The Last Unicorn*—in specific contradistinction to the portrait of a demure unicorn with velvet eyes—would be an attempt to capture—in the form of a still life, or a trompe l'oeil, or in a rhetoric of hieratic deployment, as in a knitted tapestry—this central moment when the world holds its breath in pun. For any "visual rapture" intended to illuminate Fantasy must surely grapple, somehow or other, with the great unexhaustible visual pun at the heart of the genre: that this is that: that Bondage is Loosening: that Mask is Face: that Stone is Water: that Water is Life.

He'd hounded light—not just visual light—straining every muscle of body and mind to get down to what was real, what was absolute; beauty not as someone else had seen it but beauty he could honestly find himself, and what he'd gotten was a picture of the coal pocket. . . . And then, at the edge of self-destruction, John Napper had, I saw, jumped back. He would make up the world from scratch: Let there be light, a splendid garden. (John Gardner, "John Napper Sailing through the Universe")[3]

Where the Land is parodied into Fantasyland, bad fantasy art has its home, and flourishes, then. Bad fantasy art illustrates actions and scenes and characters and icons where they are most stable, most familiar, most irrelevant: which is precisely, according to the model of the fantasy Story we have sketched, where they are vitiated by Thinning. The fixated reiterations of tableaux, the unrelenting insistence on musclebeach and cheesecake, the mortmain glare of fjord and peak, all constitute a gallery of the dead moments, the moments that signal dread and amnesia in true fantasy texts. The immobilized Fantasylands that backdrop most genre fantasy are perhaps justly portrayed in this fashion, by these decals pasted to the corpse of template; but illustrations of this sort make mock of the real thing, just as the Dark Lord, who can never create and never change, who can only parody the good, makes mock of the real thing. Until the change comes.

It may be inappropriate to describe as illustration that fantasy art which works to illuminate the cusps of the fantasy Story; it may be better to think of fantasy illumination as a form of co-creation. "Let there be light," says the illuminator, "a splendid garden." We will close with four examples of fantasy illumination. Two are from the nineteenth century, and are well known; two are from the twentieth century, and are taken almost at random from the vast well of fantasy art created over the past hundred years. The first example is a pure creation; the others arguably transform the texts they accompany, whose immanence and doubleness they manifest in ways words do not.

1. "The Fairy Feller's Master Stroke" (1855-1864) by Richard Dadd (1817-1886), an English painter who died insane, after 40 years in Bedlam and Broadmoor. I considerably modify the following comments from my entry on Dadd in *The Encyclopedia of Fantasy*.[4]

The first thing one notices upon seeing this very famous painting in the flesh is that it is, in fact, despite its enormously complicated tapestry-like texture, a very small canvas indeed. A magnifying glass could be used to advantage if one wished to do a count of the number of figures depicted. Before coming to terms with the internal hugeness of the work, the viewer must come to terms with its external tininess: even in its physical circumstances, then, "The Fairy Feller" manifests a fantasy turn: the Little Big turn, where the inside is larger than the outside. Dreams and rabbit holes are Little Big.

"The Fairy Feller" portrays an engorged landscape, within which a cross-section of the denizens of Faerie seem caught in claustrophobic Bondage (just as the physical painting itself seems caught within the bondage of its restricted compass). These denizens are depicted in various scales; some are so minute they are hardly visible; others, half-hidden within vortices of branch and vine, are huge. It is all a visual pun, a palimpsest: fairies are laid over fairies, worlds over worlds. Contradictions of perception pervade the work, which seems to hover at the edge of an explosive trompe l'oeil, but there is none in view. Instead, centrally located, the "Fairy Feller," who may be a human being, seems about to engage in some paroxysm-like act. His ax is held high. He is being viewed with what seems deep (though transfixed) apprehension by those who notice him at all, and before him, awaiting his blow, sits something vast, maybe an acorn.

Richard Dadd's own gloss on this moment is that the beings here pictured will be released from a spell when the Feller's stroke demolishes the huge nut it is aimed at; and although the end of bondage is not necessarily freedom, it may be appropriate to accept the painter's own understanding here, though it may seem somewhat demented: for no more reason, perhaps, than the sense that the denizens of Faerie show no signs of happy anticipation whatsoever. Perhaps, though, their bondage has frozen them, thinned them into rigidity. "The Fairy Feller's Master Stroke" can be seen as a consummate visual pun in which Fantasy wears Horror's frozen face, a moment of Thinning which never properly begins, and which certainly never ends.

Or it can be seen as the held breath before the loosening.

However it is interpreted, the painting—deliriously, meticulously—manifests some central suspension in the movement of fantasy. The tension is quite extraordinary. Like any great fantasy tale at its moment of resolution, "The Fairy Feller's Master Stroke" is dangerous to gaze upon.

2. In "Narcissism and the Theory of the Double," which appears as a chapter in his useful *Illuminated Fantasy* (1988), James Whitlark describes at some length John Tenniel's illustrations to Lewis Carroll's Alice books. One image selected for concentrated attention—it is from *Through the Looking-Glass* (1871)—is that of the conflict between the beamish boy and the Jabberwock. The text of "Jabberwocky" is well-known. *Illuminated Fantasy* allows us to appreciate the co-creative nature of Tenniel's illumination (Whitlark, pursuing different ends, merely states that it "stands as a complement to the text in a number of ways.") But he is clear enough:

The drawing shows a feminized figure with long hair and dresslike tunic battling a monster wearing a vest, who resembles an old man, as if the child were battling a figure of adult authority. Because Tenniel has turned the face of the pictured hero/heroine from the audience, he renders the Jabberwock-slayer's gender and identity ambiguous, being either Alice or the boy from the medieval past. Thus, the drawing strangely links the two opposite characters together, acting as a mediation between them and enhancing the psychological unity of the total book.[5]

Again, there is a punning at the heart of the illumination. It is quite unlike the affect of Tenniel's illustrations in general, which tend to maintain a calm but peculiarly morose distance from the action. Here, there is no distance. Tenniel's co-creative vision of the inner nature of the conflict waged in fact realizes (as Carroll does not) the action of the scene. The twisting labile unction of Carroll's nonsense sharpens into metamorphosis holding its breath.

3. The twentieth century is, of course, wherever one sets one's gaze, an immensity. Almost at random, therefore, I have settled upon two texts to comment on briefly. They are both books in which—unlike almost all conventional fantasy art—text and illustration interpenetrate.

The first is *The Squirrel Wife* (1971), story by Philippa Pearce, illustrations by

Derek Collard.[6] The text, which is original, is told in fairy tale mode. Young Jack lives by the edge of the forest with his evil older brother. He saves a Green Man, a fairy who conducts him into the woods, into Faerie, where everything is subject to change; there the fairy king rewards him for his sagacious kindness by promising that the baby squirrel whose forelock he encloses in a magic ring will become his wife. Soon this occurs: she is human, but squirrel-like. They escape the wicked brother and live in a village far away; but the wicked brother discovers them eventually, tells lies about them so that they must escape back to the forest. There, the fairy king offers Jack a choice: to keep the squirrel, or to keep his human wife. Being a Jack (Jacks being noted for their worldly wisdom), he chooses the wife.

Though the squirrel wife is only ambivalently human, Pearce's text is a straightforward telling of a moderately straightforward tale; and could have been illustrated with the usual irrelevant competence: with a perky Jack, a dimpled baby squirrel, a cheesy Oberon. But Collard chooses differently: his full-page illustrations, mostly in color, are done in a mosaic style, as though tesserae had been laid together, without regard for lines of perspective. As in Dadd's great painting, figures of various sizes occupy the same suspensed space, peering through the leaves of the magic heartwood glen, peering through each other. Collard outlines in black his figures, his trees, his acorns, his labyrinths of landscape; as these images do not occupy any single space, the effect is of a jigsaw puzzle whose pieces tell their own story. That story is analogous to Pearce's, but emphasizes (as Pearce does not) the uncanniness that underlies the bondages and metamorphic leaps of her tale. Through Collard, we are taken far deeper into the woods than Pearce is inclined to take us. The threat and pulse and timbre of *The Squirrel Wife*—it is a disturbing, arousing artifact—comes to us almost exclusively through the co-creation. It is an illuminated book.

4. "The Magic Wood" is almost certainly Henry Treece's best known poem. It was published in *The Black Seasons* (1945), and has haunted readers ever since with its admonition that the young boy who narrates the poem "must not go to the wood at night!" But the boy ignores his own six-times repeated injunction, goes into the woods, meets "a man with eyes of glass" who carries a stick which is a snake, who makes sounds and has the semblance of something that is widdershins, and a rat peers through his hair. He shows the boy a magic way to catch birds. When asked, the boy gives him a false name, but even so the Green Man or Wicker Man or wodewose asks him to come and "dance with the Kings from under the hill." The boy narrator refuses by saying his prayers, and as the poem closes finds himself "safe on my father's land."[7]

There is danger in the poem, but apparently a safe ending. Several decades later the poem appeared in book form as *The Magic Wood* (1992), illustrated by Barry Moser.[8] The poem, one stanza to a page, is printed over Moser illustrations, which are consistently dark, as befits a narrative that takes place in the woods at night. We see a small crewcut boy sitting close to his rural house, peering into the woods. We see the woods, speckled with tiny lights that are quite certainly eyes. We see the wodewose, his glass eyes glittering from within his foliate head, the snake writhing in his hand, his clawing fingernails. We see creatures of the night. They have metamorphosed from eyes. We see the farm again, with the boy "safe on my father's land." But the boy is in silhouette. His hair is long. He is fully grown, wodewose-like. Once you are in the woods, it may be enough simply to be asked to dance. The boy may have been gone seven years.

There is little need to add a gloss. Barry Moser's illumination of Henry Treece's poem manifestly demonstrates an intersection between visual art and the metamorphoses at the heart of the labyrinth of the fantasy story. The location of goodness in fantasy art is here.

Notes

1. David Denby, "The Current Cinema," *The New Yorker* (July 24, 2000), 86.

2. Peter S. Beagle, *The Last Unicorn* (New York: Viking Press, 1968), 197.

3. John Gardner, "John Napper Sailing through the Universe," in *The King's Indian: Stories and Tales* (New York: Alfred A. Knopf, 1974), 133.

4. John Clute, "Richard Dadd," in *The Encyclopedia of Fantasy*, edited by Clute and John Grant (London: Orbit, and New York: St. Martin's Press, 1997), 245.

5. James Whitlark, *Illuminated Fantasy: From Blake's Visions to Recent Graphic Fiction* (Rutherford, NJ: Fairleigh Dickinson University Press, 1988), 161.

6. Philippa Pearce, *The Squirrel Wife*, illustrated by Derek Collard (London: Longman Young Books, 1971).

7. Henry Treece, "The Magic Wood," in *The Black Seasons* (London: Faber and Faber, 1945); text unpaginated.

8. Treece, *The Magic Wood*, illustrated by Barry Moser (New York: HarperCollins, 1992).

9

Archaeological Fieldwork in the Paper Tiger Stacks Report #43: A Short Happy History of Fantasy Art

John Grant

The Paper Tiger Archival Collection, which holds all the materials used by the staff of Paper Tiger Books in researching and creating its many books of fantasy and science fiction art, has one great advantage: if you're able to avoid the hawk eyes of the vigilant curators, you can cut past the main stacks to reach the storage areas where are amassed the vast number of historical sf documents and memorabilia that still await cataloging. With staff numbers remaining constant over the years while the size of the collection is constantly increasing, it hardly needs a mathematician to realize that the numbers of these uncataloged items are necessarily increasing at a rate approximating, though not mathematically identical to, the exponential.

That this should be so is of course a great boon to the fantasy/sf archaeologist, particularly the fantasy/sf archaeologist engaged in that most traditional of academic pursuits: the search to attain unfair publication advantage over the other members of his or her peer group. How else but through such archaeological fieldwork could such assiduous researchers as Gary Westfahl have discovered, for example, the earliest known printed sf story, which he did in an issue of Hugo Gutenberg's *Shockinge Natural Philosophye Wonder Storyes*? How else might, say, the eminent Mr. Colin Ziegler consult his own unanswered mail?

It is in this context that I am proud to present, as my forty-third report in an occasional series, a selection of the various ancient documents I and my team of researchers have uncovered within the Paper Tiger stacks, which, taken together, in this instance have much light to shed on the history of the art of the fantastic. In particular, we are now better able to understand a few significant highlights of that long and torturous tale—to wit: the dawn of fantasy art in dim prehistory; the birth of fantasy/sf pulp *illustration* some 400 years earlier than other historians have heretofore thought; the genesis of the Flower Fairies (and possibly also of the Pokémon creatures, according to a variant view held by my associate Professor Mimi Culotte of the Taco Bell University of West Covina) in a nineteenth-century madhouse; and the truth of events during the short period when Walt Disney employed Salvador Dali with the intention of creating the first full-bloodedly surrealist animated cartoon, *Destino*—according, at least, to the first draft of the hatchet-job biography of Disney planned by his disgruntled animator (soon afterward fired) Arnold "Grunt" Boxxo, best known for the long-forgotten series of Dickey Dormouse cartoons he later did for Charles Mintz. In the "Research Conclusions" section, it will be demonstrated rigorously, complete with diagrams (unfortunately omitted from this edition), that these documentary fragments, taken together, constitute a complete history of fantastic art.

Altamira, Spain, Aurignacean Period

Uncle Og was good, if a little gamey. After eating, we womenfolk retreated to a far corner of the cave leaving the men to drink themselves into a stupor on fermented mammoth milk while we discussed Sister Nyung's most recent painting.

As is well known, the only bison our menfolk ever are able to catch are those that are become old and palsied, and which stray near to our cave in such a condition of senile febrility that one need merely give them a good push to make them fall over dead. Much the same could be said of many of our menfolk, especially the morning after a session with the fermented mammoth milk—which is to say most mornings. Two nights ago, however, one of our number, the Girl-Child LoChi, dreamt of a land where things were different: where bison were plumply muscled and virile and our menfolk likewise. In this land, which she fancifully called Cimmeria, the mighty-thewed men were swift and valiant hunters, and nightly brought home to their womenfolk great steaming feasts of fresh meat and sanguine love-trophies whose precise nature it is inconvenient to describe.

The purest fancy, all this, of course; but LoChi had told of it, laughing, over our grim breakfast of grit [this was, of course, the original *Homo neanderthalis* grit; the term has since been shortened—Ed.], and soon afterward Nyung seized her frayed twigs and her pigments, selected a round section of the cave wall, and set to work by the flickering firelight. In less than a day she had completed a painting that LoChi cheerfully agreed accorded with the bright, impossible land of her dream. There, indeed, was a broad-shouldered bison, full of meat and vigor; and there nearby was the proud-pronged hunter whose spears already decorated the beast's flanks.

Tonight all of us decided that the painting was among Nyung's finest, although, even so, imperfect. We suggested slight changes, most of which Nyung said she would consider—although, if I know my Sister, she will do precisely nothing about them.

After the critique was over, we lay about chattering idly in between picking bits of Uncle Og from between our teeth.

"Your paintings are going to be very confusing for fantasy historians of the future," I said to Nyung.

"Why so?" she replied.

"Well, your depiction of a bison is based upon LoChi's dream, is it not? We have never seen such a fine animal, except in the distance and from a rear view, and nor have we seen such a brawny, valorous hunter. The whole scene is purest wish-fulfillment fantasy."

"Get on with it," she said testily.

"Well," I continued, "they are going to be incredulous that people as intellectually unsophisticated as ourselves—who do not play Nintendo games nor watch *Who Wants to Be a Millionaire?*—are capable of conscious fantasy. They are going to say that conscious fantasy as a mode of creative thought did not exist until, shall we say, late in the century that they might as well call, for want of anything better, the 'eighteenth.' They are going to cast around for some other explanation of this painting"—I waved a hand at it—"that will more satisfactorily accord with their theories. *Any* explanation, in fact, that does not allow of our being able to creatively dream, for that would clash with their preconceptions."

"But what other explanation could they construct aside from the obvious one?" interposed LoChi, growing interested. She is a precocious child.

"I don't know," I said, "but they're bound to be able to find *something*."

"Like what?" she persisted.

Again I waved a hand, plucking a notion from the air. "Like sympathetic magic, for example," I said.

"Oh, *that*. Surely they'd not be so stupid." LoChi's nose seemed to wrinkle under its mat of fur. "Everyone knows that silly old sympathetic magic stuff doesn't work."

Nyung was looking thoughtful. "Yes," she said slowly, "but supposing we pretended to *believe* it did? Supposing I painted my pictures as a part of a pretended belief in sympathetic magic, the same way we always used to pretend to believe in the tales Uncle Og told us about his younger days—when he told us he'd run down gazelles, fought saber-toothed cats and had two women in the same night? Wouldn't that mean my paintings were just as much fantasy as they actually are? More so, if anything, because they'd be conscious fantasies based upon a conscious fantasy?"

We sat in deep silence for a moment, trying to wrestle our brains around that one.

"You know," said LoChi after a while, "even if we *did* believe in sympathetic magic, that wouldn't stop your paintings being fantasies, Nyung."

"How so?" said Nyung, beginning to look impatient. Except when she is at work on her art, her attention span is short.

"Well," said LoChi, "everyone is aware of the self-evident fact that spirits abide in trees and stones and streams, even though we none of us have ever directly seen any such; and, equally, we all know, because it is true, that the Sun is the only god worth worshipping."

"And that if you're making a face when the wind changes you're stuck with it," I said, completing the list of the basic tenets of our complicated theology.

"If Nyung painted one of the stream spirits," said LoChi, "even though we know such spirits exist, the painting itself would be an expression of a conscious fantasy, because she has never seen such a spirit and must therefore wittingly draw upon her own imagination in order to depict one."

"Those future historians are never going to swallow that," said Nyung with a laugh. "They're going to be too busy guarding the supposed intellectual superiority of twenty-first-century Man to concede that those whom they regard as lower—just because earlier—forms of humanity could ever be capable of such a sophistication."

LoChi looked sad. "You are right," she admitted. "I could even conceive of them ignoring the lesson of the words of one of their greatest sages—let's pretend he's called Darwin—when he might say something like this: 'As dogs, cats, horses, and probably all the higher animals, even birds, have vivid dreams, and this is shewn by their movements and the sounds uttered [as they sleep], we must admit that they possess some power of imagination. There must be something special, which causes dogs to howl in the night. . . .' "

I looked at LoChi with a new respect. I had never known before that she could pronounce square brackets.

"Is it not," I began, "an exercise of conscious fantasy that we can even consider the opinions of such future historians? Or would that more correctly be called the exercise of conscious science fic. . . ."

But at that moment my mate Ooble staggered drunkenly into our part of the cave, gave me a red-eyed and lustful stare, and then collapsed on the upper stratum of broken artifacts we had so carefully been laying down out of consideration for future archaeologists. His arrival effectively ended our conversation.

Just as he was passing out he turned his glare to Nyung's painting. "Looks like a woman with big . . ." he slurred before unconsciousness bested him.

Which proved we womenfolk's point, I felt, that anyone can deduce from a picture what it suits them to deduce, even if it has no relation to the facts.

Brabant, *c.* 1500

Hieronymus has gone upstairs to try to get in a bit more work on "The Garden of Earthly Delights" before sleep overtakes him—I wish he wouldn't accept these tight deadlines, but Master Wynkyn de Worde sent an urgent message from London to say that the new issue of *Amazinge* will be going to bed before year's end and must needs have a cover illo or Hieronymus will never get employ in the skiffye market again. My husband prefers doing still lifes but, as he puts it, de Worde's coin is good and there are absolutions to pay for.

Now that Hieronymus has gone upstairs, as I have said, I have a little time to spend down here with my journal, and I have determined to try to describe the way in which my husband conceives his art.

Ours is an age of devils, and the Devil. In earlier times, perhaps, Satan did not lurk at every doorstep ready to tempt, but today he does. The Good Lord could stop him from doing so, of course, but does not do so for reasons which Hieronymus and I have been told are too theologically complex for our ill-educated minds.

Sometimes, as we sup, we talk of how there might be somewhere—in this New World they talk of, perhaps, across the western sea—where the Devil does not exist at all, but we know this to be just idle fancy, of course: wherever downfallen Man is, there the Devil will inevitably be.

It was twenty years ago that Hieronymus said to me, business being a bit slow on the still lifes, "Nettie old lass, the way to get on in the world is to scare the unmentionable out of folk."

"How's that you say, Mussy?" I replied.

"Folk *like* being scared unmentionableless," he said, planting his elbow in the stew the way he always does when he's thinking hard. "Think o't, we burn witches not because it actually does us any good—except, depending upon the placing of the witch, to help with t' fuel bills in the winter—but because doing so serves to bolster our belief in witchcraft. If we stopped roasting the occasional old bat, people might start getting to thinking that there weren't really no such thing as witchcraft—or that, if there were, it weren't nothing much to worry about. Which we couldn't be having. We *want* there to be witchcraft, and we *want* it to be scaring. We *like* being frightened so long as we don't actually get hurt."

"The witches get hurt when we burn 'em," I pointed out. "Least, they act as if they do."

"All the better," said Mussy, "because that's frightening for us, too."

I thought about that a while, until I stopped.

"Same goes for the Devil," he continued. "You know and I know that the Devil is everywhere around us just hoping to be able to lure us into sins like fornicating with young Helga down at the dairy and things . . ."

"Are you leading up to something, Mussy?" I asked, but he waved me to silence.

"The question is, if the Devil weren't around, would everyone go and fornicate with young Helga anyway?"

"They already do," I said tartly, but so soft that he didn't hear me.

"In itself, fornicating with Helga is an extremely pleasant experience—or, er, so the other guys tell me. But it's made even *more* pleasurable by the fact that we—they—know it's sinful, that it's just the wiles of the devil making . . . um . . . men do it, so that actually there's a sort of nice feeling of scariness about it."

"More scary even than the notion that if these men's wives found out about it they'd beat their heads in with a rolling pin?"

"Much more, because the Devil is *unseen*, he's *intangible*. The only way we can ever see him is in our mind's eye, or in our nightmares. We can *imagine* what he looks like—and all of our imaginings are probably correct and accurate, because the Devil can as we know take any form—but we cannot actually *look at him*. That's the scariest thing about him, if you think about it."

I sighed. He'd left his carrots again, the way he always did. One of these days he'd learn better.

"So there's a big opportunity for the commercial artist," my husband insisted, "in scaring people. I could put my own imaginings of the Devil, and of Hell, and all that stuff, down on canvas and, even though they wouldn't be the same as anyone *else's* imaginings, they'd still be enough like as to shiver the spines of people. And those people'd like that just as much or maybe even better than thinking someone was casting the evil eye their way every time they got a boil."

"I'm not sure . . ." I said.

"I am," he said, and that very morrow he went off and painted a vision of Hell so deliciously harrowing that the Bishop of Brabant gave him a sack of gold and a lame cow for it, and since then our fortunes have never looked back, even though meeting the deadlines is a constant pain. I feel that perhaps professional artists of the future have a lot to learn from my dear husband. While inevitably there will be some who insist that Mussy is painting visions born of his profound religious convictions, most will realize that he has discovered a way of giving the public what the public wants by doing much of their imagining for them. That his imaginings are born from his religious beliefs has nothing to do with it: he is still aware, as an artist *must* be aware, that he is consciously creating and controlling his visions.

Mussy has now come downstairs, and I shall continue my journal another day. Before he did so he called me up to his studio to look at how his new picture is going. It is very grand—a three-quarter wraparound.

"Do you think Master de Worde will be entirely happy with exactly where that flower is being stuck?" I asked him.

"Master de Worde maintains that skiffye is a form of literature designed for intellectually mature adults," said Mussy, effectively ending the discussion.

Bethlem, 1865

"You're mad, Dadd!"

"How much did 'The Fairy-Feller's Master Stroke' fetch?"

"Er . . ."

"Precisely, doctor. So who's calling who mad?"

"Um . . ."

"They laughed at John Martin, too, you know, but look how much he fetched for 'The Great Day of His Wrath.' And he didn't do so badly, either, out of that commission he got to illustrate Milton's *Paradise Lost*, did he?"

"Ah . . ."

"People look at my paintings and they say they like them because they have a frisson of madness, but can you tell me to the nearest digit quite how many of the madmen you've treated have seen cute little fairies in arboreal surroundings? Monsters in the walls, devils under the bed—but *fairies*?"

"B-b-b-but . . ."

"The public like my fairy pix a lot better than Dicky Doyle's, and they attribute that to my supposed mania, but might it not be simply that I'm a much better painter than he is—not just his technical superior but also with a better and more fertile imagination? A better artistic 'eye' for fantasy, in other words? I know precisely what I'm painting, and I know precisely why I do it, you see: I do it because it stimulates the fantasticating part of my intellect, and thereby gives me deep pleasure. Here in Bethlem, with all my needs taken care of, I have the freedom to indulge myself in this way—and, unlike poor Dicky, I don't have to meet deadlines or conform to the idiot preconceptions or lumpen crassnesses of the marketing department. I'm sitting pretty, mate, and I'm producing great art and having a lot of fun. So who's the fruitcake?"

"But you bumped off your dad, Dadd!"

"How d'you think I set this up in the first place?"

Burbank, 1946

Walt was in a foul mood when he got in to the studio that morning, having hit both the tequila and several old ladies the night before. Sal was late, which didn't improve Walt's temper any.

"Where is that **** Spaniard?" he yelled, laying out a few lines on a discarded cel showing Bambi and Thumper cavorting in the forest. "I told the **** when I **** hired him that he'd have to **** punch the **** clock like every other **** around here!"

"Probably takes a while for him to wax his mustache in the mornings," observed Milt.

Walt withered him with a glare, no mean feat when you've got one nostril wrapped around a rolled-up dollar bill.

"What he does with his spare **** time is his own **** business," he snapped, "but in the **** time I **** pay him for he should be **** here, working on this surrie-whatsit short I **** want him to do."

"*Destino*," supplied Grim.

"Yah. Like that."

I felt it was time to get withered by a glare myself.

"Sal keeps telling us, the rest of us, that he don't want to do no surrealist cartoon. He just wants the chance to draw Mickey, like all the rest of us."

"**** that," said Walt, pulling the wings off a fly he'd caught. "He's a **** surrie whatyousaid, isn't he, the ****? I can hire a zillion young and hungry **** animators any day of the week who can **** do Mickey, which all you ****s had better remember, and if I **** wanted a **** Spaniard to **** do it as **** well I'd **** tell him so. I want him to **** do a **** surrie thingie cartoon, so every **** body will reckon I have **** cultural cachet, know what I **** mean?"

"Yeah, but . . ."

"But me no **** buts! If **** Sal were **** let loose on **** Mickey he'd do him **** melting all over a **** cactus in the middle the **** desert, or **** something, complete with all **** sorts of suggestively organic **** bits that would go down like a **** bucket of **** cold sick in **** Poughkeepsie. And it's **** Poughkeepsie that **** pays the **** bills around here. That's another **** thing you'd better not **** for **** get."

It's of little use arguing with Walt when he's in one of these moods, especially with the remains of the tequila and whatever he'd been snorting inside him, not to mention the stuff he was taking for the clap he'd picked up off of the brace of one-legged ladies of pleasure he'd stupidly bought in the midst of a drunken binge in the Whips'n'Cuffs Bar in Hollywood last month. So we called Roy and Roy called the Catamites R Us service and Walt went away and left us to carry on drawing Mickey.

While he was working with us, Sal Dali was just one of the lads, you understand: He liked a beer at lunchtime along with the rest of us, and he laughed at the same smutty jokes. But almost from the moment he arrived, hired on a short-term contract by Walt, he realized that he was on a fool's errand. "The customer is always right," he used to say to us, "but I like to pick the right customer, and this time I haven't. Walt has his own type of fantasy and I have another type, and the two don't really go together. Walt's a customer who's hired me to do what I'm good at doing, but who really wants me to do what he *thinks* I do; and that's why anything he and I try to do together is bound to end up as a disaster—a commercial disaster as well as an artistic one, and I, Salvador Dali, do not like to be associated with commercial disasters. When he allows himself to be, he's a master of fantasy, just as I am: I have seen *Snow White* and *Dumbo* and *Pinocchio* a hundred times, and I have hidden my tears when Bambi's mother dies. But he allows Poughkeepsie to tell him what his fantasy should be, so in turn he tries to tell me what *my* fantasy should be . . . and this I, Salvador Dali, will not stand for. So let me draw Mickey instead, I keep telling him: all the fantasy has been beaten out of Mickey years ago, at the demand of Poughkeepsie, so there can be no clash with my fantasy if I draw Mickey—I have to do something to while away the time I'm here, after all."

I once told Sal I'd always thought surrealism wasn't really fantasy, that it was deconstructivism, the removal of form from the world, whereas fantasy was a bringing of form *to* the world.

He looked at me with disdain over the hot dog he was eating at the time.

"At the back of your brain there is a fantasy bone," he said. "If it tingles, you know you are in the presence of fantasy. If it doesn't, you know you are not. All other definitions are nonsense."

I have been looking in anatomy books, and I know he was wrong. There is no fantasy bone at the back of the brain.

Hewitt, New Jersey, 2000

"Thank you for saying you'll take my paintings to the World SF Convention in Chicago and hang them in the art show for me."

"Not at all. It's our very great pleasure."

"Well . . ."

"Which of the abstracts have you decided to send with us?"

"Um, just a couple of small prints."

"What!? Your abstracts are the very best things you do! They're brilliant!

They're amongst the very finest fantasy art that's being produced today! I just take a look at one of them and I can feel my imagination beginning to move—*that's* what fantasy art is all about."

"Yeah, but the fans don't like them. They say they're not fantasy."

Research Conclusions

The history of fantasy art that we can piece together from these documents does not sit well with the various orthodox histories of the subject that have earlier been produced. Almost all of the famous names those histories cite have been omitted—the great illustrators of sf's Golden Age, for example, or precursors like Fuseli and Magritte and Doré—but nevertheless this version, based on primary archaeological research rather than received and regurgitated ideas, would seem to be complete in itself.

There are various lessons that can be drawn from this account:

1. Fantasy art, like all other forms of fantasy, is what you make of it.

2. Whatever form it takes, it tells the only story that is important to *you*, the viewer, the story in which both the artist and yourself are protagonists. If it does not tell this story, it is almost certainly not fantasy art except by commercial definition.

3. Conscious fantasy has existed as long as the human mind, and likely longer. Watch a cat with a cloth mouse—watch it hunt, stalk and seize an object that it knows is a toy and yet treats as if it were alive—and you watch even a far simpler brain than the human one conjuring up a conscious fantasy. Fantasy art is, though slightly younger than conscious fantasy, nevertheless still very old—approximately as old as the human ability to create a visual representation of our own thoughts.

4. Never guess at the motivations of a fantasy artist. He or she is not a two-dimensional character in a pulp story possessing only a single predominant motivation. Fantasy artists are complex people like the rest of us, and accordingly the motivations that drive them are multi-stranded and not readily subject to instant analysis.

5. If ninety-nine people out of a hundred say that something is not fantasy art, then there is every possibility—although of course no certainty—that it is the very best of fantasy art, because it is going into territory not normally associated with (generic) fantasy. Conversely, what ninety-nine people out of a hundred say is a fantasy artwork may in fact not be a work of fantasy at all, but simply a unicorn or a dragon.

6. Fantasy is a precious and important thing, and likewise fantasy art. They are too important to be circumscribed or stifled by our preconceptions of what they *should* be.

10

Wisdom and Clemency: The Collaborations of Margaret Wise Brown and Clement Hurd

Lynne Lundquist and Gary Westfahl

As one model for the dynamics of written narrative, one might propose the following: writers choose the words and phrases that will evoke in their readers' minds appropriate images of people, places, and events; and as the story proceeds, readers not only absorb the words but also experience a kind of internal motion picture, as the writer's words continually provoke corresponding mental images. For writers crafting narratives for adults, whether realistic stories or fantasies, this process is unproblematic, for two reasons. First, those writers have access to a broad range of vocabulary words (in English, at least 50,000 to 100,000 words), so they can choose words precisely to evoke precisely the right images. Second, they are writing for mature readers who have had innumerable actual and vicarious experiences, so readers can choose from a wide variety of vivid memories to locate or develop mental images of events in the text. And, with the freedom of their unlimited vocabulary and their mature audience, writers for adults face no difficulties in making their narratives entertaining.

For writers crafting narratives for children, especially fantasies, the process is more difficult, which makes it absolutely necessary to provide such stories with illustrations.

First, the range of vocabulary they can employ is severely limited, both for logical reasons (young children do not know as many words as adults) and due to editorial policies (publishers of children's books maintain "word lists" for children of various ages, and writers for children in each group may only use words that appear on that group's list). Thus, the author of a children's book cannot say that characters "ambled," "strolled," "sauntered," or "shuffled," because the only sanctioned word may be "walked," and even an adverb—"slowly walked"—may not fully convey the particular sorts of motion defined by more precise words. So, an illustrator is needed to draw characters with the proper facial expression and posture to communicate their exact style of walking.

Second, children have had relatively smaller numbers of actual and vicarious experiences, and so may not be able to summon up appropriate mental images to accompany written descriptions. This may be especially true for stories with fantastical elements, such as the surrealistic adventures of Maurice Sendak, where the author's accompanying illustrations are not merely decorative additions to, but essential components of, the stories he tells.

A third reason why illustrations are important especially pertains to books for small children and their other audience, parents. Since small children often fall in love with a certain book, and demand that it be read to them again and again and again, the plight of the poor parent, repeatedly forced to recite the same simple text, should elicit some sympathy. Creators of children's television programs like *Sesame Street* may work in some humor that only adults can appreciate, like a knowing reference to a famous movie, confident that the child will not be bothered by it; but the author of a children's book, staring at the very short list of words she is permitted to use, has less freedom to include statements or phrases that only adults would find amusing. In this case, the entertainment for adults must come from the illustrators, who are free to feature in drawings any number of small details and embellishments that can amuse adult readers and, as another way to break the monotony, provide them with something to point out and explain to their young readers during repeated readings.

It is for these reasons, not simply established custom or canny marketing, that virtually all children's books are thoroughly illustrated: the pictures are necessary to communicate aspects of the story that the writer's limited vocabulary cannot entirely communicate; the pictures are necessary to offer young readers appropriate mental images for the story; and the pictures are necessary to provide unobtrusive but appreciated entertainment for adult readers. It is logical, then, for all bibliographies of children's literature to list illustrators' names right after authors' names; in a real sense, the illustrators of children's books are their co-authors, because their contributions make an essential and distinctive contribution to the young readers' experience of the story. When considering the success or failure of works of children's literature, then, critics must examine both its text and its art; and they will consistently find, we believe, that the most successful works invariably display three characteristics: an excellent text, excellent art, and words and pictures that complement each other, suggesting they were produced in a genuinely collaborative fashion. So, more so than other forms of literature, the study of children's literature and children's fantasy demands a study of both authors' words and artists' illustrations.

However, the status of illustrator as co-author is sometimes ignored in studies of children's literature. To cite two classic fantasies for older children, critics invariably speak of "*Alice's Adventures in Wonderland* by Lewis Carroll" and "*The Wizard of Oz* by L. Frank Baum." In discussing those works, commentators may note in passing that yes, Sir John Tenniel did provide memorable illustrations for the Alice books, and yes, W. P. Denslow did provide memorable illustrations for *The Wizard of Oz*, but then they return to an almost exclusive focus on the writers and their words.

Yet we learn some interesting things from the historical record. In both cases, writer and artist exercised some control over the works: Carroll removed one chapter from *Through the Looking-Glass* simply because Tenniel refused to illustrate it,[1] and Baum's silence about the age of Dorothy Gale permitted Denslow to define her as a child of five or six, a decision that Baum evidently embraced in writing later Oz books.[2] The relationships between the writers and artists were often tempestuous, as the writer wanted to regard himself in the traditional way as the sole creator of the story, while the artist felt with some justification that he too should be credited with its creation. Carroll always resented Tenniel because he had wanted to illustrate the Alice books himself; Baum grew angry with Denslow when the artist successfully claimed joint ownership of the Oz characters and went on to create new Oz stories of his own, and their relationship ended when Denslow sued Baum to obtain royalties from a stage version of *The Wizard of Oz*. Finally, we note the peculiar endurance of their collaborative efforts: the Alice books and *The Wizard of Oz* are universally regarded as classics, while other works by Carroll not illustrated by Tenniel and other works by Baum not illustrated by Denslow have tended to fall into obscurity. One could argue that the texts of those particular books are superior, but surely their accompanying illustrations played a role in the survival and the continuing popularity of those works.

Here, we propose to examine the relationship between words and illustrations in children's literature by focusing on a less celebrated, but equally interesting, set of works: the fantasies for small children written by Margaret Wise Brown and illustrated by Clement Hurd. Although her subgenre is frequently ignored by critics of all varieties, Brown has gradually earned acceptance as a major modern writer: she has been the subject of a thoroughly researched and sympathetic biography, Leonard S. Marcus's *Margaret Wise Brown: Awakened by the Moon*,[3] and she earned an entry in John Clute and John Grant's *The Encyclopedia of Fantasy*.[4] Yet the contributions of illustrator Hurd to her two most famous books—*The Runaway Bunny* and *Goodnight Moon*—have been neglected. Their relationship in some ways paralleled those of Carroll and Tenniel, and Baum and Denslow: they worked closely together in creating their books; they eventually feuded, as Brown rejected Hurd's illustrations for *Wait Till the Moon Is Full* and enlisted another artist; and their two greatest collaborations remain perennial best-sellers to this day, while dozens of other books written by Brown and illustrated by other artists, and books by other authors illustrated by Hurd, are generally ignored and out of print.

In most respects, Marcus is a diligent and capable biographer, and he repeatedly explains how Brown esteemed her illustrators and worked closely with them in creating her books. Yet Marcus lacks an aptitude for literary criticism, as he tends to misread Brown's texts, and as a biographer of Brown, he is influenced by the implicit ideological agenda of all literary biographers: to promote and celebrate the authorial talents of their subjects. He can praise the contributions of the illustrators, but he must attribute the success or failure of any Brown book only to Brown's words, not to the effectiveness or inadequacies of the illustrations. Thus, his book unsatisfactorily deals with Clement Hurd simply as one of Brown's many artistic collaborators, not as a person of particular importance to her career, and he inappropriately downplays Hurd's contributions to Brown's most enduring works.

As Marcus describes it, the collaboration began when Brown was impressed by the "whimsical semi-abstractions on the bathhouse ceiling" of a friend's house (90), asked to meet the artist, Clement Hurd, and proposed that he illustrate one of her books. Their relationship would result in six collaborations during Brown's lifetime as well as two books illustrated by Hurd and published after Brown's death in 1952. For purposes of discussion, these books can be placed into two distinct categories. First, we will speak of their "animal fantasies," distinguished by their focus on adorable, and often anthromorphized, animals: their first collaboration, *Bumble Bugs and Elephants* (1938); the classic *The Runaway Bunny* (1942) and *Goodnight Moon* (1947); and the little-known appendage to *Goodnight Moon*, *My World* (1949). For purposes of contrast, we will include in this discussion another Brown book, *Wait Till the Moon Is Full* (1948), which was planned as a Brown-Hurd collaboration although another artist, Garth Williams, did the illustrations. Second are their "people fantasies," primarily featuring human characters and generally aimed at a slightly older audience: *The Bad Little Duckhunter* (1947), *The Peppermint Family* (1950), *The Little Brass Band* (1955), and *The Diggers* (1960).

The first Brown-Hurd collaboration, *Bumble Bugs and Elephants: A Big and Little Book*, displays a number of interesting features.[5] First, perhaps because its words were, as Marcus notes, "written to order for Hurd" (92), Brown freely announced that Hurd was the principal creator of the book, as it is credited on both the cover and title page as "Pictures by Clement Hurd and Word Pattern by Margaret Wise Brown"; only tiny print on the first page, "Copyright 1938 by Margaret Wise Brown," identifies her as its main author. To explain her modesty, one sees that the text is extremely brief, simple, and repetitive, even compared to her later books, beginning with "Once upon a time there was a great big bumble bug and a tiny little bumble bug" (2), followed by a series of similarly worded contrasts between one or more large creatures and one or more small creatures for nine contrasts in all (respectively, bumble bugs, butterflies, birds, turtles, chickens, fish, dogs, pigs, and elephants). There are some differences in the language: Brown names the large creature(s) first five times and names the small creature(s) first four times; while the large creatures are always described as "great big," the small creatures are variously described as "tiny little," "little tiny," and "little"; and the numbers of creatures involved in the contrasts may be one, two, three, "some," or "a lot," and of course "There were three little pigs" (12-13). Overall, however, *Bumble Bugs and Elephants* seems little more than a device for teaching very small children the difference between "big" and "little" by means of simple statements accompanying pictures of large and small animals, the sort of functional but forgettable book that has been regularly produced and sold to new parents for most of this century. Perhaps, as Marcus suggests, the book was "experimental" for its day (93), but that hardly qualifies it as memorable literature.

Further, attempting to present the book as precisely that, Marcus argues that "without ever developing a plot line," Brown was offering a series of pictures "of a small creature that had found its place in the world alongside a much larger one," producing a book that "was not so much a story as a game," reflecting the "emotional reality of early childhood," which "the very young might extend indefinitely by inventing big-little pairs of their own" (93-94). However, there is a narrative in *Bumble Bugs and Elephants*, in part suggested by Brown's words but mainly developed in Hurd's illustrations.

One notices first that the nine pairs of creatures are roughly arranged in order of size, beginning with bumble bugs and butterflies and ending with horses and elephants; the book not only contrasts little and big, but *travels* from little to big. Further, the first four pages each contrast a single large creature and a single small creature, and the only other objects in the pictures are natural objects like flowers, grass, trees, and clouds. But then comes a two-page spread with two big chickens and a total of nine little chickens (6-7); the world is expanding, both in size and in the number of inhabitants. The next two-page spread features not only three big fish and twelve little fish, but also a fisherman in a small boat, a sailboat, and a tugboat (8-9); people are now entering a previously unpopulated world. Then a two-page spread shows a big dog and two little dogs who are obviously pets, inside of a kitchen with a window, two paintings on the wall, a chair, and a dining-room table with a pitcher and a plate of food on it; further suggesting the influence of people in an amusing way, the big dog is standing on its hind legs with its front paws on the table, in the posture of a human being (10-11). In the following two-page spread with the pigs, there is another new development: while a farmer standing by a fence and a passing airplane further convey a populated world, the big chicken and big butterfly from previous drawings make a return appearance (12-13). So, the previously separated tableaux of big and little are now starting to come together. Similarly, the two-page spread of horses includes not only an old man in a cart holding the reins on the big horse and transporting the small horse, but also five of the little chickens and the two turtles (14-15). The final painting brings matters to a conclusion, returning to the pattern of one big creature and one small creature—a small black elephant standing on the trunk of a big white elephant—while also featuring the big bird, the big butterfly, a big pig and two of the little pigs, and a big chicken and three of the little chickens, the latter humorously perched upon the big elephant's back (16-17).

Thus, carefully examined, *Bumble Bugs and Elephants* does tell a story that resonates with the experiences of early childhood: one first has only a narrow vision of intimate relationships between oneself and larger versions of oneself; then, while growing larger, one notices more, and more variegated, residents in the world, and one finally begins to integrate perceptions of separate residents into a fuller world view. And, while one cannot discount the possibility that certain features in the art were suggested by Brown during the collaborative process, these narrative elements in an otherwise repetitive book can be largely attributed to the creative artwork of Clement Hurd.

However, Marcus notices in Hurd's illustrations only his "playful humor" and his "sure grasp of young children's need for reassurance that the world they live in is a safe and secure place"; thus, Brown subsequently "turned primarily to him to illustrate those manuscripts of hers that investigated the child's elemental feelings of attachment to home" (93). One manuscript along those lines, *The Runaway Bunny*, would soon become their second collaboration, and their first masterpiece.[6]

In discussing this remarkable book, Marcus most egregiously reveals his inadequacies as a critic. He notes that Brown borrowed the basic idea and structure of the book from a medieval love ballad, replacing a suitor pursuing his beloved with a mother pursuing her rebellious child, and he explains the book's appeal by arguing that the bunny's mother serves "as a reassuring bridge between real and imaginary worlds, for while the bunny child escapes into a succession of other-than-human guises . . . his mother nearly always overtakes him by adopting a familiar human form" (149-50). He additionally speculates that the "bunny child's rejection of the here-and-now" reflected the book's "private meaning" for Brown, her growing impatience with mentor Lucy Mitchell, and her desire "like the wayward bunny child, to see how far astray she might go and still remain within her teacher's protective ken" (151).

Yet in seeing this book as a way to "bridge" the "real and imaginary worlds" and as an expression of Brown's quest for freedom, Marcus is, first of all, obviously misreading the text, which unambiguously conveys the message that young children should avoid wild imaginary worlds and embrace familiar real worlds, and that they should abandon all their dreams of freedom and accept, at least for now, complete parental control. Almost inarguably, *The Runaway Bunny* is a story about suppressing one's yearnings for freedom, not a story about achieving some sort of partial freedom or gradually developing a desire for freedom.

Yet Marcus's second and more grievous error is that he says almost nothing about Hurd's illustrations for *The Runaway Bunny*, even though they constitute a major reason for the book's success. Examining Brown's text in isolation, the mother bunny can sound strident, even dictatorial, as she responds to each of her child's dreams of escape with a grim resolve to pursue and capture the child regardless of his actions. Here is a typical exchange:

> "If you become a mountain climber," said the little bunny, "I will be a crocus in a hidden garden."
> "If you become a crocus in a hidden garden," said his mother, "I will be a gardener. And I will find you." (19)

Considering the flat determination of the statement "I will find you," and envisioning what a gardener might actually do to a crocus in a garden, one could readily see the mother as a tyrannical and unsympathetic figure. However, readers do not get that impression due to the humor and colorful creativity of Hurd's drawings. For example, in the painting after this exchange, the mother bunny appears wearing denim overalls, a wide-brimmed hat, and carrying a basket and hoe—all the accoutrements of a human gardener—walking toward an array of large, brightly colored flowers, with a little white bunny inconspicuously lurking inside of one pink flower (20-21). Any aura of oppressiveness, then, is instantly dissipated by the wit and splendor of the following illustration.

Throughout *The Runaway Bunny*, in fact, Hurd's color paintings continually balance the earnestness of Brown's words with gently satiric humor. Thus, his illustrations perfectly exemplify the three important roles that pictures play in children's books. First, they provide descriptions that the limited vocabulary of the text cannot convey: while the mother bunny can say "I will be a mountain climber" (15), only Hurd's illustrations can provide her with the rope, walking stick, hat, and backpack that Brown could not describe in words (16-17). Second, they illustrate scenes that young readers may have trouble visualizing: when the text grows more abstract and the mother bunny says "I will be a tree that you come home to" (23), it may be hard for children to figure out what this would involve—but Hurd draws a tree with bushy green leaves in the shape of a rabbit, perfectly explaining her transformation (24-25). Finally, they provide sly humor for adults to enjoy and perhaps discuss with their children: the mother bunny as fisherman tries to catch the little bunny with a fishing pole baited with a carrot (12-13); the little bunny as sailboat has huge ears shaped like sails, with a little red flag on top (28-29); and the circus features not only the bunny trapeze artist and tightrope walker but also a ringmaster, poodle, monkey, horse, and two clowns (32-33). The overall effect is that Hurd's illustrations lighten the didacticism and potential oppressiveness of the text, making the book especially delightful to both children and parents.[7] One could even make the heretical suggestion that it is Hurd's paintings, more than Brown's words, that have made the book a classic.

However, one must acknowledge the genius of both Brown's text and Hurd's illustrations for their next, and most successful, collaboration, *Goodnight Moon*.[8] Here, Marcus is not far off the mark when he describes this famous book as "A little elegy and a small child's evening prayer . . . a supremely comforting evocation of the companionable objects of the daylight world" conveying a "sense of the fantastic as an aspect of the everyday" (187-88). One objects only to his additional notion that the book represents some sort of "ritual preparation for a journey beyond that world, a leave-taking of the known for the unknown world of darkness and dreams" (187), since the focus of the story is so overtly on the child's acceptance of, and reconciliation with, the confined world of his bedroom. In fact, the book not only provides a sharp contrast to *The Runaway Bunny*, but also serves as its sequel. First, it is the story of a little child who has outgrown his desire to run away from home and has learned instead to love being at home. Second, and perhaps more important, it is the story of a previously powerless little child who has not accepted his home but has in some sense gained mastery over it, as he addresses and personifies all its objects.

In fact, Hurd's illustrations cunningly establish the close relationship between the two books: on the left side of the room (from the reader's perspective) a copy of *The Runaway Bunny* lies on the top shelf of a bookcase, and above it in a picture frame is the scene from *The Runaway Bunny* where the mother bunny as fisherman is fishing for her son, complete with most of the picture's details, like the hip boots, the fallen tree, and (if one looks very carefully) the carrot bait dangling in front of the little bunny in the river. On the right-hand side of the room, on the boy's nightstand, lies a copy of *Goodnight Moon* itself, presumably his favorite bedtime book. Further suggesting this shift is that the mother bunny, the parental figure who dominated the world of *The Runaway Bunny*, sits and knits on the left side of the room, while the little boy in bed, who takes over the world of *Goodnight Moon*, is on the right side. Thus, by slowly moving one's eyes from the left to the right in each picture (as most readers would naturally do), the reader repeatedly is literally moving away from the world of *The Runaway Bunny* and into the world of *Goodnight Moon*.

It is in their astounding attention to detail that Hurd's illustrations both command, and reward, such close examination. On one hand, the repeated illustrations of the same room from slightly different angles reinforce the entire theme of the book, as the room gradually becomes as familiar and comforting to readers as it is to its occupant. On the other hand, in addition to the different perspectives, there are ingenious variations. While all repeated readers of *Goodnight Moon* will notice some of its surprises, and while several of them have been previously noted by commentators, the number and variety of little stories being told by means of Hurd's sequential illustrations are truly remarkable.

Consider, for example, how carefully Hurd records the passage of time. In the eight color paintings of the room, the time on the clock on the mantlepiece is 7:00, 7:10, 7:20, 7:30, 7:40, 7:50, 8:00, and 8:10; when the clock on the nightstand is visible, it records the same time (5, 8-9, 12-13, 16-17, 20-21, 24-25, 28-29, 32-33). So, we are seeing snapshots of the room taken every ten minutes, and we know the boy's precise bedtime ritual: he is put into pajamas and into bed at 7:00; at 7:20, his mother comes to sit in the room and keep him company while he continues to rest; and at 8:00, the lights are turned out, the mother leaves the room, and the boy goes to sleep. The passage of time is also recorded by the movements of the Moon in the window to the left of the mantlepiece. At 7:10, the first time we observe that window, the Moon is just beginning to be visible in the lower left corner of the window; at 7:20, we can see almost half of the Moon in the corner; next, in the one of the black-and-white illustrations before the next color painting, presumably representing some time between 7:20 and 7:30, the Moon has risen a bit more, so that we can now see about three-quarters of it; by 7:30, almost the entire Moon is visible, centered behind the left window bar; at 7:40, the Moon has risen and has almost moved beyond the left window bar; we cannot see it at 7:50, but at 8:00, the Moon is still higher and now starting to inch behind the right window bar; and at 8:10, the Moon is now very high and centered behind the right window bar.

Thanks to Hurd's meticulous creativity, then, *Goodnight Moon* becomes an especially memorable book because every time one looks at it, despite the seeming sameness of the illustrations, there is another aspect of the scene to focus on, often leading to new and delightful discoveries. During one reading of the book, a reader might decide to pay attention to the progress of the room's white mouse. At 7:00, the mouse is sleeping beside the firewood to the right of the mantlepiece; at 7:10, while near his original position, he is awake and watching the cats playing on the central carpet; at 7:20, he is still watching the cats and has boldly moved a bit closer to them; at 7:30, he has moved to the left side of the room, has climbed on the rack with the mittens and socks (perhaps to keep away from the cats), and is looking up at the picture of the cow jumping over the moon above the mantlepiece; at 7:40, he has now climbed on top of the bookcase and is looking down at the cats intently; at 7:50, he has moved back to the center of the room and sitting directly in front of the fireplace, staring at the fire; and at 8:00, he has climbed up onto the table to the right of the boy's bed and he is about to nibble the boy's mush! Finally, at 8:10, the mouse has gotten up on the window sill of the window to the right of the mantlepiece and is looking off into the sky—and we notice that there is now significantly less mush in the boy's bowl, indicating that the mouse has just enjoyed a hearty dinner.

While the mouse's adventures may be the most entertaining, the kittens are also worth examining. At 7:10, when they are first seen, the kittens sit expectantly in the middle of the carpet; they know that the knitting mother will soon arrive, and they know that she will let them play with a ball of yarn. Sure enough, they begin to play with the ball of yarn at 7:20 and are still doing so at 7:40, the next time they are observed. Then, at 8:00, the kittens expectantly look up at the mother; they know it is about time for her to depart, which will leave them a nice warm chair to sleep in. And sure enough, at 8:10, both cats are sleeping on the vacated chair. Watching the cats thus confirms that what we are witnessing is indeed an exactly timed nightly ritual in the boy's life.

At times, Hurd's attention to detail is amazing. Most readers will see the boy's brush displays the word "Bunny," identifying it as his brush, and will notice how the room gradually gets darker in each picture. However, few if any will notice that in the picture over his bed of the three bears in chairs, the picture shown in *their* room, barely discernible in various renderings, is the same picture of the cow jumping over the Moon that hangs in the middle of the boy's room! Hurd also cleverly shows the boy's attachment to both his room and his mother: at 7:00, he is looking to his left, at 7:20, when his mother has arrived, he is looking at his mother; at 7:30, he looks behind him; at 7:40, he looks back at his mother; at 7:50, he looks to his left; at 8:00, he looks back at his mother; and at 8:10, the dimness of the room makes it hard to tell, but the bunny is either fast asleep or staring at the chair where his mother had just been sitting. Thus, the boy is balanced in his interest in his room and his interest in his mother.

A reader might also approach the book as a challenging puzzle, examining each picture to see if there are any mistakes or inconsistencies in his multiple renditions. The only major problems involve the cover painting for *Goodnight Moon*, which not only shows the Moon in the wrong position—it is far too high, and too far to the left, for the indicated mantlepiece time of 7:00—but also has three other errors: the window curtains are green and red, not green and yellow; the golden fireplace equipment to the left of the fireplace is omitted; and the picture of the cow jumping over the Moon does not include the three buildings below the cow. However, we have only been able to find one small discrepancy in the paintings within the book:

in the 7:20 illustration, the curtain rod on the left is yellow and the one on the right is red; but in the 7:40 and 8:10 paintings, both of them are red.

While all of these details make *Goodnight Moon* an especially involving picture book, they also reinforce the book's stance as a rebuttal to the rebelliousness of *The Runaway Bunny*. Being in the same room for hours at a time, day after day, may seem like a terribly monotonous existence that would understandably make a little bunny want to run away; but Hurd's illustrations show that such a confined existence can be interesting in its own way, if the child is attentive to its intricacies and subtle changes. *Goodnight Moon*, then, shows the child of *The Runaway Bunny* that a little bunny does not have to run away in order to discover a fantastic new world; such a fantastic world is literally within his room.

However, children cannot stay at home forever, and to see *Goodnight Moon* as a sequel to *The Runaway Bunny* invites the idea of a third book that would serve to complete the trilogy, as it were. Following William Blake's progressive scheme of innocence, experience, and organized innocence, one might say that *The Runaway Bunny* is about being rebelliousness, *Goodnight Moon* is about accepting supervision, and the projected third volume would be about some sort of supervised rebelliousness, as the bunny who has overcome his wild desire to go off on his own and learned to accept and dominate his own little world is now gently introduced to the independent life that he will someday have to lead. In fact, Marcus reports, Brown and Hurd at the time did see *The Runaway Bunny* and *Goodnight Moon* as their "classic series" and, immediately after the latter was published, they began to plan their "next installment," which was to be entitled *Wait Till the Moon Is Full* (229).

However, after Hurd had completed one painting for the book, Brown inexplicably decided to hire another artist, Garth Williams, to illustrate the book. Marcus's theory is that Brown made the substitution only because Williams seemed to get along with her new lesbian girlfriend, Michael Strange, while Hurd and his wife clearly disliked her. Regardless of why the decision was made, however, the results were disastrous.

If one considers *Wait Till the Moon Is Full* as the envisioned continuation and culmination of *The Runaway Bunny* and *Goodnight Moon*, one immediately notices some changes in the overall format of the series that appear to be ill-advised.[9] First, in contrast to the small, wide shape of *The Runaway Bunny* and *Goodnight Moon*, this book is larger and taller, making it less attractive and accessible to little people with little hands. Second, while the two books illustrated by Hurd almost always provided a new picture to accompany every new sentence, the format of larger pages with larger pictures demands more words on every page of text, so children may be obliged to listen to several sentences while staring at the same picture. Finally, while *The Runaway Bunny* and *Goodnight Moon* alternated monochromatic illustrations with full-color illustrations, the pictures in *Wait Till the Moon Is Full* are entirely monochromatic, except for the frontispiece and one final picture, necessarily making the experiences of looking at the pictures sequentially rather less interesting. Presumably, these all represent decisions mutually agreed upon by

Brown and Williams, so they must be considered equally to blame.

Another decision—to substitute raccoons for rabbits—seems even more unwise, since raccoons lack the warm emotional resonances that were skillfully exploited by Hurd in the previous books. It is also incongruous because, while Brown altered the main text to describe mother and child as raccoons, the references to rabbits in the two songs sung by the mother were retained—so that a raccoon mother strangely sings songs that most often mention rabbits, and sometimes mention other creatures, but mention raccoons only once.

All of these problems might have been minimal if Garth Williams's illustrations for *Wait Till the Moon Is Full* had been brilliant and creative; however, this is simply not the case. Marcus describes his pictures as "wonderfully accomplished," offering both "whimsy" and "tenderness" (231), but one finds none of the wit and attention to detail that characterized Hurd's drawings. The predominant color in Williams's pictures is gray, and the predominant impression is dullness. The mother raccoon seems to lead an extraordinarily dull life, engaged in one chore after another, carried out with a rolling pin, scrub board, iron, ironing board, and sewing machine that are identical to those used by human mothers. The boy raccoon endures a similarly dull existence of eating porridge in a high chair, washing his hands in a basin, and listlessly carrying about his two toys, a ball and a little raccoon on rollers. This last feature—one of the few details added by Williams's illustrations—displays an extraordinary lack of imagination: would a human little boy play with a little toy human on wheels? Surely, giving the child some other sort of toy, or a greater variety of toys, would be both more appropriate and more entertaining. Overall, then, as the children being read to start to lose interest in the monotonously realistic, brown-and-gray illustrations, adult readers of this book, unlike adult readers of *The Runaway Bunny* and *Goodnight Moon*, will find nothing amusing or striking in the illustrations to hold their interest.

However, the gravest problem in Williams's approach to the work is surely his final, full-color illustration. Throughout the story, the boy raccoon has been portrayed as anxious to get away from home and experience the nighttime world, not unlike the boy bunny in *The Runaway Bunny*; as the mother summarizes, the boy has wanted "to go out in the woods and see the night and know an owl and how dark is the dark and see the moon and how big is the night and listen to the Whip poor Will and stay up all night and sleep all day and see that the moon isn't a rabbit and what color is the night and see a bird fall out of his nest and fly away in the moonlight and find another little raccoon to play with" (32). Yet this child calmly acquiesces when his mother repeatedly tells him "Wait till the Moon is full," accepting that it will be best to postpone his adventure until his mother feels the time is right.

However, by the time he is finally permitted outside, Williams's illustrations suggest that he has forgotten about all of his desires and ambitions except the last one, to find a playmate. For in the next-to-last illustration, as the boy raccoon walks out into the nighttime world, he is bizarrely carrying *a baseball bat* under his arm; and once he is finally outside in the nighttime in the final color illustration, he is observed spending his time *playing baseball* with another raccoon and two rabbits. He is not looking at the full moon, or at the owl that is a tiny detail in the background; there is no "Whip poor Will" or "bird fall[ing] out of his nest" to observe; instead of displaying any interest at all in this new environment, the boy raccoon simply holds his bat on his shoulders and stares intently at the baseball that is being thrown for him to swing at and hit. The other pleasures of nighttime life experienced by the animal children in the painting are similarly stultifying—three rabbits are playing with a jump rope, and a squirrel is swinging on a swing. Further, while the whole concept behind the book presumably is that the boy will find some freedom from oppressive parental control by venturing out into the night, Williams's illustration portrays the boy as still firmly under the thumb of his mother, who sits only a few feet away from his baseball game, knitting, and chatting with a rabbit mother who is also knitting. Given that he is paying no attention to the outdoor world and is simply playing a game while his mother watches, his situation has really not changed very much at all.

In sum, the final painting not only fails to reflect the true spirit of the text, but it actually betrays the text: a story about a child's desperate desire to escape from parents and explore the wide world has been depicted only as a child's modest transition from a rigidly supervised indoor environment to a rigidly supervised outdoor environment. The boy raccoon finds no freedom, no stimulating new experiences, but only a new place to play his games, a place that otherwise does not interest him. What was the point of waiting till the moon was full, when the end result for the little raccoon was only more of his same dull existence?

Marcus recognizes that *Wait Till the Moon Is Full* is related to *The Runaway Bunny* and *Goodnight Moon*, stating that the book represents Brown's return to the "compelling theme" of the other two books, "the small child's gradual development from a condition of absolute dependence to one of increasing self-possession" (230). However, he cannot grant that the book's failure stemmed primarily from its inferior illustrations; rather, he must condemn Brown's text because it does not have the "emotional intensity" and "overall integrity" of the other two books (230, 231). While there may be some truth in those observations, these problems might have been overcome if *Wait Till the Moon Is Full* had been accompanied by some warm and clever Hurd illustrations.

In any event, since this book clearly was not going to serve as a follow-up to the successful *Goodnight Moon*, another obvious strategy would be necessary: to bring Hurd back as illustrator to work on another collaboration with Brown featuring pictures of bunnies. This duly occurred with the 1949 publication of *My World*.[10] This book represents the closest thing to a genuine continuation of *The Runaway Bunny* and *Goodnight Moon*, and given the ongoing popularity of those two books, *My World* might well be opportunistically republished today as a "lost" sequel to those books. However, despite the superficial similarities between *My World* and its noteworthy predecessors, the book is, in its way, just as disappointing as *Wait Till the Moon Is Full*.

The book might be summarized as an expanded version of *Goodnight Moon* that deals with the boy's entire daily routine and his entire house, not merely the nightly rituals of bedtime. As in *The Runaway Bunny* and *Goodnight Moon*, two-page color illustrations alternate with two pages of black-and-white illustrations. The first seven two-page illustrations show the six rooms of the house, and the final illustration provides an exterior view. The boy as narrator mentions various objects that he owns, in contrast to objects that are owned by others, each description introduced by word patterns like "Mother's chair, My chair" (6) and "Daddy's slippers, My slippers" (7), usually followed by a comment or two: "My soap. Daddy's soap. My soap will make soapsuds, I hope" (20-21). There is a recognizable chronological sequence of events: first, in the evening, his mother is reading to the boy in the parlor (4-5); later, his father looks at him while he sleeps on his crib (checking his pocket watch, which says 10:10) (8-9); the next morning, around 7:20 according to the kitchen clock, the boy and his parents have breakfast (12-13); the boy then goes to work in the garage with his father, who appears to be a car mechanic (16-17); the boy and his parents then wash up for dinner in the bathroom (20-21); they eat dinner in the dining room with another bunny couple and their little daughter (24-25); the next morning, the mother reads to the boy in his bedroom (28-29); and the boy then goes outside to swing on a swing in his front yard (32-33). Only the odd mention of a fishing trip with his father between bath time and dinner time (22-23) disrupts the flow of events (though the scene was perhaps inserted to explain the fish that is being served for dinner on the following pages).

While resemblances are not always exact, the book is also filled with deliberate visual references to *Goodnight Moon*. The parlor recalls the boy bunny's bedroom, with his mother on a chair on the left, a roaring fireplace in the middle, and a round table with a lamp on it to the right. While this boy's bedroom is smaller and more spartan, and has a crib instead of a bed, there is an open window displaying a full moon. The family's breakfast seems to consist of bowls of mush. The fishing father wears big black boots and a satchel on his waist, like the fishing mother in *The Runaway Bunny* whose picture is on the boy's bedroom wall; and that very same picture also adorns the dining-room wall in this house. When the boy wakes up in the morning, he is holding a big red balloon, just like the red balloon in the room of *Goodnight Moon*.

However, despite its superficially expanded worldview, *My World* in fact reads more like a "prequel" to *Goodnight Moon* than a sequel, in that its child-narrator seems younger and less advanced than the preternaturally mature child-narrator of *Goodnight Moon*, and for that reason the book is less resonant for children and their parents. Part of the problem is that Brown's text lacks the crucial element of direct address that made *Goodnight Moon* so charming and, in its way, empowering: the child of *My World* simply observes, but manifestly does not control, his world. In addition, the story surely would have been more cohesive and satisfying if Brown had shaped it into a narrative of a single typical day, from morning to night, which would not have been difficult at all. The absence of such a clear pattern further suggests a child who has not fully understood, and gained a sense of power over, his daily life.

However, Hurd's illustrations also reinforce the impression that the world of *My World* represents a dissatisfying regression, not a progression, from the world of *Goodnight Moon*. Possibly to save money, the illustrations are not fully colored, but only have various shades of yellow, orange, red, and brown, inevitably making the environments depicted seem less fully realized. In addition, Hurd displays a child who must sleep in a crib, not a child who sleeps in a bed, and a child who must eat at the dinner table in a high chair, not a child who is trusted to eat at a table by his bed. Following up on Brown's comment "In my book I only look" (3), Hurd displays a floor strewn with blocks showing various letters and little words like "cat," "dog," "run," "to," and "boy" (4-5), suggesting a child who has not yet learned to read, and he is also a child who does not have a book next to his bed. Hurd also makes no effort to unify the story through his art in the ways that made *Goodnight Moon* so memorable. For example, the family has a dog and cat, and the little bunny has a teddy bear, but their occasional appearances are unremarkable and cannot be tied together to form a clever storyline. Perhaps some suppressed but lingering bitterness over his dismissal from *Wait Till the Moon Is Full* was making Hurd a bit halfhearted in his dedication to this new project.

Still, *My World* does offer a few touches of the old Hurd wit. While the little bunny is sleeping in his crib, we see his teddy bear riding on the hobbyhorse and looking up at the full moon, as if taking the opportunity to enjoy itself while beyond the boy's notice. In the breakfast scene, the mother is standing by a stove with a pan that, on close examination, is frying carrots, not bacon. In the garage, three wrenches resembling the letter "I" hang next to an adjustable wrench resembling an "F," a pair of pliers resembling an "X," and a hammer resembling a "T." If you rearrange the letters a bit, the tools spell out "I FIX IT," which is precisely what the father is doing to the car in the picture and what the boy is attempting to do to his toy car. In the bathroom, a hanging towel displays a "B" for "bunny." And, following the scene showing the father catching a big fish and the little bunny catching a little fish, we see the dining room scene with the big fish lying on a platter in the center of the table, while the little fish is in the mother's hand as she looks down at the cat eagerly reaching for its anticipated treat. Still, none of these sporadic details serve to compensate for the other problems in Brown's text and Hurd's illustrations.

The way we have characterized *My World*—a flawed text by Brown combined with halfhearted illustrations by Hurd—would also serve to describe the last two Brown-Hurd collaborations during Brown's lifetime, *The Bad Little Duckhunter* and *The Peppermint Family*, both books that Marcus does not even bother to mention. Both are written for somewhat older children, featuring more complex story lines, longer sentences, and more words per page, and as such may represent a form that Brown was less comfortable with. And, since neither story had anything to do with "the child's elemental feelings of attachment to home," they would appear to be poorly suited to Hurd's talents, as proved to be the case.

The Bad Little Duckhunter involves a determined little man with a rifle whose efforts to shoot a duck are repeatedly thwarted by natural forces.[11] First, a "Mother Duck" is upset when he points his gun at a duck and "nipped him in the pants" (7), which causes his bullet to hit a mosquito instead. The angry "Mother Mosquito" (11) then gets her children to bite the man in the neck, which sends his next errant bullet up into the wind; but since "A Mother Wind was teaching her little winds to blow that morning" (15), she becomes angry as well and instructs her little winds to blow at him. Further errant bullets disturb "a Mother Wave" (18), a "Mother Grass Blade" (22), and "a big fat Mother Cloud" (24), which leads to vengeful splashes, swishing grasses, and rain. The frustrated hunter then wonders, "Where is the pleasure in shooting ducks!" (30), and after noting that he is now surrounded by pleasant winds, grasses, mosquitoes, and ducks, asks "Why shoot?" (32) and appears ready to coexist peacefully with the natural world.

Even before considering Hurd's illustrations, one sees that there are significant problems in Brown's text. Although the original idea for this book might have struck Brown as clever, the execution of the formula is plodding at best, and although the reactions of the ducks and mosquitoes are reasonable enough, the subsequent involvements of the plants and personified natural phenomena seem more contrived than imaginative, as Brown strains to keep the wheels of the storyline turning. The book further suffers from its heavy-handed message and abrupt ending.

Understandably, Hurd provides uninspired illustrations for this uninspired work. Again, the book does not have full color illustration, as only reds and greens are employed. The duckhunter is drawn too crudely to be involving—drawing people was never one of Hurd's strengths—and the opportunities for clever depictions of the unlikely characters in this drama are entirely neglected. Recalling how imaginatively Hurd dealt with the mother bunny transformed into a raging wind and a tree in *The Runaway Bunny*, one is disappointed to see that the winds, waves, grass blades, and clouds are drawn in a dully realistic manner, lacking faces or any attributes of animate life. Only the last two color drawings in the book reflect any creativity or attentiveness to the text, as Hurd shows the duckhunter in a bucolic field gradually surrounded by various adorable little creatures—a bear, birds, squirrels, fish, a turtle, and even a family of white rabbits that recall, one more time, *The Runaway Bunny*. Along with a final black-and-white drawing showing the duckhunter with two ducks on leashes and accompanied by a rabbit, turtle, and bird, these final pictures contrive to endow *The Bad Little Duckhunter* with a concluding warmth and sense of closure that the text itself really fails to provide.

While *The Bad Little Duckhunter* at least has a discernible message, however poorly it is presented, one cannot say the same for *The Peppermint Family*.[12] While Mrs. Gloria Peppermint awaits the birth of their baby, her husband announces that he must go to the North Pole—in order to do some fishing and capture some polar bears, we eventually learn. When his wife asks only that he first provide her with a name for their baby, he tells her that she must send him a letter addressed to "Mr. Peppermint, North Pole" (7) when the baby arrives, and he will mail back the name he has chosen. She follows his instructions, and the letter is delivered to him after "it traveled by ship. And it traveled by train. It traveled by bus and by hydroplane. And soon. . . . in a big balloon" (21-22). He then stops fishing for a moment to write down and mail the name he has decided on, which is soon revealed to be "Chocolate Peppermint" (30). Mr. Peppermint then returns home and promises his wife that he will "Never again" travel "so far away" (34).

To explain why this story is unappealing, one might speculate that, in today's more enlightened times, the very idea of a man abandoning a pregnant wife to go fishing at the North Pole, even in the context of a childish fantasy, is more risible than charmingly eccentric. Even in 1950, however, readers must have wondered, "What is the point of this story?" Perhaps Brown believed it would serve as a pretext for a series of clever illustrations incorporating peppermint motifs, but there are limited possibilities for entertainment in this plan, as Hurd's illustrations demonstrate.

Dealing this time with a limited palette of reds and blues, Hurd shows us, among other things, pictures with red-and-white-striped borders; Mrs. Peppermint wearing a red-and-white-striped skirt; Mrs. Peppermint painting red and white stripes on her baby's furniture in a room with red-and-white-striped wallpaper; red-and-white-striped trim on her letter and envelope; a red-and-white-striped balloon delivering the letter; Mr. Peppermint sitting on a red-and-white-striped cushion while fishing at the North Pole; and the new baby wearing red-and-white-striped pajamas next to a red-and-white-striped rattle. But none of this is striking or amusing. About the only truly imaginative variation on the theme is at the North Pole, where two fish caught by Mr. Peppermint have red and white stripes (23). Again, Hurd attempts to make the concluding scene special, as Mr. Peppermint's captured polar bears add an interesting touch to a final tableau of Mr. Peppermint and his wife dancing with their baby surrounded by pictures of peppermint candy; but since readers have no reason to care about these strange people, the picture is entirely lacking in emotional resonance.

Although *My World, The Bad Little Duckhunter,* and *The Peppermint Family* provided little grounds for optimism regarding the future of the Brown-Hurd relationship, the writer and artist may have been able in later works to recapture the magic of *The Runaway Bunny* and *Goodnight Moon.* We will never know, however, because Brown suddenly died two years after *The Peppermint Family,* at the age of forty-two, of complications following surgery to remove an ovarian cyst. However, as Marcus reports, she did leave "Immense caches of unpublished manuscripts" (285), some of which were chosen for posthumous publication and usually assigned to artists who have previously worked with Brown. Two of these were illustrated by Hurd. *The Little Brass Band* was written to be read aloud while accompanied by an orchestra and first appeared as a record in 1948, but anyone reading the story could guess that, since its thin story is manifestly designed to introduce the sounds of various musical instruments. In Brown's words, a number of musical instruments—a trumpet, drum, bassoon two horns, flute, clarinet, and oboe—gather one by one outside of a town, then march through the town playing music to entertain the residents before leaving the town and separating. With no sound effects, the story is ineffectual to say the least, but might have been mildly entertaining with imaginative drawings of anthropomorphic instruments marching and playing. However, Hurd unwisely elected to emulate the look of a medieval tapestry and placed all instruments in the hands of human musicians, contradicting the text and imposing a mundane realism on the fantastic tale. The flat drawings, colored with an unappealing combination of dark green, yellow, orange, and red, are interesting in only two respects. First, before the text refers to the rising sun, each picture is predominantly dark green; then, after the sun rises, all but one of the pictures are bright yellow; finally, after the sun sets, the dark green returns until the final drawings are almost entirely dark green, with only stars and thin outlines of objects visible. Thus, the book reflects the changing times of day in a manner reminiscent of the darkening room of *Goodnight Moon*. Second, in two pictures of the road outside of the town, one can see two little white rabbits, looking very much like the rabbits of *The Runaway Bunny*—a faint and touching reminder of former glories.

The final Brown book illustrated by Hurd, *The Diggers*,[13] might be regarded as an unintentional summary of their entire career, since it opens promisingly with scenes of animals but concludes disappointingly with a focus on people. In an opening sequence of two-page illustrations, various creatures are seen digging: a mole (6-7), a dog (8-9), a worm (10-11), and a rabbit and a mouse (12-13). Brown's descriptive language begins in each case with "Dig Dig Dig Dig," followed by one or more lines of verse about the animal's digging activities. Then the story abruptly shifts from the natural to the human world, first with a scene of a pirate digging a hole to bury treasure (14-15), then with the extended story of a determined human digger that occupies the rest of the text: the man spends a week digging a hole, announces his dissatisfaction with the small scale of his work, enlists the help of a steam shovel, and begins the process of digging a huge tunnel under the city and under a river, which a train then travels through (16-27). After the train surfaces for a brief glimpse of the natural world—a "bright green country" of "ducks and geese and donkeys and cows and sheep and fields of galloping horses" (28), another obstacle is encountered—a mountain—which requires another visit from the steam shovel to dig a tunnel through the mountain. The process completed, the book concludes with further ambitions to dig: " 'That was easy,' said the steam shovel. 'I'll dig a hole to China someday' " (34).

In defense of Brown's text, it does present the interesting argument that the large construction projects of humans represent not a break with nature, but rather a continuation of a long-standing natural impulse to dig. Still, the point might have been made more engagingly with a text that primarily described animal diggers, with human diggers as a coda; there was no need to devote so much space to the story of a single human digger. Further, while the animals have a stated or implicit purpose for their digging—usually to make themselves a home, though the dog is burying a bone—the man in Brown's story seems obsessed with digging purely for the sake of digging: driving a train through his big hole is not his announced goal, but only an afterthought, and his final plan to dig a hole to China is manifestly purposeless. Perhaps the message is that animals maintain a sense of proportion in their modest activities, while humans get carried away with grandiose ambitions, but the celebratory tone of Brown's descriptions of the man's activities suggests no irony of this kind.

However, as with other later collaborations, Hurd must also shoulder some of the blame for this book's failure. With illustrations that are primarily orange, with touches of green, this book is the least attractive of all the Brown-Hurd books. Hurd's drawings of the man look amateurish, and there is nothing remarkable about his drawings of the animals. Hurd further fails to take advantage of the possibilities in Brown's text. As the quotation above indicates, Brown wrote about the steam shovel as a character, suggesting that it might be drawn in a cleverly anthropomorphic manner, but Hurd draws it realistically and prosaically places a human operator at the controls. When first describing the steam shovel, Brown says that it was designed to unearth such things as "dinosaur bones," "cavemen's homes," and "buried gnomes" (20)—language that cries out for accompanying illustrations; but Hurd ignores the passage and shows nothing of the kind. The pirate is burying the "gold . . . diamonds and rubies he stole" (14), but Hurd ignores the colorful language and shows only an undifferentiated blur of small objects; and when Brown refers to the "ducks and geese and donkeys and cows and sheep and fields of galloping horses," Hurd doesn't bother to show any geese and shows only one donkey.

Again, one must search hard for a few signs of Hurd's talents: the rabbit shown is of course the white mother bunny from *The Runaway Bunny* (12); in one scene of the dedicated human digger, Hurd adds two mice looking intently at him (19), cleverly suggesting that the human diggers are attracting the interested attention of their animal predecessors; and Hurd makes striking use of charcoal in his penultimate drawing of a modern railroad racing down the tracks (32-33), conveying a powerful impression of blurred, dynamic energy unlike anything else that he drew for Brown's works.

After the heirs to Brown's estate decided that no additional unpublished manuscripts merited publication, the Brown-Hurd relationship seemed to be over; but two decades after Brown's death, there did occur another collaboration. While *Goodnight Moon* had remained a perennial success over the years, its predecessor *The Runaway Bunny* had not fared as well, perhaps because its illustrations were not as well executed as those in *Goodnight Moon*. Someone must have believed that, for Hurd was commissioned to redo every drawing and painting for a new, 1972 edition of *The Runaway Bunny*.[14] For the most part, Hurd merely copied his earlier pictures, using a finer line, adding nuances to the black-and-white drawings, and using brighter colors for the color paintings. In a few cases, he reversed or repositioned some of the figures. And, whether it was Hurd's or someone else's decision, the concluding "Song of the Runaway Bunny" was wisely removed. While these changes are unspectacular, two of the new color paintings are significantly different in the 1972 edition, in ways worth discussing.

First, repainting the scene in which the mother bunny imagines herself the human mother of her transformed boy, Hurd subtly alters the living room to recall *Goodnight Moon*. Two nondescript wall paintings of vegetables and a male bunny are replaced with the familiar picture of the cow jumping over the Moon; the fireplace equipment is moved to the left-hand side of the fireplace, as in the *Goodnight Moon* room; a previously unseen ball of yarn and two mice are now visible on the floor; the square fireplace is changed to the rounded shape of the fireplace in the *Goodnight Moon* room; and the solid blue pajamas of the boy bunny are replaced with the blue-striped pajamas of the boy in *Goodnight Moon*. In these ways, Hurd is visually emphasizing the link between *The Runaway Bunny* and *Goodnight Moon* that he and Brown always believed in.

Second, while the original concluding painting appeared to take place during the daytime, with the mother bunny and her child at ground level inside a hollow tree trunk, the redone painting takes place at nighttime, with stars and a full moon visible in the sky, and the mother bunny and son are seen in a cutaway picture completely underneath the tree, with other trees now in the background. This new version recalls Marcus's description of the rejected painting Hurd prepared for *Wait Till the Moon Is Full* in response to Brown's description: "a nocturnal forest landscape with moon and clouds and a cutaway view of the subterranean world where a rabbit family had their own" that Hurd subsequently labeled "his finest single piece of illustration work" (230). What we may be seeing, then, is not simply Hurd's reworking of his 1942 painting for *The Runaway Bunny* but also a new version of his fondly remembered work for *Wait Till the Moon Is Full*, additionally tying *The Runaway Bunny* to the third book in their series that never properly materialized.

The final item in the Brown-Hurd relationship came in the 1980s, when Hurd prepared and published *The Goodnight Moon Room*, a three-dimensional rendering of the room he had repeatedly and so carefully painted in 1947.[15] In Brown's book, the boy's direct address of the objects in his world seemed designed to bring them to life, and in a sense, this three-dimensional artifact finally accomplished just that. Not really a new collaborative work, *The Goodnight Moon Room* is best appreciated as a singular tribute to the enduring power of their greatest collaboration.

So, how does one summarize the story of the Brown-Hurd collaborations? As is often the case, it is the story of a rise and fall: first, three works of increasing quality that illustrate author and artist working in harmony to achieve together something greater than either could have achieved individually; then a crisis that scars the relationship; and finally, a few failed attempts to recapture the magic that they once possessed. While we can speculate about a possible longer relationship that would have yielded more works like *The Runaway Bunny* and *Goodnight Moon*, we may be best advised to simply appreciate the two masterpieces they did create, and to approach other fantasies for children with greater appreciation for both their authors and their artists.

Notes

1. As discussed in "A Suppressed Adventure of 'Alice' Surfaces after 107 Years," no author given, *Smithsonian*, 8:9 (December, 1977), 50-57.

2. As discussed in Michael Patrick Hearn's third note to Chapter Two of *The Annotated Wizard of Oz* by L. Frank Baum, pictures by W. W. Denslow, introduction, notes, and bibliography by Hearn (New York: Clarkson N. Potter, Inc., 1973), 100.

3. Leonard S. Marcus, *Margaret Wise Brown: Awakened by the Moon* (Boston: Beacon Press, 1992). Subsequent Marcus page references in the text are to this edition.

4. Lynne Lundquist, "Margaret Wise Brown," in *The Encyclopedia of Fantasy*, edited by John Clute and John Grant (New York: St. Martin's Press, 1997), 144.

5. Clement Hurd, illustrator, and Margaret Wise Brown, author, *Bumble Bugs and Elephants: A Big and Little Book* (New York: William R. Scott, Publisher, 1938). Note: this book and all the children's books discussed here are unpaginated, so we have in each case counted the pages ourselves, beginning with the first page following the inside front cover as page one. Thus, all the page numbers from children's books provided in the text of this chapter represent our own paginations, although we omit the brackets usually placed around such page numbers to reduce clutter.

6. Margaret Wise Brown, author, and Clement Hurd, illustrator, *The Runaway Bunny* (New York: Harper & Row, Publishers, 1942).

7. Related to the issue of the need to sometimes "lighten" Brown's texts, Marcus tells the story of an editor-instigated change in the original text: feeling that "And so he did" ended the story "too abruptly"—though one might also say "too harshly," as the words convey only the little bunny's complete, abject surrender to his overbearing mother's wishes—editor Ursula Nordstrom asked Brown to provide "a touch of whimsy," which she did with the addition of " 'Have a carrot,' said the mother bunny" (Marcus 150). Our argument here is that in other cases, it was Hurd's illustrations that provided that essential "touch of whimsy."

8. Margaret Wise Brown, author, and Clement Hurd, illustrator, *Goodnight Moon* (New York: Harper & Row, Publishers, 1947).

9. Margaret Wise Brown, author, and Garth Williams, illustrator, *Wait Till the Moon Is Full* (New York: Harper & Brothers, 1948).

10. Margaret Wise Brown, author, and Clement Hurd, illustrator, *My World* (New York: Harper & Brothers, 1947).

11. Margaret Wise Brown, author, and Clement Hurd, illustrator, *The Bad Little Duckhunter* (New York: William R. Scott, 1947).

12. Margaret Wise Brown, author, and Clement Hurd, illustrator, *The Peppermint Family* (New York: Harper & Brothers, 1950).

13. Margaret Wise Brown, author, and Clement Hurd, illustrator, *The Diggers* (New York: Harper & Row, 1960).

14. Margaret Wise Brown, author, and Clement Hurd, illustrator, *The Runaway Bunny*, Revised Edition with New Illustrations (1942; New York: Harper & Row, 1972).

15. Clement Hurd, illustrator, *The Goodnight Moon Room* (New York: Harper & Row, 1984).

11

"And What Happened After": How J. R. R. Tolkien Visualized, and Other Artists Re-Visualized, the Denizens of Middle-Earth

Beatrix Karthaus-Hunt

J. R. R. Tolkien, proclaimed the "author of the century" by Tom Shippey,[1] brought several special talents to the creation of his fantasy worlds in addition to writing skill and a great imagination. First, he was a scholar by profession who held a number of academic positions, among them a Merton Professorship of English Language and Literature at Oxford University (1945-1959).[2] His principal professional focus was the study of Anglo-Saxon and its relation to linguistically similar languages such as Old Norse, Old German, and Gothic with special emphasis on the dialects of Mercia, that part of England in which he grew up and lived; but he was also interested in Middle English, especially the dialect used in the *Ancrene Wisse*, a twelfth-century manuscript probably composed in western England.

Second, not only was Tolkien was an expert in the surviving literature written in these languages, but he also had an unusual ability to simultaneously read the texts as literature and as linguistic sources; this has been described as "his unique insight at once into the language of poetry and the poetry of language."[3] Already at an early age he had been fascinated by language, particularly the languages of Northern Europe, both ancient and modern. From this affinity for language came not only his profession, but also his private hobby, the invention of languages. By 1946, he had developed Adûnaic, the language of Númenor, while he finished *The Lord of the Rings*, which is said to be his fifteenth invented language.[4]

Finally, although he lacked formal training or credentials, Tolkien was an enthusiastic and talented amateur artist, although he is only sporadically noticed as an illustrator in his own right. He not only paid attention to detail as he constructed the geography, history, genealogy, and linguistic and cultural diversity of *The Lord of the Rings*, but also in his drawings of those landscapes.[5] Many of his drawings have surfaced in posthumous publications of unpublished works like *Mr. Bliss*, as well as compilations like *Pictures by J. R. R. Tolkien* and *J. R. R. Tolkien: Artist and Illustrator.*[6]

Employing his scholarly background, linguistic abilities, and artist's eye, Tolkien created a major series of works involving the denizens of his imagined Middle-Earth—*The Hobbit, The Lord of the Rings*, the posthumously published *The Silmarillion*, and other posthumous compilations—as well as lesser known tales like *Farmer Giles of Ham*. As everyone knows, his stories have spawned a vast literary output in form of trilogies, such as *The Gormenghast Trilogy* by Mervyn Peake, romance novels, such as *The Worm Ouroboros* by Eric Rucker Eddison, and even an erotic parody called *Bored of the Rings* by Henry N. Beard.[7] However, Tolkien not only inspired literary endeavors but also musical interpretations and visual depictions: the musical play entitled *The Hobbit* by Allan Jay Friedmann and David Rogers, rock songs such as "The Battle of Evermore" by Led Zeppelin with an allusion to Edgar Allan Poe's famous poem "The Raven," figurines to popular games such as Middle-Earth Role Playing and Dungeons and Dragons, as well as poster art, comic books, coloring books, animated cartoons for television and film, photo novels, calendars, book illustrations, dust jackets, and a live-action film trilogy.[8] The numbers of illustrators of Tolkien's fantasy worlds, including Tolkien himself, are immense, but they have largely gone unnoticed in the elitist confines of art history.

Here, I will focus on the visual representation of some of the fantastic types and characters which populate Tolkien's Middle-Earth as illustrated in comic books and book illustrations. Three of these types—the well-known Hobbit, the evil Orc, and the "tree-ish" Ent—are essentially genuine inventions by Tolkien that previously had not inhabited fairy tales, legends, or myths while other more common fantasy figures such as wizards, dwarves, dragons, elves, and trolls refer back to a well-established literary tradition.[9] The names of "Hobbit" and "Orc" as terms owe their introduction into *The Oxford English Dictionary* solely to Tolkien, while only the "Ents" have suffered omittance by it up to now.[10] Nonetheless, Tolkien's neologisms draw often on medieval, if not ancient literary sources as will become evident when compared to his descriptions of them. From tracing the etymology of the words "Hobbit," "Ent," and "Orc," I will then turn to explore the development of their visual representation as imagined by Tolkien and executed by a number of artists whose works enjoy a greater visibility in the current fantasy book market, thereby showing the present iconography of a fantasy typology.

John Ronald Reuel Tolkien was born of English parents at Bloemfontein, South Africa on January 3, 1892 and died in England on September 2, 1973.[11] His entire childhood was spent in England, to which the family returned permanently in 1896 upon the death of his father. After graduating from Oxford University in 1915, he joined the British army and saw action in the Battle of the Somme. He was eventually discharged after spending most of 1917 in the hospital suffering from "trench fever," thus inadvertently escaping the Great War alive.[12]

As a scholar, linguist, and artist, Tolkien was drawn to the entire "Northern tradition," which inspired him to wide reading of its myths and epics and of those modern authors who were equally drawn to it such as William Morris, the founder of the Arts and Crafts Movement in England, and George MacDonald, a Scottish writer mostly known today for his children's books. His broad knowledge inevitably led to the developments of various opinions about myth, its relation to language, and the importance of stories, interests that were shared by his friend, C. S. Lewis.[13]

In *The Lord of the Rings, The Hobbit,* and *The Silmarillion,* Tolkien sought to maintain the fiction that these writings were actually ancient manuscripts written by Frodo and Bilbo, respectively, of which he was merely the editor and translator. In addition to explicit descriptions, it is implicit in the way in which many sections of *The Lord of the Rings* outside the story are written.[14] Thus, the "Prologue: Concerning Hobbits" is plainly written as though by a modern editor describing an ancient time: "Those days, the Third Age of Middle-Earth, are now long past, and the shape of all the lands has been changed; but the regions in which Hobbits then lived were doubtless the same as those in which they still linger: the North-West of the Old World, east of the Sea."[15] Tolkien's intention was to create Middle-Earth as our own world, which took place in an imaginary time. Beside the passage in the "Prologue," he made this fully explicit in his "Notes on W. H. Auden's Review of *The Return of the King*" dating from around 1956.[16] Not only is Middle-Earth our own world but also the people inhabiting it are ourselves, morally as well as physically: "I have not made any of the peoples on the 'right' side, Hobbits, Rohirrim, Men of Dale or of Gondor, any better than men have been or are, or can be. Mine is not an 'imaginary' world, but an imaginary historical moment on 'Middle-Earth'—which is our habitation."[17]

Tolkien's Hobbits

Hobbits, who inhabit Earth in an imaginary past, are also called "Halflings" and regarded as a subgroup of humans in three variants.[18] There are several statements to this effect made by Tolkien such as this one:

The Hobbits are, of course, really meant to be a branch of the specifically *human* race (not Elves or Dwarves)—hence the two kinds can dwell together (as at Bree), and are called just the Big Folk and Little Folk. They are entirely without non-human powers, but are represented as being more in touch with "nature" (the soil and other living things, plants and animals), and abnormally, for humans, free from ambition or greed or wealth.[19]

The origin of their name has sparked various debates.[20] Apparently, the name is traceable to several origins, although Tolkien could not remember precisely when he had written the first sentence for *The Hobbit.*[21] In *The Return of the King,* he gave the etymologically grounded explanation that "holbytla," stemming from an Old English root, means "hole-builder," but he strongly objected to any linkage between "hobbit" and "rabbit."[22] Donald O'Brien has argued that the word "hobbit" is derived from the Scottish "simple perfect active/participle adjectival forms of 'hubbet, hobbet' of the verb 'hub' defined to mean 'to suspect or accuse of dishonesty, hold guilty of a crime,' approximating Bilbo's career as a burglar."[23]

O'Brien's conclusion is interesting, but not too surprising in Bilbo's instance since it is supported by the fact that Bilbo himself as well as Thorin Oakenshield and his company of dwarves viewed him as a thief or burglar, but hobbits are not characterized by thievery.[24] In an interview in 1968, Tolkien surmised that he might have associated the word "Hobbit" with Sinclair Lewis's novel *Babbitt*, since "Babbitt has the same bourgeois smugness that hobbits do. His world is the same limited place."[25]

Tolkien was careful in constructing not only the name for his hobbits but also their appearance. His general concern for art as craft is expressed in his tale *Leaf by Niggle* first printed in 1945, which might explain his painstaking attention to detail.[26] Niggle, the title figure, spends a long time painting a single leaf, while trying to catch its exact shape and sheen with the glistening of dewdrops on its edges. However, he has to forsake his painting of the big tree due to constant interruptions at his task or in order to lend assistance to his neighbor. During a mysterious course of events, he is enabled to finish the painting in cooperation with his neighbor while the painting acquires a world of its own. In this story of the much-hindered painter Niggle, Tolkien not only acknowledges the societal constraints imposed by everyday life on artists and the necessity for an economically stable living, but also insists that a work of art attains an identity which is separate from its creator. In his essay "On Fairy Stories" also from 1945, Tolkien relates in his view of life that

[t]here are hunger, thirst, poverty, pain, sorrow, injustice, death. And even when men are not facing hard things such as these, there are ancient limitations from which fairy-stories offer a sort of escape, and old ambitions and desires (touching the very roots of fantasy) to which they offer a kind of satisfaction and consolation. . . . But the "consolation" of fairy-tales has another aspect than the imaginative satisfaction of ancient desires. Far more important is the Consolation of the Happy Ending.[27]

Nonetheless, he condemned probably one of the most famous animated cartoon producers of the fantastic of the twentieth century, when writing to his publisher Allen & Unwin on May 13, 1937: "As for the illustrations. . . . It might be advisable, rather than lose the American interest, to let the Americans do what seems good to them—as long as it was possible (I should like to add) to veto anything from or influenced by the Disney studios (for all whose works I have a heartfelt loathing)."[28] It has been argued that Tolkien might have changed his mind had he viewed Walt Disney's first full-length animated cartoon, *Snow White and the Seven Dwarfs*, which had its premiere in Los Angeles on December 21, 1937, in the same year when *The Hobbit* first appeared in print in Great Britain, though this assumption remains doubtful.[29] In spite of his plead for "the good catastrophe," he objected to any kind of "mollified versions of Grimm" that omit the gruesomeness and horror of fulfilling the creed for justice in the end: in the Grimm brothers' recorded version of *Snow White* the evil stepmother has to dance in burning hot shoes until she dies.

Aside from his aversion against the "Disney studios," Tolkien did have definitive ideas about the outer appearance of hobbits. He described Bilbo for a commission of illustrations in a letter to Houghton Mifflin dating from March or April 1938, as

a fairly human figure, not a kind of "fairy" rabbit as some of my British reviewers seem to fancy: fattish in the stomach, shortish in the leg. A round, jovial face; ears only slightly pointed and "elvish"; hair short and curling (brown). The feet from the ankles down, covered with brown hairy fur. Clothing: green velvet breeches; red or yellow waistcoat; brown or green jacket; gold (or brass) buttons; a dark green hood and cloak (belonging to a dwarf). Actual size . . . say about three feet or three feet six inches.[30]

The height of hobbits seems to mislead Tolkien illustrators into depicting them as too child-like. This problem becomes even more complex when attempting to render their age differences. Ted Nasmith, a Canadian illustrator of three of Tolkien's calendars and the Houghton Mifflin 1998 edition of *The Silmarillion*, has complained that

since hobbits are equivalent in size to our small children, that is, anywhere from two to four feet in height, it's all too easy to portray them as child-like. Consider that their beardless rosy-cheeked jollity and curly headedness is so easily associated with healthy, rosy-cheeked children, who historically would often have long curly locks of hair, whether boy or girl.[31]

Tolkien's own rendition of Bilbo in his rather spacious hobbit hole at Bag-End circumvents the obstacle of the child-like height combined with an adult appearance by avoiding altogether to picture him in company with humans in his drawing entitled "The Hall at Bag-End, Residence of B. Baggins Esquire."[32] The drawing was later colored in by H. E. Riddett in 1976, faithfully rendering Bilbo's hair in brown, his breeches in a faint dark green with his waistcoat in a light greenish yellow, standing in the middle of the hall while he lights his pipe with a green hood on a dresser in the lower left-hand corner.[33]

The twin brothers Greg and Tim Hildebrandt from New Jersey, largely known for their three Tolkien Calendars of 1976, 1977, and 1978 and their illustration of children's books, have admitted to the problematic rendering of some of Tolkien's fantasy types, yet they claim that "the images they create, with few exceptions, are true to the descriptions in [*The Lord of the Rings*]. They feel that they must make fantasy real and not cartoonlike."[34] They refer to photographs of life models in costumes or to clay figurines before finishing an art piece, which assist them in creating a three-dimensional quality in their work. Most striking in their art is their dramatic use of light and shade, a chiaroscuro reminiscent of the Italian Baroque painter, Tintoretto, as can be seen in the painting of "Bilbo in Rivendale."[35] An aging Bilbo indicated by his white curls with an only little wrinkled face—an interpretation of the supposed life-lengthening effect of the One Ring—surrounded by books and other paraphernalia is portrayed sitting at his desk with a feathered pen in his hand while staring out at an invisible point some distance in front of him. Apparently deep in thought about the tale of his adventures or the composition of a poem, Bilbo's face is lit by a candle on the top of the desk, which casts a soft light about a rather low room throwing shadows off the objects around him. In this depiction Bilbo makes an alert impression on the viewer, although Tolkien hints often at his sleepiness.[36] In another painting by the brothers entitled "The Wedding of the King," the staging of models becomes more apparent in the frozen scene when Aragorn receives Arwen Undómiel in Minas Tirith. At this point it should be noted that both paintings dramatize events that have not been recorded explicitly by Tolkien. The brothers have ventured to portray Frodo at the wedding in company of humans, elves, and dwarfs, allowing the viewer to judge the scaling of the figures more closely.[37] Frodo, dressed in white and set to the right in the middle ground beside the wizard Gandalf, is only slightly smaller than the cloaked dwarf Gimli with a hunched back to the left, but more than half the size of Gandalf. Nonetheless, despite the portrayal of Frodo's hairy feet, his slightly pointed but large ears and the expression of marvel on his face, the size of his hands and head appear noticeably and disproportionately large in comparison to his delicate stature giving him, unfortunately, a midget-like appearance. To depict the right height of hobbits is doubtless difficult when placing them in the company of other fantasy figures; however, the stumbling block in "The Wedding of the King" seems mainly a misconception of the Brothers Hildebrandt who "made the Hobbits look like English working-class people" whereas, especially in the case of Bilbo and Frodo—not to mention the almost aristocratic lineage of Meriadoc and Peregrin—Tolkien has clearly stated that they were regarded as "gentlehobbits" in the Shire.[38] Nasmith has already commented that

[u]nfortunately, it seems that even among the most widely published interpretations of Tolkien there is this persistent tendency to misconceive hobbitry. This includes the Hobbits of Ralph Bakshi's "Lord of the Rings" film; the Bilbo of the new edition of "The Hobbit" illustrated by Michael Hague; and, most notorious for me, the hobbits of the Brothers Hildebrandt.[39]

However, David Wenzel, an illustrator from Connecticut of the comic book series of *The Hobbit* from 1989 to 1990 with an excellent text adaptation by Charles Dixon, solves the problem of scale without much hesitation by putting Bilbo right next to Gandalf on the front cover of the first issue of the series, who is followed by dwarves walking up a hill on the back cover.[40] Though Ted Nasmith viewed Gandalf's eyebrows as impossible to depict, to which the Hildebrandt Brothers would almost certainly have agreed—Gandalf is described as having long eyebrows that extended beyond the rim of his hat—Wenzel is able to render accurately here those same said eyebrows.[41] The figure of Bilbo in front of his hobbit hole with Gandalf to the left is clothed in blue pants, not in prescribed greenish velvet, and with a colorful embroidery around the hem of his yellow shirt, green coat pockets and sleeves of a somewhat Celtic resemblance and depicted as "a fairly human figure . . . fattish in the stomach, shortish in the leg . . . [with a] round jovial face. . . . The feet from the ankles down [are] covered with brown hairy fur."[42] In size, Bilbo appears throughout the sequential storytelling in company smaller than the dwarves and never taller than half the size of Gandalf, while in smaller picture frames Wenzel's facial portrayals of Bilbo with a big reddish nose indicative of character and wrinkles around the eyes make it impossible to mistake him for a child.[43]

Toward the end of the first comic book of the series *The Hobbit* by Dixon and Wenzel, Bilbo meets his counterpart Gollum.[44] Tolkien described Gollum as "a small slimy creature . . . [with] two big round pale eyes in his thin face . . . large feet . . . [and] long fingers."[45] In his short article "Who's Afraid of the Big, Bad Gollum?," Arden R. Smith points to the unusual height of some of the early depictions of Gollum, who was beyond all doubt also a hobbit.[46] Apparently, illustrations to translations of *The Hobbit*—as in a Portuguese example from 1962—show him "fully clothed" with "webbed feet . . . and a beard—a big, bushy, black beard" and juxtaposed next to Bilbo's hobbit height to be "about 6 feet," whereas a Japanese edition from 1965 depicts Gollum as "an unclothed, reptilian sort of creature with frog-like fingers and toes. Furthermore, he is approximately 10 feet tall."[47] These illustrations are based on the second edition of *The Hobbit*, which appeared before 1966 and does not mention that Gollum is "a small slimy creature" explaining these, if not misguided, certainly individualistically imaginary depictions of him. It was only after Tolkien had begun writing *The Lord of the Rings* that it occurred to him to tie *The Hobbit* as a "prequel" to it and, subsequently, forced him to rework and add to the characterization of Gollum, which had been wanting before.

Tolkien's Orcs

The creatures referred to as orcs in *The Lord of the Rings* were first invented during the writing of *The Book of Lost Tales*, also called the "pre-*Silmarillion*."[48] Orcs and goblins are different names for the same race of creatures.[49] Of the two, "orc" is the correct one. This has been a matter of widespread debate and misunderstanding, mostly resulting from the usage of "goblin" in *The Hobbit*; Tolkien had changed his mind when writing *The Lord of the Rings*, but the confusion in the earlier version was made worse by inconsistent backward modifications in it. The actual source of the word "orc" is found in *Beowulf*, an Old English epic poem believed to have been composed in the early eighth century: "orc-nass," translated as "death-corpses." In 1936, when C. S. Lewis's *The Allegory of Love* was published, it contained the first published reference to Tolkien's "orcs": "[T]he 'literary' poets . . . [will] take up the extravagances of popular romances with a smile . . . [and] will write of giants and 'orcs,' of fairies and flying horses, of Saracens foaming at the mouth."[50]

Regarding the origin of the orcs, a race of slaves bred from twisted elves, a fundamental concept for Tolkien was that Evil cannot create, only corrupt.[51] He rejected the Manichean concept that, though the material body may be evil, still grants that within each person's mind a particle of "divine" light might be imprisoned, which could be released by the practice of religion.

Since the outer appearance of orcs—or, as written in *The Hobbit*, goblins—is not described until *The Lord of the Rings*, David Wenzel must have turned to the latter in order to obtain a more specific description of them.[52] Orcs are not quite man-high and "crook-legged," but strong. They are said to have long arms, huge shoulders, squinted eyes, and are "clad in black mail" with helmets. Their skin is supposedly black as wood, appearing as though it had been charred by flame or of "greenish scales." They are fearful of light for it weakens and burns them. The jagged fangs in their wide mouths are yellow. Still, this information is somewhat scant and only during close encounters with orcs does Tolkien almost grudgingly reveal any details at all.

In the scene at the inquest of the dwarves and Bilbo as prisoners of the Great Goblin, the sequence of picture frames leads rapidly to the goblins' discovery of the hated sword Orcrist, also known to them by the name of "Goblin-cleaver" or "Biter," which was in Thorin's possession.[53] Visually building toward the catastrophe, the last picture frame on the page below is virtually filled with the facial contortions of the Great Goblin, who, enraged, exposes his yellowish fangs and red tongue, which form a contrast to his blotchy dark green skin. The color contrast together with the text bubble above heightens the tension of a cataclysmic foreboding.

Wenzel's dramatic use of color, essential for the sequential narration of comic books, was almost completely abandoned in the illustrations by Alan Lee from Dartmoor in southwest England, who has painted dozens of cover illustrations for imaginative fiction. Lee discovered the fantasy world of Middle-Earth as an art student.[54] His illustrations for Tolkien's books and calendars with particular emphasis on landscape painting are executed in watercolors of delicate, misty hues. He was commissioned by George Allen & Unwin to illustrate *The Lord of the Rings* for the centenary edition to celebrate J. R. R. Tolkien's birth.[55] The task involved fifty watercolor paintings, all of which are untitled and, perhaps for this reason alone, the customary index of illustrations, which such a large number should have merited, has been omitted. The familiarity with the text of *The Lord of the Rings* remains the sole basis for identifying each illustrated scene.

The image across from page 448 of the centenary edition, or the twentieth illustration of the book, is one of the few in this edition to depict two scenes divided only by a gray outline, which also binds them together in an upright rectangular frame.[56] The larger scene on top represents, seen from their backs, Legolas, the elf, identifiable by his bow and quiver of arrows with Aragorn kneeling beside him, both gazing at the open steppe with the cloudy sky above, while only the dwarf Gimli with a broad-bladed ax in his belt over a shirt of steel-rings faces the viewer, his head searchingly turned to the lower right-hand corner. This depiction is recounted in the text next to it on page 448:

Slowly the downs drew near. It was still an hour before noon when they [Legolas, Aragorn, and Gimli] reached them: green slopes rising to bare ridges that ran in a line straight towards the North. At their feet the ground was dry and the turf short, but a long strip of sunken land, some ten miles wide, lay between them and the river wandering deep in dim thickets of reed and rush. Just to the West of the southernmost slope there was a great ring, where the turf had been torn and beaten by many trampling feet. From it the orc-trail ran out again, turning north along the dry skirts of the hills. Aragorn halted and examined the tracks closely.[57]

Aragorn, Gimli, and Legolas are in search of Merry and Pippin, their two companions who have been kidnapped by orcs and are depicted in the smaller scene below, which could almost be viewed as a decorative boarder to the image above. Here the orcs are shown from their shoulders up with their heads in profile carrying Pippin and Merry off on their backs, Merry distinguished by the bandage around his head. The two scenes visualize two simultaneous actions, which reach a reflection in Pippin's vision: "Every now and again there came into his [Pippin's] mind unbidden a vision of the keen face of Strider [Aragorn] bending over a dark trail, and running, running behind. But what could even a Ranger see except a confused trail of orc-feet?"[58]

Lee's sparing use of color contrasts makes the faces of the hobbits look pale and the orcs' gear appear washed out, but his soft shading in tones of gray, brown, and olive makes the visages of the orcs more pronounced and differentiated from each other. Pictured with the pointed ears of elves—a remainder of their former selves— jagged teeth, hideous noses, warty skin, and deformed jaws, Lee has succeeded in rendering the orcs' physiognomies with such an intense ugliness bordering on the absurd, that it is comparable only to that of the bystanders in Hieronymus Bosch's famous oil painting "Christ Carrying the Cross," housed in the Musée des Beaux-Arts in Ghent nowadays, as the very embodiment of evil.[59]

Tolkien's Ents

During the War of the Ring the strange giants called ents came in the battle against the orcs and men of Isengard. Half men, half trees, they were twelve to fourteen feet tall.[60] Treebeard "is the oldest of the Ents, the oldest living thing that still walks beneath the Sun upon this Middle-Earth."[61] The expression "ent" is actually derived from an Old English word *ent* meaning "giant," but the *ents* of this tale are not in form or character derived from Germanic mythology. *Entings* are the "children of Ents."[62]

Carl F. Hostetter and Patrick Wynne have laid out a convincing etymological origin of the word "ent." According to Hostetter and Wynne in their article "Stone Towers" in which they trace the origins of various elements of Tolkien's languages and mythologies, the pre-Celtic word *ond* means "stone."[63] This leads them to point to Alois Walde, author of the *Vergleichendes Wörterbuch der Indogermanischen Sprachen* (1927-1932), which lists *ond-, nd-* as an Indo-European root meaning "stone, rock,"

whose descendants include Sanskrit *adri-* "stone, rock, hill" and Middle Irish *ond* or *onn* "stone, rock"; but more remarkable still is Walde's citation of a theory that the Old English word *ent* "giant" derives from the same root. In light of this theory, which Tolkien was very likely aware of given his creation of the Ents, it seems probable that the Sindarin word for Ent, *onod.* . . . is cognate with Q *ondo* "stone." Though it may seem bizarre that Ents should be etymologically linked with stone, such an association is attested in Anglo-Saxon poetry. After their establishment in Britain, the Anglo-Saxons were supposedly awed by the great stone buildings and roads that the Romans had built and then abandoned as their empire collapsed. The Anglo-Saxons called these stone works, far beyond their technological abilities, the *eald enta geweorc* "the old work of Ents," and *orthanc enta geweorc* "skillful work of Ents," the legacy of an ancient and vanished race of stone-working giants. In light of this, it is significant that Tolkien's Ents have the ability to break stone with ease, as Treebeard boasts to Merry and Pippin. . . .

"We can split stone like the roots of trees, only quicker, far quicker, far quicker, if our minds are roused! . . . [W]e could split Isengard into splinters and crack its walls into rubble."[64]

Hostetter's and Wynne's argument about the etymological connection between ents and stone finds additional support in the following passage when Treebeard explains to the hobbits: "You do not know, perhaps, how strong we are. Maybe you have heard of Trolls? They are mighty strong. But Trolls are only counterfeits, made by the Enemy in the Great Darkness, in mockery of Ents, as Orcs were of Elves. We are stronger than Trolls. We are made of the bones of the earth."[65] At this point it may be worth noting that trolls, mockeries of ents, turn to stone when exposed to sunlight. And in fact, as stingy as Tolkien is in his descriptions of orcs, the more generous is he in the portrayal of Treebeard as an

almost Troll-like figure . . . very sturdy, with a tall head, and hardly any neck. Whether it was clad in stuff like green and grey bark, or whether it was its hide, was difficult to say. At any rate the arms, at a short distance from the trunk, were not wrinkled, but covered with a brown smooth skin. The large feet had seven toes each. The lower part of the long face was covered with a sweeping grey beard, bushy, almost twiggy at the roots, thin and mossy at the ends. . . . [The eyes] were brown, shot with a green light.[66]

Alan Lee's depiction of Treebeard shows a close-up of his face, unusual in its closeness to the depicted object and unique among all of his illustrations of the centenary edition, which might have partly been caused by Tolkien's careful description.[67] Treebeard's pose is of one who rests on one arm while gesturing with a "large knob-knuckled" hand of the other arm in front of his face during a conversation as indicated by his parted lower lip. His facial hair is given the appearance of twigs ending in a soft shaggy grayish-white beard, which runs over his supporting hand while the skin is rendered in the texture of shining dark gray bark. The glowing, yet sad-looking eyes with the light brown irises meet Pippin's lyrical words of them "like sun shimmering on the outer leaves of a vast tree, or on the ripples of a very deep lake."[68] The text on the page across the image concerns the mourned loss of the Entwives as related by Treebeard to Merry and Pippin. Lee's illustrations are based on complex reconstructions of narrated descriptions and events executed in sparingly applied contrasts of subtle watercolors, which give them the effect of a dimmed view into the past.

Conclusion

J. R. R. Tolkien was master both of words and of the mythopoeic vision; he was epic poet and modern writer. Since his death in 1973, artists working in the genres of book illustrations, comic books, and animated films have begun to treat both aspects of Tolkien's gift by rendering his work into another powerful Mimesis, the visual image. The images discussed here are examples of a development emerging from the desire to transport Tolkien's imaginary figures into a visual reality, first akin to static history paintings as in the case of the Brothers Hildebrandt, and accompanied by an increasing degree of close reading of Tolkien's text. The comic book illustrations of David Wenzel in collaboration with Charles Dixon achieve the next level of movement through sequencing the pictures, which dramatize the action in vivid colors, but—although accurately—render the figures as types in necessarily a flat outline. Alan Lee, less interested in the depiction of movement and, more appropriately for book illustrations, in the rendition of vistas into the fabulous, juxtaposes parallel events and follows the author's imagination as closely as possible into character portraiture. The last step that remains should be taken by film art, shifting from a typified version of Tolkien's fantasy world to nothing less than a detailed character and scrupulous script rendition. Perhaps, then, in the much-anticipated forthcoming live-action adaptation of *The Lord of the Rings*, we shall see the final stage in this long and fascinating process.

Notes

1. T. A. Shippey, *J. R. R. Tolkien: Author of the Century* (New York: HarperCollins, 2000).

2. Tolkien was staff member of the *New English Dictionary* from 1918 to 1920, reader, and later Professor of English Language at Leeds from 1920 to 1925, and Rawlinson and Bosworth Professor of Anglo-Saxon at Oxford from 1925 to 1945. See Humphrey Carpenter, *J. R. R. Tolkien: A Biography* (London: George Allen & Unwin Ltd., 1977), 365-67.

3. Mary Salu and Robert T. Farrell, eds., *J. R. R. Tolkien, Scholar and Storyteller: Essays in Memoriam* (Ithaca: Cornell University Press, 1979), 13.

4. Although the language of the Rohirrim was a real language, Entish, Khudzul (Dwarvish), and the Black Speech, the language of Mordor, were among the languages developed by Tolkien. See Salu and Farrell, 12. For an entire dictionary devoted to Tolkien's invented languages, see Ruth S. Noel, *The Languages of Tolkien's Middle-Earth* (Boston: Houghton Mifflin Co., 1980).

5. For a collection of maps to the geography of Tolkien's Middle-Earth, see Karen Wynn Fonstad, *The Atlas of Middle-Earth* (Boston: Houghton Mifflin Co., 1991).

6. For examples of Tolkien's art, see Christopher Tolkien, ed., *Pictures by J. R. R. Tolkien* (London: George Allen & Unwin, 1979); J. R. R. Tolkien, *Mr. Bliss* (London: George Allen & Unwin, 1982); Wayne G. Hammond, "Art by J. R. R. Tolkien," in *J. R. R.*

Tolkien: A Descriptive Bibliography (Winchester: St. Paul's Bibliographies, 1993), 369-83; and Wayne Hammond and Christina Scull, *J. R. R. Tolkien: Artist and Illustrator* (London: HarperCollins, 1995).

7. It should be noted that "*The Lord of the Rings* is often erroneously called a trilogy, when it is in fact a single novel, consisting of six books plus appendices, published for convenience in three volumes." See Douglas A. Anderson, "Note on the Text," *The Fellowship of the Ring: Being the First Part of "The Lord of the Rings"* by J. R. R. Tolkien (Boston: Houghton Mifflin Co., 1987), v.

8. See Ruth Perry, *A Musical Play: The Hobbit* (Chicago: The Dramatic Publishing Co., 1972); Marsha Elkin, *Lord of the Rings Coloring Book* (Cambridge, MA: NESFA, 1972); Lin Carter, *Middle-Earth: The World of Tolkien Illustrated*, illustrated by David Wenzel (New York: Centaur Books Inc., 1977); Chris Conkling, *The Lord of the Rings: A Saul Zaentz Production, a Ralph Bakshi Film* (Los Angeles: Fotonovel Publications, 1979); Anne Cemmire, ed., "BAYNES, Pauline (Diana) 1922-," *Something About the Author: Facts and Pictures About Authors and Illustrators of Books of Young People* vol. 59 (Detroit: Gale Research Inc., 1990), 10-20; Philip Smith, *The Lord of the Rings and Other Bookbindings of Philip Smith* (London: Stephen Austin and Sons, 1970). On Tolkien in the media, see Gene Hardy, "More Than a Magic Ring," in *Children's Novels and the Movies*, ed. Douglas Street (New York: Frederick Ungar Publishing Co., 1980), 131-40; A. K. Reed, "The Greatest Adventure Is What Lies Ahead: Problems in Media and Mythology—An Analysis of the Rankin/Bass Production of Tolkien's *The Hobbit*," *Journal of Popular Culture* 17.4 (Spring 1984), 138-46; Alex Lewis, "An Interview with Ted Nasmith, Tolkien Illustrator," *Amon Hen* 98 (July, 1989), 22.

9. Donald O'Brien, "On the Origin of the Name 'Hobbit,' " *Mythlore* 16.2 (60) (Winter 1989), 32-38.

10. On the entry for "Hobbit," see James A. H. Murray, Henry Bradley, and W. A. Craigie, eds., *The Oxford English Dictionary* vol. VII (Oxford: Clarendon Press, 1989), 275. On the entry for "Orc," see vol. X, 896.

11. For an interesting narration of Tolkien's life, see Daniel Grotta, *The Biography of J. R. R. Tolkien: Architect of Middle-Earth* (Philadelphia: Running Press, 1992).

12. About the literary dimensions of the trench experience during World War I, see Paul Fussell, *The Great War and Modern Memory* (New York: Oxford University Press, 1977). It was during this time that Tolkien began *The Book of Lost Tales*.

13. On the inspiring friendship between Tolkien and C. S. Lewis, see Humphrey Carpenter, *The Inklings: C. S. Lewis, J. R. R. Tolkien, Charles Williams, and Their Friends* (New York: Ballantine Books, 1978).

14. *The Fellowship of the Ring*, 23-24.

15. *The Fellowship of the Ring*, 11.

16. Humphrey Carpenter, ed., *Letters of J. R. R. Tolkien* (London: George Allen & Unwin Ltd., 1981) 238-44, #183.

17. *Letters of J. R. R. Tolkien*, 244, #183.

18. "*Hobbit.* Do not translate, since the name is supposed no longer to have had a recognized meaning in the Shire, and not to have been derived from the Common Speech (= English, or the language of translation)." Jared Lobdell, ed., *A Tolkien Compass: Including J. R. R. Tolkien's Guide to the Names in "The Lord of the Rings"* (La Salle, IL: Open Court, 1975), 168. "*Halfling.* Common speech name for *Hobbit*. It is not actually an English word, but might be (that is, it is suitably formed with appropriate suffix). The sense is 'a half-sized man/person.' Translate with similar invention containing the word of 'half' in the language of translation. The Dutch translation used *Halfling* (presumably an

intelligible derivative of *half*, though not in use in Dutch any more than in English)." Lobdell, 167. See also: *The Fellowship of the Ring*, 12-13.

19. *Letters of J. R. R. Tolkien*, 158, #131, footnote.

20. For further information on Hobbits and the controversy of their origin, see Bonniejean Christensen, "Tolkien's Creative Technique: 'Beowulf' and 'The Hobbit,' " *Mythlore* 15.3 (57) (Spring 1989), 4-10; O'Brien, 32-38; and Richard Crawshaw, "The Origins of Hobbits," *Amon Hen* 111 (August, 1991), 31-33.

21. *Letters of J. R. R. Tolkien*, 215, #163.

22. J. R. R. Tolkien, *The Return of the King: Being the Third Part of "The Lord of the Rings"* (Boston: Houghton Mifflin Co., 1987), 408. On the "hobbit-rabbit"-linkage, see O'Brien, 35-36.

23. O'Brien, 37.

24. J. R. R. Tolkien, *The Hobbit or There and Back Again*, illustrated by the author (Boston: Houghton Mifflin Co., 1978), 201.

25. O'Brien, 35-36.

26. J. R. R. Tolkien, "Leaf by Niggle," *Tree and Leaf* (London: George Allen & Unwin Ltd., 1964), 71-91. For another perspective on Tolkien's opinions of art, see Corbin S. Carnell, "Large Aims and Modest Claims: The Inklings on Art," *The Bulletin of the New York C. S. Lewis Society* 18.3 (207) (January, 1987), 1-2.

27. J. R. R. Tolkien, "On Fairy-stories," *Tree and Leaf* (London: George Allen & Unwin Ltd., 1964), 58 and 60.

28. *Letters of J. R. R. Tolkien*, 17, #13.

29. Jessica Yates, "The Other 50th Anniversary," *Mythlore* 16.3 (61) (Spring 1990), 47-50.

30. *Letters of J. R. R. Tolkien*, 35, #27.

31. Ted Nasmith, "On Illustrating Tolkien," *Mallorn: The Journal of the Tolkien Society* 26 (September, 1989), 28. For biographical information on Ted Nasmith, see Alex Lewis, 21-24.

32. " 'The Hall at Bag-End, Residence of B. Baggins Esquire.' The original [drawing] was published in the first impression of *The Hobbit*, 1937 (in Chapter 11, *On the Doorstep*)." Christopher Tolkien, ed., unpaginated.

33. "The coloured version by H. E. Riddett was first published in the English De Luxe edition and in the new Dutch translation (both 1976), and appeared also in *The J. R. R. Tolkien Calendar 1979*," Christopher Tolkien, ed., unpaginated.

34. Ian Summers, *The Art of the Brothers Hildebrandt* (New York: Ballantine Books, 1979), 11. For an interesting summary of the Hildebrandts' career, see Summers, 3-12.

35. See Grotta, 16.

36. *The Fellowship of the Ring*, 242-43; *The Return of the King*, 264, 266-67, 309.

37. See Grotta, 44.

38. Summers, 11; *The Fellowship of the Ring*, 30.

39. Nasmith, 28.

40. For a short account of David Wenzel's career, see Charles M. Collins, ". . . About David Wenzel," in *Middle-Earth: The World of Tolkien Illustrated*, 62-3. See also Robb Walsh, *Kingdom of Dwarfs*, Illustration and Concept by David Wenzel (New York: Centaur Books Inc., 1980). For Wenzel's illustration, see J. R. R. Tolkien, *The Hobbit or There and Back Again* adapted by Charles Dixon, illustrated by David Wenzel, Book One of Three (Forestville, CA: Eclipse Books, 1989), front cover.

41. Nasmith, 30. *The Hobbit* (1978), 13.

42. See note 31.

43. For examples of the size and age rendering of Bilbo in comparison to his companions, see *The Hobbit* Book One of Three (1989), 7, 8, 25-26.

44. For Wenzel's depictions of Gollum, see *The Hobbit*, Book One of Three (1989), 43-44.

45. *The Hobbit* (1978), 67.

46. Gandalf's opinion alone: "I guess they were of hobbit-kind; akin to the fathers of the fathers of the Stoors" should suffice to settle this question, but it is also confirmed in several other places. See *The Fellowship of the Ring*, 62.

47. Arden R. Smith, "Who's Afraid of Big, Bad Gollum?," *Vinyar Tengwar* 17 (May, 1991), 23.

48. J. R. R. Tolkien, *The Book of Lost Tales*, Part I (New York: Ballantine Books, 1992), 268, 270, 273-76, 279.

49. Tolkien himself on the etymology of "orc": "*Orc*. This is the supposed to be Common Speech name of these creatures at that time; it should therefore according to the system be translated into English, or the language of translation. It was translated 'goblin' in *The Hobbit*, except in one other place; but this word, and other words of similar sense in other European languages, are not really suitable. The *orc* in *The Lord of the Rings* and *The Silmarillion*, though of course partly made out of traditional features, it is not really comparable in supposed origin, functions, and relation to the Elves. In any case *orc* seemed to me, and seems, in sound a good name for these creatures. It should be retained.

"The adjective is spelt *orkish*. The Grey-elven form is *orch*, plural *yrch*. I originally took the word from Old English *orc* (Beowulf 112 *orc-nass* and the gloss *orc* = *pyrs* ('ogre'), *heldeofol* ('hell-devil'). This is supposed not to be connected with modern English *orc*, *ork*, a name applied to various seabeasts of the dolphin order." See Lobdell, 171.

50. Cited in Joe R. Christopher, "A Literary Friendship," *Mythprint* 30.8 (156) (August, 1993), 7.

51. For a summary of the history and development of the orcs, see David Day, *Tolkien: The Illustrated Encyclopedia* (New York: Macmillan Publishing Co., 1992), 214-17.

52. *The Fellowship of the Ring*, 338-39. J. R. R. Tolkien, *The Two Towers: Being the Second Part of "The Lord of the Rings"* (Boston: Houghton Mifflin Co., 1982), 48, 50, and 52.

53. See *The Hobbit*, Book One of Three (1989), 35. For further information on the sword Orcrist, see *The Hobbit* (1978), 44, 51, 61-62.

54. For a short summary of Alan Lee's artistic career, see the dust jacket: J. R. R. Tolkien, *The Lord of the Rings*, illustrated by Alan Lee (Boston: Houghton Mifflin Co., 1991). Also see Harper Prism, ed., *Tolkien Calendar 1999: Illustrated by Alan Lee* ([s. l.]: A Division of HarperCollins Publishers, [1998]), last page, no page numbering. See also: David Larkin, ed., *Faeries*, Illustrated by Brian Frond and Alan Lee (New York: Harry N. Abrams, Inc., 1978).

55. See *The Lord of the Rings* (1991).

56. See *The Lord of the Rings*, no page numbering [opposite of page 448].

57. *The Lord of the Rings*, 448.

58. *The Two Towers*, 52.

59. For further examples of illustrations of orcs by Alan Lee, see *The Lord of the Rings*, no page numbering [opposite of pages 768, 848, 929, 960].

60. For the history and development of the ents, see Day, 200-202.

61. *The Two Towers*, 102. For more concise information on Treebeard, see also Day, 269-70.

62. "*Ent*. Retain this, alone or in compounds, such as *Entwives*. It is supposed to be a

name in the language of Vale of Anduin, including Rohan, for these creatures." Lobdell, 165.

63. Carl F. Hostetter and Patrick Wynne, "Stone Towers," *Mythlore* 19.8 (74) (Autumn 1993), 48-49.

64. Hostetter and Wynne, 49.

65. *The Two Towers*, 89.

66. *The Two Towers*, 66.

67. See *The Lord of the Rings*, no page numbering [opposite of page 496].

68. *The Two Towers*, 66.

12

Conan the Oxymoron:
The Civilized Savage of
Robert E. Howard and Frank Frazetta

David Hinckley

The story of how the fantasy of "sword and sorcery" emerged as a significant force in its field is not unlike the metanarrative that reverberates throughout the subgenre itself: an outsider, sneered at as a barbarian by sophisticated members of the establishment, contrives to force his way into, and even dominate, civilized society. When authors like Edgar Rice Burroughs and Robert E. Howard were writing their colorful adventures for the pulp magazines, they had no idea that, someday, their works would be displayed in prominent bookstores and subjected to literary analysis by university professors; yet that is precisely what has happened. The history of their subgenre is not exactly unknown, but I wish in this chapter to recast that history within a particular framework, and to argue that the modern triumph of sword and sorcery fantasy can be primarily attributed to two men: Robert E. Howard, who first hit upon the ideal avatar for this type of narrative in creating Conan the Barbarian, and Frank Frazetta, whose memorable artwork perfectly reflected and helped to popularize Howard's champion.

Gary K. Wolfe once argued that the fundamental theme of science fiction is the interface, or conflict, between the known and the unknown; I will first suggest here that the fundamental theme of sword and sorcery is the interface, or conflict, between the civilized and the savage. Such a juxtaposition is suggested by the very name of the subgenre, which references the sword—humanity's most ancient weapon, and still the weapon of choice for peoples not yet civilized—and sorcery— a sophisticated discipline that typically demands a long apprenticeship with an experienced sorcerer and extensive readings of ancient texts, as occurs only in civilization. The subgenre's adventures, then, characteristically involve civilized people encountering barbaric lands, barbaric people encountering civilized lands, or—as we shall see—people and lands that in some ways combine barbarism and civilization.

The precise origins of sword and sorcery can be endlessly debated, and several authors might be plausibly nominated as the form's true progenitor. However, if one goes searching through the literature of the past 200 years in search of civilized people experiencing exciting adventures in exotic and fantastic lands, the figure of H. Rider Haggard would invariably be prominent. More so than other writers of his day, Haggard nurtured in his British and American readers a fascination with distant, foreign realms whose inhabitants displayed strange, ancient powers and hinted at deep mysteries hidden from Western eyes. His most famous novels—*King Solomon's Mines* and *She*—have endured in the popular imagination by means of endless reprintings and a series of film adaptations. Yet Haggard can seem stodgy and uninvolving to modern readers, in part because his heroes are invariably standard-issue European males like Quatermain: they might gaze longingly at exotic foreign women like Ayesha, She-Who-Must-Be-Obeyed, and form friendships with noble savages like Umslopogaas, but in the end they always retain their civilized identity, abandon their savage lovers and comrades, and return to their stately European lives. Thus, while there are encounters between civilization and savagery in Haggard's numerous novels, there are no true interactions.

Edgar Rice Burroughs improved upon Haggard by employing as his principal hero Tarzan, who is an English aristocrat by birth who later serves in the House of Lords, but who is also a child of the jungle raised by intelligent apes. However, while Tarzan is both civilized and barbaric, he comes to lead a precisely bifurcated life. In his early encounters with civilization in *Tarzan of the Apes* and *The Return of Tarzan*, Tarzan sometimes acts like a savage among Western companions, but he soon learns to dress and act like any other English gentleman: he makes speeches in the House of Lords without arousing comments, and those who visit his African plantation find a normally dressed, well-spoken nobleman known as Lord Greystoke. When a crisis arises in the jungle, however, he strips off his stylish clothes and reaches for his loincloth and knife to become Tarzan the Ape-Man, in a transformation that precisely anticipates Clark Kent entering a phone booth to change into his Superman suit. So we observe in Tarzan a figure who is *alternately* civilized and barbaric, in response to changing situations and needs.

It was the inspired idea of Robert E. Howard to take the final step and create a hero, Conan the Barbarian, who is *simultaneously* civilized and barbaric. Conan is a walking contradiction, a sophisticated savage, a savage sophisticate. He functions well in both the wilderness and high society but never changes his clothes or manner of behavior in moving from one world to another; he is always the same Conan, always acting in exactly the same way.

And what sort of person is Conan the Barbarian? On one hand, he is perfectly savage: no scion of a highly civilized, noble family, Conan is born and raised a barbarian, the product of a race that evolved separately from the dominant Hyborians. We are told that Conan is a "barbarian of barbarians," and "the vitality and endurance of the wild were his, granting him survival where civilized man would have perished."[1] Not only because of his feral and difficult life, but also because of the genetic advantage of natural selection, Conan appears to be made of "sterner stuff" than his Hyborian counterparts, and therefore he is simply more durable, a superman. Howard's use of evolutionary theory represents a fundamental departure from Burroughs in that his hero is not a natural aristocrat, but rather a barbarian descended from countless generations of savages who, if a kind of superhero, is the evolutionary culmination of the natural laws governing his world rather than a miraculous exception. To emphasize his savage nature, Howard often describes Conan with animal similes and metaphors: his name among the black pirates of what is now northern Africa is "Amra," meaning Lion (echoing Burroughs's allusive word for lion, "Numa"), and Howard constantly likens Conan's strength and speed to that of a lion, a tiger, or a wolf. Like Tarzan, Conan is said to have the senses and instincts of a wild beast, and he regularly displays an animalistic appetite for "wenching," strong drink, and vast quantities of food—although he seems never to have contracted a sexually transmitted disease, and his flat waistline belies the gallons of wine or ale he guzzles whenever the opportunity presents itself, usually while devouring a "joint of beef" large enough to "satisfy a lion."

On the other hand, although this sort of barbarism is linked throughout the Conan stories with positive traits like health, animal vigor, vitality, and virility—in contrast to the faint whiff of corruption ("softness") that invariably accompanies even the best of civilizations—Conan himself also embodies some of the attributes of civilization. This barbarian has learned enough about money to covet it, and his appetites for material wealth at times match his appetites for women, alcohol, and food. Conan regularly displays a strong fascination with the acquisition of treasure—or at least the adventure involved in attempting to acquire it. In addition, while Tarzan in his loincloth prefers to travel by himself through the jungle, communing only with the animals he can speak with, Conan the Barbarian always longs to be with, and to enjoy power over, his fellow men, mostly realized when he plays the role of a martial "football coach" and leads a wild horde to raze some hapless city to the ground for plunder. These desires for wealth and power over other men, in a sense, define Western civilization, so it is not surprising that a barbarian with such urges drives himself to eventually conquer and rule the Hyborians, becoming not only an integral part of their civilization but actually its dominating influence. Conan the Barbarian then functions as a revitalizing force for the civilized Hyborians, as the mightiest Hyborian kingdom, Aquilonia, prospers greatly under his even-handed reign.

In sum, Conan is an oxymoron, or an incarnation of opposite forces in one being. He is the exposer of civilized hypocrisy yet the defender of civilized achievements, the restorer of the natural order against the forces of darkness yet himself a ferocious killer, and the champion of the gods of light yet the toppler of thrones and the slayer of thousands. To epitomize all the contradictory impulses that govern Howard's Conan, one might examine the rousing conclusion of "The Pool of the Black One":

"A kiss?" she cried hysterically. "You think of kisses at a time like this?"

His laughter boomed above the snap and thunder of the sails, as he caught her up off her feet in the crook of one mighty arm, and smacked her red lips with resounding relish.

"I think of Life!" he roared. "The dead are dead, and what has passed is done! I have a ship and a fighting crew and a girl with lips like wine, and that's all I ever asked. Lick your wounds, bullies, and break out a cask of ale. You're going to work ship as she never was worked before. Dance and sing while you buckle to it, damn you! To the Devil with empty seas! We're bound for waters where the seaports are fat, and the merchant ships are crammed with plunder!"[2]

On one hand, Conan proclaims his undying appetites for alcohol and carnal pleasures and a primal commitment to "Life!" above all else. On the other hand, Conan does not seek, as Tarzan might, to commune with nature by himself—in "empty seas"—but rather delights in having "a fighting crew" around him that he can take to "waters where the seaports are fat" and he can obtain "plunder." Even as he demonstrates again his fundamental, savage impulses, he also demonstrates the desires for comradeship and material wealth that serve to create civilization.

We begin to see, then, just why Howard's character has proven to be so appealing to readers. Tarzan must spend most of his days living like any other European gentleman, sipping his tea with the demure Jane, with only occasional opportunities to venture into the jungle and be his true savage self; Conan, however, can constantly both live within a civilized society and freely indulge in all of his animal passions. For that reason, it surely seems that it would be more *fun* to be Conan than to be Tarzan. Further, while Tarzan maintains a clear separation between the civilized worlds of London and his African plantation and the wild worlds of the uncharted jungle, Conan's passion to bring together other men under his command makes, to some extent, a wild world into a civilized world, and his ascension to the throne of Aquilonia makes, to some extent, a civilized world into a wild world. Himself an exhilarating combination of opposites, Conan similarly transforms his environments into exhilarating combinations of opposites, making his adventures an incessant, colorful jumble of savage pleasures and civilized pleasures, unlike Tarzan's controlled journeys from civilization to savagery and back to civilization again.

If Conan thus represents an ideal hero for stories of sword and sorcery that involve a mixing of savagery and civilization, one might ask, why did the Conan stories of Robert E. Howard remain relatively obscure for decades until their rediscovery in the 1960s? One might argue, simply, that Conan's time had come, that the tumultuous social upheavals in America and Europe during that time, reflecting among other things a renewed commitment to the natural environment and the simple life, predictably engendered new interest in an heroic figure from outside civilization who could also immerse him in and revitalize civilization. No doubt, there is some truth in such an explanation, or similar explanations that might be devised. Yet there is one other factor involved in Conan's successful return to center stage in the 1960s; and that is, for the first time, his adventures were accompanied by the entrancing, evocative artwork of Frank Frazetta.

After two decades of drawing mainly for comic books and comic strips, ranging from *L'il Abner* to *Playboy*'s *Little Annie Fanny*, Frazetta would have seemed an unlikely candidate to emerge as the premiere artist of fantasy paperback covers in the 1960s. But in a sense Frazetta's time had also come, given the special qualities of his artistic style. In her introduction to *The Fantastic Art of Frank Frazetta*, Betty Ballantine identifies two features of Frazetta's work as especially noteworthy. First is the dynamic vigor of his art: "His painting is intensely alive, vibrant, even when the figures are in repose. It is perhaps this quality of life, of energy, which most signally sets Frazetta's work apart from all others in comparable fields. . . . His work is all sinuosity and movement." It is in this way that Frazetta's art displays a savage power. "Yet," as Ballantine goes on to say, "the trappings that surround all this vivid life are well done too, the textures of stone and bone and leather, of heavily wrought metals, of armor."[3] Frazetta also excels, in other words, in depicting the accoutrements of civilization. In displaying his great skill in conveying both the "quality of life, of energy" and the "trappings that surround all this vivid life," Frazetta also made use of an awareness of focus, drawn from still photography and film, so that he might strikingly portray one figure in sharp focus and leave another nearby figure blurry and out of focus; yet he could also impose an aura of connectedness between such disparate figures by choosing and effectively employing a single dominant color, usually a subdued one, in the painting as a whole. In all these respects, Frazetta was ideally prepared to depict scenes from the literature of sword and sorcery, with its emphasis on the juxtaposition or blending of savagery and civilization, and the 1960s were the time when the works of major authors in this tradition, like Haggard, Burroughs, and Howard, were being brought back into print.

To understand why Frazetta displayed, in my view, a special affinity for Howard's Conan, one might usefully consider Frazetta's artwork in the context of the three literary progenitors of sword and sorcery that I have identified. Unfortunately, to my knowledge, Frazetta has never been assigned to illustrate any of Haggard's works; however, we can gain a sense of what may have resulted if we examine his cover for the Ace paperback edition of Burroughs's *The Land That Time Forgot*, depicting the moment in the novel when heroic Bowen Tyler and a companion (probably the engineer Olson) first venture into the land of Caspak to encounter its strange, primitive creatures.[4] The painting is so uncharacteristic of Frazetta's classic style that one must consult Robert B. Zeuschner's definitive *Edgar Rice Burroughs: The Exhaustive Scholar's and Collector's Descriptive Bibliography of American Periodical, Hardcover, Paperback, and Reprint Editions*, checking the book's stock number, to confirm that the artist was Frazetta.[5] Instead of foregrounded, nearly naked figures, two rather small men serve as the focus of attention, both completely dressed in shirts and pants. Instead of a flashing sword or bloody mace, the first man is pointing a large pistol at the nondescript large reptile that he confronts. And, instead of a striking overall emphasis on one dominant, but muted color, the painting is a gaudy combination of primary colors, with a bright blue sky in the background, a bright red and a darker blue shirt for the men, and a yellowish-orange reptile. Only a dark, snakelike creature slithering in dark branches above the main scene, almost unnoticeable at first, recalls Frazetta's more famous compositions. From this painting, we conclude that Frazetta is simply not inspired by scenes of civilized people like Haggard's Quatermain venturing into uncivilized realms with loaded guns in their hands; rather, he is excited by figures who are themselves uncivilized, displaying large expanses of naked flesh and brandishing more primitive weapons. It is little wonder, then, that Frazetta did considerably better in painting the covers of the other two books in the Caspak series, *The People That Time Forgot* and *Out of Time's Abyss*, since Burroughs's adventure gradually primitivized his protagonists, bringing them into contact with cavepeople, and allowing Frazetta to illustrate, respectively, a beautiful naked woman being abducted by apemen and a loinclothed man and woman facing a tyrannosaurus, mammoth, and other ancient creatures amidst a huge flood.[6]

So, if Frazetta has this predilection for savage people and savage realms, one would assume him to be an ideal artist for Burroughs's Tarzan; and, in fact, his covers for several Tarzan novels were what first garnered widespread attention to the artist. Yet for all their polish, there is, to my eye at least, a certain languid quality to some of Frazetta's paintings of Tarzan. Consider, for example, "Apeman," a black-and-white illustration reproduced on page 19 of *The Fantastic Art of Frank Frazetta*. Here, Tarzan in his loincloth is soaring through the jungle, holding a voluptuous, almost naked woman, with a large pyramid outlined in the background. Knowing that Burroughs's Tarzan is a virtuous married man, we assume that the jungle lord is rescuing the woman from some dangerous situation in the vicinity of the pyramid; yet the drawing conveys no sense of imminent peril. Tarzan and the woman appear suspended in midair, not rushing in desperate haste, touring the jungle rather than escaping from its menaces. Another example would be Frazetta's cover painting for Richard A. Lupoff's *Edgar Rice Burroughs: Master of Adventure*.[7] Here Tarzan stands with his back to the viewer, arms raised in a triumphant gesture, while great apes and a leopard sit behind him. As in the preceding painting, there is no sense of danger in the scene, which appears almost a pastoral depiction of an apeman in harmony with his natural environment. We can recognize, then, the problem that Frazetta faced in depicting Tarzan. When wearing the loincloth, Tarzan is a completely savage man in a completely savage environment; hence, his adventures provide few opportunities to depict sharp contrasts between savagery and civilization, to present conflicts or juxtapositions of opposing qualities. But Robert E. Howard's Conan would offer precisely these sorts of stimulating opportunities in abundance.

It is first interesting to consider the uniform that Frazetta develops for almost all of his portraits of Conan (even though the stories themselves are not that consistent in describing his apparel). Conan typically wears a horned helmet and carries a round shield. His arms and chest are almost entirely naked (except perhaps for a necklace of animal teeth), but he wears armor around his waist and private parts and large boots on his feet. There are sheaths near his waist to hold a large sword and an ax (one of which he is usually brandishing), and a knife is strapped to one leg. By placing Conan in such apparel, Frazetta iconographically portrays him as a man who is both savage and civilized in equal proportions. His body, with almost mathematical precision, is 50 percent naked and 50 percent armored. The bulging muscles of his arms, chest, and legs announce that he is perfectly capable of fighting with his bare hands, when the need arises, but he also carries metal weapons as another way to inflict harm on his opponents. Both a barbarian and a civilized soldier, then, Conan must have represented to Frazetta a more interesting figure to portray than Tarzan.

In examining some individual paintings, we can further see how Conan's adventures provided unique opportunities to visually explore the contrast between savagery and civilization at the heart of sword and sorcery. At times, Conan's savage nature comes to the forefront. In "Man-Ape" (on page 79 of *Fantastic Art*), Frazetta illustrates a scene from Howard's "Rogues in the House," first published in *Weird Tales* in 1934. The story is told largely from the point of view of a young nobleman, Murilo, who has hired the barbarian as an assassin. In the climactic battle Conan must confront Thak, a pre-human anthropoid, half-man, half-beast (rather like one of Burroughs's "great apes"). Choosing a primitive method of attack, Conan leaps upon Thak from ambush, and despite his advantage of surprise, only narrowly succeeds in killing the powerful creature with the help of his knife. In Frazetta's painting, we first notice the unusual detail of Conan's familiar round shield, hanging on the wall. To fight in this stealthy manner, Conan must abandon the civilized protection of a shield and function more like an animal. The amber darkness of the painting heightens the resemblance between the antagonists—here, two savages fighting each other—and the blazing blue of Conan's eyes conveys an unusual, animalistic ferocity. This is Conan at his nearest approach to Tarzan, a nearly naked antagonist armed only with a knife and his muscular strength.

In contrast, Frazetta emphasizes Conan as a representative of civilization in "Berserker" (page 41 of *Fantastic Art*) one of several pictures that portrays Conan as a soldier, contending against an army. (This is also one of Frazetta's most famous paintings, having served both as the cover for the 1967 Ace paperback edition of *Conan the Conqueror* and as an album cover for the Southern rock band Molly Hatchet.) In this battle scene, Conan relies upon his round shield and large sword to combat his many opponents. Frazetta also adds an armored and taloned figure of Death in the lower right-hand corner, referencing the Four Horsemen of the Apocalypse that will someday destroy civilization, here part of the horde that Conan is in the process of defeating. A similar scene is portrayed in "Indomitable" (page 77 of (*Fantastic Art*), based on Howard's story "Beyond the Black River" (originally published in *Weird Tales* in 1936). Here, Conan is battling against more primitive barbarians than himself—the savage, nearly naked Picts—and fittingly he is wearing more armor than usual, to emphasize he is in this instance a defender of civilized values. His opponents include the Picts's leader, a demonic wizard, his swamp demon half-brother, and a strange reptilian monster darting its venomous head at Conan's leg. Clearly, Conan here is presented as an opponent of natural forces, not their embodiment.

We can now begin to understand why Conan and his adventures proved so stimulating to an artist like Frazetta. Since Conan represents a combination of contradictory traits, he is potentially attuned to, and potentially in conflict with, every person or being he encounters; yet, of course, the more exciting artistic possibilities will reflect conflict. Thus, while scenes of the purely savage Tarzan in the savage jungle can seem overly harmonious, even bucolic, there are always interesting disparities between Conan and those around him that can be exploited for powerful artistic effect. In "Chained" (page 89 of *Fantastic Art*), Conan is stripped of his usual weapons and placed in chains astride a gigantic, menacing snake, emphasizing his civilized vulnerability to immense, uncontrolled natural forces. However, in "Apparition" (page 39 of *Fantastic Art*), Conan stands with all his armor and weaponry, rendered in sharp clarity, to display civilized strength in the face of natural forces, here represented by an uncannily illuminated female figure who appears nude even though physiological details are conspicuously absent, emphasizing her basically unnatural quality. The vaguely cloak-like object she holds billowing aloft merges with the murky background, through which can be dimly seen the head of a gigantic, ursine monstrosity, but the blurriness of these figures only serves to make them seem weak in contrast to the foregrounded Conan, armed to the teeth.

Still, although these two paintings also appear to emphasize Conan as an avatar of civilization, Frazetta's paintings do not always lend themselves to interpretation as depictions of Conan's "savage" side or his "civilized" side; often, the two aspects of Conan appear in Frazetta's work to be in perfect balance. Consider one of his most striking portrayals of Conan, "The Snow Giants" (pages 45 and 47 of *Fantastic Art*), illustrating a scene from Howard's "The Snow Giant's Daughter" (originally published in *Weird Tales* in 1934). On one hand, the painting offers breathtaking natural beauty and grandeur in its snowy winter landscape and a Matterhorn-like peak in the background, and Conan and his opponents, two demigods known as the Ice Giants, all reveal improbably large expanses of naked flesh, even though no one could really dress like that in sub-zero temperatures. On the other hand, the armor and weapons of Conan and the Ice Giants are rendered with meticulous clarity and realism, so much so that Ballantine's compilation saw fit to include both the entire painting and a close-up reproduction of one of its figures, to fully display the splendid detail of their accoutrements. In this painting, the bright red hair of the Ice Giants, suggesting primitive passion, and their status as demigods might suggest that the scene represents a battle between nature, as symbolized by the Ice Giants, and civilization, as symbolized by Conan. However, since all three figures appear to stand in semi-naked harmony with their scenic environment, one could also view them as personifications of warring elements in nature; or one could focus on their elaborate weaponry and interpret the scene as a battle between older and newer levels of civilization. Despite its disparate elements, then, the picture has a satisfying organic unity, blending together savagery and civilization in the manner of Conan himself.

A final illustration worth discussing in this context is "The Barbarian" (page 91 of *Fantastic Art*). Frazetta attempts in this painting (which also served as the cover of the Sphere edition of the first Conan book, *Conan the Adventurer*) a kind of pictorial tribute to the invincible barbarian hero in all his contradictory glory. Conan is depicted leaning on his great phallic longsword atop a grisly pile of human and non-human remains, with a beautiful—and of course unclothed—woman clinging to his leg. In the background swirl a great death's-head and other vaguely monstrous shapes, mingled with hints of city walls and ruins. Amid all of this stands the barbarian, inscrutable, a scar—or is it a grim smile?—turning up the corner of his mouth, an image of unquenchable life amid the ruins of past and present battles. In both the background of the painting and the mound upon which Conan stands, there is conveyed the impression of everything blurring together—the human and inhuman, the dead and the alive, the primal and the civilized—while in the center stands Conan, here (as in "Apparition") the only figure rendered in sharp clarity, who emerged from precisely these sorts of contrary influences but nevertheless achieved a degree of solidity in his own consistent but oxymoronic personality.

After appearing in the paperback editions of the 1960s, accompanied by Frazetta's illustrations, Conan the Barbarian has remained an important figure in popular culture, and other images of Howard's barbarian have achieved their own prominence—most notably, the Conan of Barry Smith's *Conan* comic books, the muscular figure of Arnold Schwarzenegger portraying Conan in two major films of the 1980s, and the equally muscular figure of Ralph Moeller portraying Conan in a short-lived television series in the 1990s. But these and other portrayals have continued to reflect, in my view, the strong influence of Frazetta's pioneering paintings, and the peculiar combination of savage and civilized man that Frazetta so effectively portrayed has remained a key element in all perceptions of the character. Thus, on one hand, it was surely, at first, for comedic effect that the brutal Conan was enlisted by American educators in a campaign to encourage children to read by means of a series of educational comic strips featuring "Conan the Librarian," who incongruously sits at a library desk in barbarian garb and speaks bluntly about the value of reading books to inquiring children. On the other hand, there is also something strangely appropriate in having Conan, who so often represented and defended civilization in his own adventures, now representing and defending our own print-based civilization being threatened by its own, domestic barbarians taking the forms of cartoons, computer games, music videos, and the like.

And what of the larger subgenre of sword and sorcery, which has also continued to thrive? Sword and sorcery fantasy, I would argue, is an attempt to return through the vehicle of imagination to an atavistic way of seeing that fuses the natural sublime celebrated by Romanticism with the civilized, horrific sublime of Gothic fiction, viewing history and prehistory as the record of an endless struggle between the opposing forces of light and darkness, order and chaos, and struggling to achieve some sort of synthesis between them. As arguably the first popular writer to explore these impulses in a manner that also suggested a way to satisfyingly resolve these disparate urges, Robert E. Howard merits recognition, for the influence of Conan and his world on subsequent writers of greater technical skill and broader sensibility has been considerable indeed. Of equal significance is Frank Frazetta's pioneering work in visually portraying these sorts of conflicts in his illustrations for Howard's adventures, achieving in his art the same sort of satisfying synthesis that Howard achieved in his stories and helping to convey to a larger audience the full, fascinating implications of Howard's vision.

The immense popularity of this particular kind of fantasy over the last thirty years suggests that it speaks to a strong and deeply rooted cultural need, felt by readers of many different sorts. The themes of sword and sorcery, as tentatively explored here, provide definite clues as to what these needs might be. The intense concern with physical strength, virility and clearly defined sexual roles shows that sword and sorcery may in part be a means for the male members of a once-patriarchal society to escape their fears of a loss of identity, emasculation, in a world where traditional ideas of sexual identity are threatened. For similar reasons, the confrontation of barbarism and civilization in sword and sorcery might appeal to male members of a once-dominant racial and cultural group unsettled by our society's burgeoning multiracialism and multiculturalism, or heterosexual males disturbed by the new prominence of gay and lesbian activism. In all cases, sword and sorcery might function as a reaffirmation and revalidation, as it were, of ancient and traditional values—but not, one must stress, simply a rejection of newer, more civilized values, inasmuch as Conan both represents ancient savagery and becomes a part of advanced civilization. However hesitantly, then, sword and sorcery does not (in the manner of, say, survivalist fiction) flatly repudiate our brave new world; rather, it strives to understand and embrace the civilized values of a new age from the perspective of a unrepentant old barbarian.

Even more broadly, the fantasy of sword and sorcery asserts the meaningfulness of human activity in a universe bedeviled by chaos, suffering, and death, suggesting that humans can indeed achieve their impossible dreams and synthesize their opposing desires. If we are all partly barbarians, and if we are all partly creatures of civilization, then Conan the Barbarian is a figure that everyone can identify with; and sword and sorcery fantasy, as powerfully represented by Howard's stories and Frazetta's artwork, may be precisely the sort of literature that many people desperately need during these troubling and confusing times.

Notes

1. Robert E. Howard, "The Slithering Shadow," in *Conan the Adventurer*, by Robert E. Howard, edited by L. Sprague de Camp (1966; London: Sphere Books, 1975), 91. Story originally published in the September, 1933 issue of *Weird Tales*.

2. Robert E. Howard, "The Pool of the Black One," in *Conan the Adventurer*, 192. Story originally published in the October, 1933 issue of *Weird Tales*.

3. Betty Ballantine, "Introduction," *The Fantastic Art of Frank Frazetta* (New York: Rufus Publications, 1975), 10. Note: since the book is unpaginated, the page numbers in notes and in the text are the result of my own personal count of pages, beginning with the first page after the inside front cover as page one, though I omit here and later the brackets usually employed to identify unofficial page numbers.

4. Edgar Rice Burroughs, *The Land That Time Forgot* (New York: Ace Books, 1973). Story originally published in the August, 1918 issue of *Blue Book*.

5. Robert B. Zeuschner, *Edgar Rice Burroughs: The Exhaustive Scholar's and*

Collector's Descriptive Bibliography of American Periodical, Hardcover, Paperback, and Reprint Editions (Jefferson, NC: McFarland & Company, Inc., 1996), 87.

6. Edgar Rice Burroughs, *The People That Time Forgot* (New York: Ace Books, 1973); Burroughs, *Out of Time's Abyss* (New York: Ace Books, 1973). Stories originally published in the October, 1918 and December, 1918 issues of *Blue Book*.

7. Richard A. Lupoff, *Edgar Rice Burroughs: Master of Adventure*, revised and enlarged edition (New York: Ace Books, 1968).

A Bibliography of Works of and about
Science Fiction and Fantasy Art

The following is a selective bibliography of works of and about science fiction and fantasy art; some offer extended textual analyses, while others primarily provide numerous reproductions of representative works. We have generally excluded works focused on a single artist, as well as works that focus on the art of science fiction film, television, and comic books. While all contributors to the volume have assisted in compiling this bibliography, special thanks should go to John Grant and John Clute for a number of helpful suggestions.

Aldiss, Brian W. *Science Fiction Art*. New York: Bounty Books, 1975.

Aldiss, Brian W., and Peter Nicholls. "Illustration." In *The Encyclopedia of Science Fiction*. Edited by John Clute and Peter Nicholls. New York: St. Martin's Press, 1993, 611-13.

Anzaldi, Antonio, and Massimo Izzi. *Fanatasia*. Rome: Gremese International, 1995.

Ash, Brian, editor. *The Visual Encyclopedia of Science Fiction*. New York: Harmony Books, 1977.

Barron, Neil, editor. *Fantasy and Horror: A Critical and Historical Guide to Literature, Illustration, Film, TV, Radio, and the Internet*. Lanham, MD: Scarecrow Press, 1999.

Bleiler, Everett F. "Magazine Illustrators." In *Science-Fiction: The Gernsback Years*. By Everett F. Bleiler with the assistance of Richard Bleiler. Kent, OH: Kent State University Press, 1998, 598-620.

Brosterman, Norman. *Out of Time: Designs for a Twentieth-Century Future*. New York: Abrams, 2000.

Bryant, Mark, and Simon Heneage, editors. *Dictionary of British Cartoonists and Caricaturists 1730-1980*. London: Scolar Press, 1994.

Caldwell, Steven. *Aliens in Space: An Illustrated Guide to the Inhabited Galaxy*. New York: Crescent Books, 1979.

Carter, Lin. *Imaginary Worlds: The Art of Fantasy*. New York: Ballantine Books, 1975.

Clute, John. "Great Illustrators." *Science Fiction: The Illustrated Encyclopedia*. New York: Dorling Kindersley, 1995, 240-41.

Davenport-Hines, Richard. *Gothic: Four Hundred Years of Excess, Horror, Evil and Ruin*. New York: North Point Press/Farrar, Straus and Giroux, 1998.

Dean, Martyn, editor. *The Guide to Fantasy Art Techniques*. Text by Christ Evans; based on interviews between the artists and Martyn Dean. New York: Arco Publishing, 1984.

del Rey, Lester. *Fantastic Science Fiction Art 1926-1954*. New York: Ballantine Books, 1975.

DiFate, Vincent. *Infinite Worlds: The Fantastic Visions of Science Fiction Art.* Foreword by Ray Bradbury. New York: Penguin Studio: Wonderland Press, 1997.

————. "Science Fiction Art: Some Contemporary Illustrators." In *The Science Fiction Reference Book.* Edited by Marshall B. Tymn. Mercer Island: Starmont House, 1981, 33-55.

Edwards, Malcolm, and Holdstock, Robert. *Realms of Fantasy: An Illustrated Exploration of Ten of the Most Famous Worlds in Fantasy Fiction.* Garden City, NY: Doubleday, 1983.

Eichenberg, Fritz. *Dance of Death: A Graphic Commentary on the Danse Macabre through the Centuries.* London: Abbevill Press, 1983.

Eisler, Steven. *Space Wars: Worlds and Weapons.* Foreword by Chris Foss. New York: Crescent Books, 1979.

Evans, Arthur B. "The Illustrators of Jules Verne's *Voyages Extraordinaires.*" *Science-Fiction Studies*, 25 (July, 1998), 241-70.

Foss, Chris. *Science Fiction Art.* Illustrated by Chris Foss. Introduction by Brian W. Aldiss. London: Hart-Davis, MacGibbon, 1976.

Frank, Jane, and Howard Frank. *The Frank Collection: A Showcase of the World's Finest Fantastic Art.* London: Paper Tiger, 1999.

Frewin, Anthony. *One Hundred Years of Science Fiction Illustration.* 1974. New York: Pyramid Books, 1975.

Gaunt, William, editor. *Painters of Fantasy from Hieronymus Bosch to Salvador Dali.* London: Phaidon, 1974.

Grant, John, and Ron Tiner. *The Encyclopedia of Fantasy and Science Fiction Art Techniques.* Philadelphia: Running Press, 1996.

Grunenberg, Christoph, editor. *Gothic: Transmutations of Horror in Late Twentieth Century Art.* Boston: The Institute of Contemporary Art/The MIT Press, 1997.

Gunn, James. *Alternate Worlds: The Illustrated History of Science Fiction.* Englewood Cliffs, NJ: Prentice-Hall, 1975.

Haining, Peter. *A Pictorial History of Horror Stories: 200 Years of Spine-Chilling Illustrations from the Pulp Magazines.* London: Treasure Press, 1985. Originally published in 1976.

Hammacher, Abraham Marie. *Phantoms of the Imagination: Fantasy in Art and Literature from Blake to Dali.* Translated by Tony Langham and Plym Peters. New York: H. N. Abrams, 1981.

Hardy, David A. "Art and Artists." In *The Encyclopedia of Science Fiction.* Consultant editor Robert Holdstock. London: Octopus Books, 1978, 122-41.

————. *Visions of Space: Artists Journey Through the Cosmos.* Limpsfield: Dragon's World, 1989.

Hargreaves, Joyce, with Malcolm Ashman. *Fabulous Beasts.* Woodstock, New York: Overlook Press, 1997.

Harrison, Harry. *Great Balls of Fire! An Illustrated History of Sex in Science Fiction.* London: Pierrot Publishing Limited, 1977.

Harrison, Harry, and Malcolm Edwards. *Spacecraft in Fact and Fiction.* New York: Exeter Books, 1979.

Hartmann, William K., Andrei Sokolov, Ron Miller, and Vitaly Mjagkov, editors. *In the Stream of Stars: The Soviet/American Space Art Book.* New York: Workman, 1990.

Holdstock, Robert, and Edwards, Malcolm. *Lost Realms: An Illustrated Exploration of the Lands Behind the Legends.* Limpsfield: Dragon's World, 1984.

Jones, Bruce, and Armand Eisen, editors. *Sorcerers: A Collection of Fantasy Art.* Foreword by Ken Kesey. Kansas City: Ariel Books, 1978.

Jude, Dick. *Fantasy Art of the New Millennium*. London: HarperCollins, 1999. Published in America as *Fantasy Art Masters: The Best Fantasy and SF Art Worldwide*. New York: Watson-Guptill, 1999.

Kyle, David. *The Illustrated Book of Science Fiction Ideas and Dreams*. London: Hamlyn, 1977.

———. *A Pictorial History of Science Fiction*. London: Tiger Books, 1986. Originally published in 1976.

Langford, David, with Josh Kirby. *A Cosmic Cornucopia*. London: Paper Tiger, 1999.

Larkin, David, editor. *Fantastic Art*. New York: Pan/Ballantine, 1973.

———, editor. *The Fantastic Kingdom*. With biographical notes by Margaret Maloney. London: Pan Books, 1974.

———, editor and introducer. *Once Upon a Time: Some Contemporary Illustrators of Fantasy*. New York: Peacock Press, 1976.

MacGregor, John. *The Discovery of the Art of the Insane*. Princeton, NJ: Princeton University Press, 1989.

Malone, Robert, with Jean-Claude Suares. *Rocketship*. New York: Harper & Row, 1977.

Marantz, Sylvia, and Kenneth Marantz. *Artists of the Page: Interviews with Children's Book Illustrators*. Jefferson, NC: McFarland, 1992.

Martineau, Jane, editor. *Victorian Fairy Painting*. London: Royal Academy of Arts/Merrell Holberton Publishers, 1997.

Meyer, Susan E. *A Treasury of the Great Children's Book Illustrators*. New York: Abrams, 1983.

Miller, Ron. *The Dream Machines: An Illustrated History of the Spaceship in Art, Science, and Literature*. Original illustrations by Ron Miller and Rick Dunning. Foreword by Arthur C. Clarke. Malabar, FL: Krieger Publishing Co., 1993.

Miller, Ron, compiler. *The Space Art Poster Book*. Harrisburg, PA: Stackpole Books, 1979.

Overden, Graham, editor. *The Illustrators of Alice in Wonderland and Through the Looking Glass*. Revised edition. With an Introduction by John Davis. New York: St. Martin's Press, 1979.

Peppin, Brigid. *Book Illustrators of the Twentieth Century*. New York: Arco Publishing, Inc., 1984.

———. *Fantasy Book Illustration 1860-1920*. London: Studio Vista, 1975. Also published as *Fantasy: The Golden Age of Fantastic Illustration*. New York: Watson-Guptill, 1975.

Petaja, Emil, compiler and editor. *The Hannes Bok Memorial Showcase of Fantasy Art*. San Francisco: SISU Publishers, 1974.

Plummer, Kathleen Church. "The Streamlined Moderne." *Art in America*, 62, (January/February, 1974), 46-51.

Post, J. B. *An Atlas of Fantasy*. New York: Ballantine Books, 1979.

Robinson, Frank M. *Science Fiction of the 20th Century: An Illustrated History*. With technical assistance by John Gunnison. Portland, OR: Collectors Press, 1999.

Rottensteiner, Franz. *The Fantasy Book: An Illustrated History from Dracula to Tolkien*. New York: Collier Books, 1978.

———. *The Science Fiction Book: An Illustrated History*. London: Thames and Hudson, 1975.

Sackmann, Eckart. *Great Masters of Fantasy Art*. Translated by Hugh Beyer. Berlin: TACO, 1986.

Sacks, Janet, compiler. *Visions of the Future*. Edited by Pat Hornsey and Julie Davis. Secaucus, NJ: Chartwell Books, 1976.

Sadoul, Jacques. *2000 A.D.: Illustrations from the Golden Age of Science Fiction Pulps.* Chicago: Henry Regnery, 1975.

Sant, Montse, and Cabral, Ciruelo. *The Book of the Dragon.* London: Paper Tiger, 1992.

Sargent, Pamela, and Miller, Ron. *Firebrands: The Heroines of Science Fiction & Fantasy.* London: Paper Tiger, 1998.

Schlobin, Roger C. *The Aesthetics of Fantasy Literature and Art.* Notre Dame, IN: University of Notre Dame Press, 1982.

Sheckley, Robert. *Futuropolis.* New York: A&W Visual Library, 1978.

Sherwin, Mary, Ellen Asher, and Joe Miller, editors. *The New Visions: A Collection of Modern Science Fiction Art.* Introduction by Frederik Pohl. Garden City, NY: Doubleday, 1982.

Suares, Jean-Claude, and Richard Siegel. *Fantastic Planets.* Text by David Owen. Danbury, NH: Addison House, 1979.

Suckling, Nigel. *Dream Makers: Six Fantasy Artists at Work.* Limpsfield: Dragon's World, 1988.

———. *Heroic Dreams.* Limpsfield: Dragon's World, 1987.

Suckling, Nigel, with Bob Eggleton. *The Book of Sea Monsters.* London: Paper Tiger, 1998.

Suckling, Nigel, with Linda and Roger Garland. *The Book of the Unicorn.* Limpsfield: Dragon's World, 1996.

Suckling, Nigel, and Matthews, Rodney. *Countdown to Millennium.* London: Paper Tiger, 1997.

Summers, Ian, editor. *Tomorrow and Beyond: Masterpieces of Science Fiction Art.* New York: Workman Publishing Co., 1978.

Tiner, Ron. "Illustration." In *The Encyclopedia of Fantasy.* Edited by John Clute and John Grant. New York: St. Martin's Press, 1997, 492-95.

Vallejo, Boris. *Fantasy Art Techniques.* New York: Arco Publishing, 1985.

Weinberg, Robert. *A Biographical Dictionary of Science Fiction and Fantasy Artists.* Westport, CT: Greenwood Press, 1988.

———. *Horror of the 20th Century: An Illustrated History.* Portland, OR: Collectors Press, 2000.

Whitlark, James. *Illuminated Fantasy: From Blake's Visions to Recent Graphic Fiction.* Rutherford, NJ: Fairleigh Dickinson University Press, 1988.

Wuckel, Dieter, and Bruce Cassiday. *The Illustrated History of Science Fiction.* New York: Ungar, 1989.

Index

About the Contributors

GREGORY BENFORD, Professor of Physics at the University of California at Irvine, is the well-known author of many science fiction novels, including *Timescape*, *Cosm*, *The Martian Race*, and *Eater*, as well as the nonfictional *Deep Time: How Humanity Communicates Across Millennia*.

JOHN CLUTE served as co-editor of the award-winning *The Encyclopedia of Science Fiction* and *The Encyclopedia of Fantasy* and is also the author of *SF: The Illustrated Encyclopedia*, *The Book of End Times*, two collections of reviews and essays, and the science fiction novel *Appleseed*.

JOHN GRANT was co-editor of *The Encyclopedia of Fantasy* and has also published numerous works of fiction and nonfiction, including the fantasy novel *The World* and *The Encyclopedia of Walt Disney Animated Characters*. He is currently the Commissioning Editor of Paper Tiger Books, a leading publisher of science fiction and fantasy art books.

KIRK HAMPTON is the author of *The Moonhare*, a "Wakean science fantasy," a forthcoming novel entitled *Limbo*, and several conference papers co-authored with Carol MacKay.

HOWARD V. HENDRIX is the author of the novels *Lightpaths*, *Standing Wave*, *Better Angels*, and *Empty Cities of the Full Moon*, as well as the critical study *The Ecstasy of Catastrophe*, and numerous stories, articles, and reviews. He is also a university professor and academic administrator.

DAVID HINCKLEY, who teaches at the University of California, Riverside and the University of Redlands, has presented several conference papers and contributed entries to *McGill's Guide to Science Fiction and Fantasy Literature*.

BEATRIX KARTHAUS-HUNT is a doctoral student in the Comparative Literature Department of the University of California, Riverside, with an interest in science fiction and phot-text books in the period from the beginning of World War I to the end of World War II.

LYNNE LUNDQUIST, who teaches in the Theatre and Dance Department of California State University, Fullerton, contributed three entries to *The Encyclopedia of Fantasy*, and her work has appeared in *Extrapolation* and the critical anthology *Immortal Engines: Life Extension and Immortality in Science Fiction and Fantasy*.

CAROL MACKAY, Associate Professor of English at the University of Texas at Austin, is the author of *Soliloquy in Nineteenth-Century Fiction* and *Creative Negativity*, and is the editor of *The Two Thackerays* and *Dramatic Dickens*.

KATHLEEN CHURCH PLUMMER teaches at the University of California, Davis, lecturing on the decorative arts and interiors while also working and exhibiting as an artist in watercolor, collage, and printmaking.

GEORGE SLUSSER, Professor of Comparative Literature at the University of California at Riverside, has written several books about science fiction authors, and he has also co-edited numerous critical anthologies. In 1986, he received the Pilgrim Award from the Science Fiction Research Association for his lifetime contributions to science fiction scholarship.

SAMUEL H. VASBINDER, an Assistant Professor in the Fine Arts with the Malone College Fine Arts Department, Canton, Ohio, has published numerous articles and a book on Mary Shelley's *Frankenstein*.

GARY WESTFAHL, who teaches at the University of California at Riverside, is the author, editor, or co-editor of ten books about science fiction and fantasy, most recently *Science Fiction, Children's Literature, and Popular Culture: Coming of Age in Fantasyland* and *Science Fiction, Canonization, Marginalization, and the Academy*. He also writes a column for the science fiction magazine *Interzone*.